AMERICAN Hangman

MSGT. JOHN C. WOODS

The United States Army's
Notorious Executioner in
World War II and Nürnberg

AMERICAN Hangman

MSgt. John C. Woods

The United States Army's Notorious Executioner in World War II and Nürnberg

Col. French L. MacLean, US Army (Ret.)

SCHIFFER MILITARY

4880 Lower Valley Road • Atglen, PA 19310

Designed by Justin Watkinson
Type set in Impact/Minion Pro/Univers LT Std

ISBN: 978-0-7643-5815-9
Printed in China

Published by Schiffer Publishing, Ltd.
4880 Lower Valley Road
Atglen, PA 19310
Phone: (610) 593-1777; Fax: (610) 593-2002
E-mail: Info@schifferbooks.com
www.schifferbooks.com

For our complete selection of fine books on this
and related subjects, please visit our website at
www.schifferbooks.com. You may also write
for a free catalog.

Schiffer Publishing's titles are available at special
discounts for bulk purchases for sales promotions
or premiums. Special editions, including personalized
covers, corporate imprints, and excerpts, can be
created in large quantities for special needs.
For more information, contact the publisher.

We are always looking for people to
write books on new and related subjects.
If you have an idea for a book, please contact
us at proposals@schifferbooks.com.

Old soldiers never die, they just fade away

There is an old mess hall, not far away,
Where we get pork and beans, three times a day.
Ham and eggs we never see, even when we're on KP,
And we are gradually fading away.

Old soldiers never die, never die, never die,
Old soldiers never die, they just fade away.

Privates, they love their beer, three times a day.
Corporals, they love their stripes, and that ain't hay.
Sergeants put you through the mill, they just drill and drill and drill,
And they will drill until they fade away.

Old soldiers never die, never die, never die,
Old soldiers never die, they just fade away.

Young soldiers shine their shoes, three times a day.
Young soldiers go on leave, they know the way,
Young soldiers say good-bye, kiss the girls and make them cry,
Then the girls all wonder why, they fade away.

Old soldiers never die, never die, never die,
Old soldiers never die, they just fade away.

Washington and Grant and Lee were all tried and true,
Eisenhower, Bradley, and MacArthur too,
They will live for evermore, till the world is done with war,
Then they'll close that final door, fading away.

Old soldiers never die, never die, never die,
Old soldiers never die, they just fade away . . . fade away . . . fade away . . . fade away . . . fade away.

CONTENTS

DEDICATION

This work is dedicated to three members of "the Greatest Generation."

OBERMAYER. HERMAN OBERMAYER "Obe." Loving husband, father, grandfather, great-grandfather, and friend, died peacefully in his sleep on May 11, 2016, at his home in Arlington, Virginia. He was ninety-one. He was married for fifty-eight years to the love of his life, Betty Nan L. Obermayer, who passed away in 2013. Mr. Obermayer's rich life spanned the worlds of journalism, publishing, and politics in both the United States and abroad. He was owner and publisher of the *Long Branch* (NJ) *Daily Record* from 1957 to 1971 and of the *Northern Virginia Sun* from 1963 to 1989, and he lived in the Washington area since 1971. He counseled newspapers in emerging democracies for the U.S. State Department from 1990 to 2002 in Hungary, Poland, Lithuania, Latvia, Estonia, Ukraine, Moldova, Slovenia, Macedonia, Russia, Croatia, and Serbia.

He also wrote several significant books: *Soldiering for Freedom: A GI's Account of World War II* about his experiences as a U.S. Army soldier in the European Theatre, published in 2005; *Rehnquist: A Personal Portrait of the Distinguished Chief Justice of the U.S.* about his friendship with the renowned justice, a 2009 work that was translated into Chinese and became a best seller in China; and *Jews in the News: British and American Newspaper Articles about Jews 1665 through 1800*. Additionally, he donated his collection of 3,100 original newspaper articles to the Folger Shakespeare Library in Washington. While publisher of the *Northern Virginia Sun*, he wrote a weekly column about his life, politics, and philosophy. In 1983 and 1984, he served as a judge for the prestigious Pulitzer Prize.

Obe Obermayer was born in Philadelphia, PA, on September 19, 1924, where he graduated from Central High School. He graduated cum laude from Dartmouth College in 1946 as an English major, studying under the poet Robert Frost. His college years were interrupted by World War II, during which he served as a staff sergeant in the European Theatre from 1943–1946 and was awarded the Rhineland Campaign Star. He attended the Nuremberg Trials. As a teen, he became an Eagle Scout, and as an adult he was a member of the Executive Council of the Monmouth County (N.J.) Boy Scout Council from 1958–1971 and on the Executive Committee of the National Capital Council of the Boy Scouts of America from 1971–79. He also worked with the Jewish Policy Center and served on the National Board of the Jewish Institute for National Security Affairs (JINSA) since 1996 and the National Council of the American Jewish Committee (AJC). From 1989 to 2006, he was on the board of *Commentary*, a monthly magazine focused on religion, Judaism, politics, social and cultural issues.

Mr. Obermayer was an active member of many other clubs and organizations, including Temple Rodef Shalom (Falls Church, VA), the Washington Golf & Country Club (Arlington, VA), Cosmos Club (Washington, DC), Mont Pelerin Society, National Press Club (Washington, DC), Dartmouth Club (New York City, NY), Rotary Club, and Sigma Chi.

He is survived by his four daughters, Helen Levy-Myers of Reston, VA, Veronica Atnipp of Houston, TX, Adele Malpass of New York City, NY, and Elizabeth Weintraub of Rockville, MD; eleven grandchildren and one great-granddaughter (*Washington Post*, May 13, 2016).

I lost my hero on Tuesday, July 28, 2015, when he passed away at St. Mary's Hospital in Decatur, Illinois. He also happened to be my father, Myron D. MacLean. Born on September 4, 1923, in

Peoria, "Mac" was a true son of the Great Depression; his father was a coal miner who died of heart failure at age forty-eight, when Dad was thirteen—today we would probably ascribe the death to black lung disease. His mother taught grade school. Childcare centers didn't exist in those days, so when Dad was five or six, his father would take him to the mine and he would sleep in a mine shaft, next to the canary.

Now the man of the family, Dad graduated from Peoria High School before attending Bradley University for two years prior to serving as an infantryman in Company B, 1st Battalion, 39th Infantry Regiment, in the Hürtgen Forest and Battle of the Bulge in World War II. "Mac" always claimed he made corporal; mother insisted that he topped out at private first class. At any rate, he was wounded several times, received a Silver Star and Combat Infantryman's Badge, and—after his last wound—when he regained consciousness, he was looking down the business end of a German paratrooper's assault rifle. The Germans took his boots, and since it was January 1945, his feet became frostbitten. Years later, my brother, David, and I would watch *Hogan's Heroes* on television, and the young lad made the mistake of asking Dad if that was what a prisoner of war camp was like; he received a scowl as an answer. As a reminder, every morning when we were in school, Dad would wake us up about 6:00 a.m., throwing open the door with a bang, flipping on the overhead light, wrenching the curtains back to reveal the sun, and loudly screaming in German, "Raus . . . Raus," the same words the German barracks sergeant in Stalag 6G would yell at the prisoners of war to get them outside for roll call.

After the war, Dad got his degree in 1947 from the University of Illinois, as the returning World War II GIs majored in fraternities, football, and females. Sixty-three years later he pled ignorance as to where the university library was located.

To paraphrase the movie *Rudy*, Dad was "5 foot nothin', 100 and nothin'," and yet I saw him smash drive after drive, each one straight as an arrow and close to 300 yards on the golf course, while I caddied for him. I remember one memorable round when he carded a 69—no mulligans, no winter rules, no TV tap-ins, no kicking the ball out of the rough when nobody's looking, because he said it was more important to do the right thing when no one was looking than it was when they were—just a pure 69. I think he won two bucks that morning, and I know he paid me four. He liked Jack and Tiger, but he loved Arnie—living and dying with his hero during charge after charge on the final day of a major.

Dad also loved Caterpillar Tractor Company; he loved his granddaughters, Heather and Megan; and most of all he loved my Mom, Julie Lane MacLean. They had been married almost sixty years when she passed away in 2008; also on July 28. For the last several years of her life, the saints at Decatur Memorial Hospital provided her with a restful life, while Dad went over for every meal to help her eat—knowing that she would never again be able to say the words "Thank You." And later, the wonderful people at St. Mary's did the same for Dad, making his last hours peaceful.

Knowing that I would never be able to swing a golf club like Dad, I went to West Point—as did David—in part to see if I could catch "the old man" as a soldier. After thirty years in the Army, I realized that I was chasing a champion that I could never catch, let alone surpass. And I am happy in that knowledge, because that's the way it is supposed to be with your hero.

Sergeant and Military Police (MP) guard Richard A. Mosley served at the Loire Disciplinary Training Center, during which time he escorted seven condemned men to the gallows, three of them hanged by MSgt. John C. Woods. The son of Irish immigrants, Mosley was born in Pineville, Kentucky, on February 22, 1904. He joined the Navy in World War I but received a discharge for being underage. He spent five years at the University of Illinois, studying electrical and mechanical engineering, and was subsequently the foreman for an automobile service center.

Although Richard Mosley was partially blind in one eye, he entered the Army at Los Angeles on August 1, 1942, and became a powerhouse engineer. After arriving in Great Britain on June 1, 1943, he was transferred to new duties as a military specialty 635—disciplinarian, an appropriate duty since he stood 6'5" tall and weighed 203 pounds, with a 46" chest and a 34" waist. On March 1, 1945, he became a first sergeant in the 1008th Engineer Services Battalion. Mosley was discharged at Ft. MacArthur, California, on August 31, 1945. He was awarded the Good Conduct Medal, the World War II Victory Medal, and the European–African–Middle Eastern Campaign Medal with a Bronze Service Star for Northern France. Mosley lived in Hanford, California, until his death on January 5, 1953. He is buried at Grangeville Cemetery in Armona, California.

However, this is only part of the story. Richard Mosley asked for the transfer out of the Seine Disciplinary Training Center, for the simple reason that his duty of escorting prisoners to the gallows and watching them be executed was killing him. He could not sleep at night, waking up frequently with severe pain in his kidneys and bladder—beginning just five days after his first execution duty—as documented in *The Fifth Field: The Story of the 96 American Soldiers Sentenced to Death and Executed in Europe and North Africa in World War II*.

Family members of Sgt. Richard A. Mosley contacted the author with additional information about a year after *The Fifth Field* was published.

Richard Mosley had died in 1953, but not as I had presumed, of natural causes. The actual cause of death was a suicide. For decades after his death, his widow, Lela Ann (Askew) Mosley, and his children questioned themselves as to whether they may have contributed to the decision to end his life. Unfortunately, Mrs. Mosley died in 1992, and Sgt. Mosley's son, Richard A. Mosley Jr., died in 2013, just months before the book was published.

Sgt. Richard A. Mosley did not take his own life over family issues. He did not take his own life over financial issues. During his time as a guard, Sgt. Mosley displayed numerous acts of kindness toward condemned prisoners; a witness to one execution, an old Frenchman, recalled in 2011 in person to the author how Sgt. Mosley let a condemned man smoke a last cigarette before climbing the dreaded thirteen steps of the gallows far, far from home. No, Sgt. Richard A. Mosley— the hardscrabble kid from Pineville in southeast Kentucky at the crossing of the Cumberland River by the Wilderness Road, where coal was king and the deep mines took the lives of far too many young men—was too tough a man to let a passel of kids or monthly bills get to him.

But watching, and participating in, the hangings of young man after young man—many from difficult backgrounds such as his own, that was a different matter. He could transfer out of the unit, but he could not transfer out of his mind what he had seen and done there. Richard A. Mosley was a classic case of posttraumatic stress disorder, and he was unable to get the help he needed before it overwhelmed him.

So Lela Ann and Richard Jr.: be thou at peace.

FOREWORD

An Expert's View

MSgt. John C. Woods was truly one of those men who had a job as a soldier that no other soldier wanted: to execute by hanging those men who had been condemned to death by courts-martial or military tribunal. *American Hangman* tells the story of these hangings, of which there were a total of ninety. But the book also is a biography of Woods, who perhaps not surprisingly was an unusual individual.

The author, Col. (Ret). French L. MacLean, is ideally suited to write the story of Sergeant Woods and these military executions, since his earlier book, *The Fifth Field*, was the first to examine in any detail the death sentences carried out by the US Army in Europe in World War II. It took Col. MacLean twelve years to write *The Fifth Field*, and, in the course of researching this book, he learned that John Woods was the hangman (or assistant hangman) for thirty-six of these executions. This means that *American Hangman* is inexorably linked to *The Fifth Field*; the books are companions.

In reading this fascinating history of hangings and a hangman, the reader should keep a few thoughts in mind. First, this was a different Army and a different America. Few Americans questioned the appropriateness of the death penalty for murder, and, while more might question whether death was fitting for rape, most did not. In short, a hanging was expected where a life had been taken or a woman violated. Second, the reader should remember that in cases where the victim (or victims) were civilians in areas only recently liberated from Nazi rule, the US Army was worried that local civilians might see the Americans as little different from their previous occupiers. As historian Antony Beevor writes in *D-Day: The Battle for Normandy*, some 70,000 French civilians had been killed during the Allied invasion of France. Towns and villages had been flattened by bombing. The future looked bleak. The French appeared willing to accept this death and devastation because they were rid of the Germans, who had behaved badly in France during the occupation. But when American GIs committed murders and rapes, did this mean that one set of occupiers had simply been replaced by another? Gen. Dwight D. Eisenhower, the senior US commander in Europe, did not want the French to think that German SOBs had been replaced by American SOBs, and this explains, at least in part, why Eisenhower did not hesitate to approve the hangings that John Woods would carry out.

As for Woods, it was a dirty job, but someone had to do it. But as MacLean shows, Woods got the job as hangman because he lied about his experience and, in learning how to hang the condemned "on the job," Woods botched more than a few executions. That said, a little suffering for those who had been condemned to death might well be deserved, especially the ten Nazis, hanged by Woods, who had committed such evil acts as part of the Final Solution.

As for Woods's mysterious death in Eniwetok, MacLean presents crucial new historical evidence that shows the Army report was flawed and that at least one person thought it might have been murder—a revenge killing carried out by German scientists working on the atoll. As with many excellent teachers, MacLean leaves it up to the readers to make up their own minds after looking at the evidence in this fine book.

Fred L. Borch, Colonel, US Army, Ret.
Regimental historian and archivist
Judge Advocate General's Corps, US Army

FOREWORD

In a perfect world I would not be writing this book; that accomplishment would belong to Herman "Obe" Obermayer. My opinion is based on two facts: First, "Obe" was not just aware of John Woods; he actually knew and carefully observed the hangman at the height of his profession and was a firsthand witness to what Woods said and how he interacted with others. Second, as you will shortly read, "Obe" was a much-better writer than I will ever be; this was perhaps because he studied literature at Dartmouth under Robert Frost—Pulitzer Prize and Congressional Gold Medal winner—while US Army major Robert F. Foley had the nearly impossible task of starting to turn me into a second lieutenant at West Point in 1970. To be honest, I had the better deal, since Maj. Foley had received the Medal of Honor.

We do not live in a perfect world, but fortunately I was able to work with Mr. Obermayer for several years before his passing—assisting him to research aspects of the final months of MSgt. Woods's life. "Obe" had been planning a biography of John Woods and knew of my work on Woods with respect to *The Fifth Field*. While he mentioned that he had crafted a 10,000-word outline for submission to a publisher, I never saw that document—I am sure much to the detriment of this book.

So let us do the next best thing. A foreword, according to the *Chicago Manual of Style*, is usually written by someone other than the author or editor, usually someone eminent. In November 1946 at Dartmouth College, "Obe" wrote the most definitive period description of Army hangman MSgt. John C. Woods ever created. His description below is why you should read this book.[1]

CLEAN, PAINLESS, AND TRADITIONAL
BY HERMAN J. OBERMAYER

At 2:36 on October 16, 1946, and during the ninety minutes before that, an alcoholic, ex-bum Army sergeant was one of the most important men in the world. In the gymnasium of a dull, greystone courthouse in the midst of the ruins of Nurnberg he deftly tied ten hangman's knots, fitted ten black hoods, and ten times tripped a simple lever.

MSgt. John Woods, the official European Theater of Operations hangman and possessor of one of the Army's most unusual spec numbers, was a friend of mine. Not a personal friend but a business friend. A year ago I was the clerk who

typed the papers which ordered Woods to execute those American soldiers who, in haste or drunkenness, had raped or murdered frauleins.

He had one of those shockingly typical faces that you never forget. It was not like anything I had seen before, but as soon as I saw it my mind made that face part of a *Time* cover where it was framed with a heavy noose. It did not come out of Frankenstein or Dracula or Dick Tracy but of the most sordid part of real life. In the upper center of his round, leathery, weather-beaten face, his two owlish eyes were deeply set; his crooked yellow teeth, foul breath, and dirty neck showed a lack of attention to his toilet. His thinning hair, weathered face, and tired posture made him look every bit of his forty-four years.

He was short, obviously muscular and strong. Here was a man who you were sure had handled a pick and shovel at some point in his career and if challenged could use his fists. If he had worn a celluloid eye shade, he would have looked like one of the men who deals cards in a tough gambling house. His dress was always sloppy. His dirty pants were always unpressed, his jacket looked as though he had slept in it for weeks, his Master Sergeant stripes were attached to his sleeve by a single stitch of yellow thread at each corner, and his crumpled hat was always worn at the improper angle. Although he never raised his voice or threw chairs around bars, he was tough and everybody who had any contact with him knew it.

I spent two days with John Woods in Frankfurt last year and a month ago had no trouble picturing that man who, after hanging ten men in ninety minutes, rubbed his hands together and with hard, steady eyes calmly told a reporter, "I wasn't nervous. I haven't any nerves." He liked his job, not because he enjoyed hearing the unforgettable crack, but because, by his standards, it was a cinch. He worked less than thirty days a year, was treated like an important personality, and in his master sergeant's pay he had a regular salary while most hangmen, like clothing workers, are paid for piece work. The Nurnberg detail was just another job to for him. I'm sure his approach to it was much more like that of the union workman who stands on the slaughtering block in a Kansas City packing house than that of the proud French fanatic who guillotined Marie Antoinette in the Place de la Concorde.

We met for the first time last November, when he was passing through Frankfurt on his way to Heidelberg to dispose of a few Germans who had been condemned by an American Military Government court. He was expected on the morning train, but when I met the train, he wasn't there. This was surprising, as a Brig. Gen. had specially requested that he be given a berth on the "For Officers Only" Paris–Frankfurt sleeper, but MSgt. Woods and T/4 Mickey Rooney didn't have to obey officers. Everybody in headquarters was upset as the execution could not go on without him, and although the scheduled time for an execution is supposedly secret, Goering and all other prisoners seem to know exactly when it will take place. A stay makes the maintenance of discipline and morale very difficult.

As soon as I told Gen. Wessels that Sgt. Woods was not on the train, he became the tough, efficient headquarters' general described in Hanson Baldwin dispatches. Within ten minutes he was giving orders, placing long-distance telephone calls on special trunk lines, making first lieutenants check enlisted men's rec halls for the irreplaceable sergeant, and muttering so that everybody could hear it, "That ungrateful son of a bitch."

Sgt. Woods finally arrived by jeep early in the afternoon. His shoes were caked with mud, and his face was dirty and unshaven after a long ride from Le Mans to Frankfurt. Without combing his hair, changing his dirty clothes, or asking permission of Gen. Wessels's aide or secretary, he nonchalantly walked through the offices of three lieutenants to the general's office. It had the atmosphere of a throne room instead of an office of a minor executive in a large headquarters with its heavy velvet hangings, large raised desk flanked on either side by allied flags, and a green runner which ran from the door to the desk across an oriental rug. You wondered whether the improper gesture on entering room 301, Burgerstrasse Building, was a genuflexion or a salute.

When Sgt. Woods opened the door, the general got up from behind his desk, walked toward the door, extended his hand, and with a friendly smile across his face said, "Good to see you Woods. Where have you been?" He cockily answered with that I-know-my-way-around-don't-mess-with-me air that he wasn't sure what kind of rope they had in Heidelberg so he brought along his favorite hemp in a jeep. To satisfy a whim, he had deliberately disobeyed an order from the provost marshal general, and without telling anyone but a sergeant at Le Mans, he had taken a necessary jeep and driven from the Loire Disciplinary Training [Center] for five days. Nobody reprimanded him; the general only questioned him about how he felt after the long ride and jokingly asked why he was so interested in his work that he preferred K-rations in a jeep to a hot meal in a fancy diner. Then Gen. Wessels told me to take the day off to make sure that Sgt. Woods had everything he wanted in Frankfurt.

Woods had enough points to go home and get out of the Army. He spent twelve years in the Army, fought in North Africa, and landed on Utah Beach early on D-day morning, but he was considering reenlistment. The authorities knew that he had offers from United States jails which paid almost as much as the $160 a month he received as a master sergeant with four hitches, and the brass tried to make the position of European Theater of Operations hangman more attractive than his civilian offers. Generals, colonels, everybody in authority, even the Army's most chicken officers pampered Woods.

The thing all men overseas wanted most was to go back to the States, but after that the thing the men in the European Theater requested most often was a furlough to either Denmark or Switzerland. Sgt. Woods like everybody else wanted a furlough to Switzerland, but he did not have to sweat out lists, priorities, allotments, or the whims of personnel officers. One day Colonel [Morris T.] Warner, the commanding officer of the Loire DTC, telephoned from Le Mans to Frankfurt to say that Woods had applied for a Swiss furlough. He also wanted to know if there was anything the men in headquarters could do to expedite it. As soon as Gen. Wessels had this information, he called SHAEF G-1, who passed a priority order down through channels, and in less than a week after he applied, John Woods had a Swiss furlough.

When he came to our office in November, everybody wanted to see him. He was already legendary, and a personal impression of the theater hangman is the sort of stuff that makes good reading in letters home. Not everybody envied him, but everybody was interested in seeing him. We all speculated on why he had chosen his particular profession, what his wife was like, and how he lived with himself. The girls stared at him, tried to discuss the technical points of hanging, and didn't very effectively suppress giggles when he came into the room. Instead of treating John Woods like just another GI, they treated him like a cross between an escapee from a midway freak show and a minor war hero. He wasted little time with our overloved, overtoasted, none-too-demure WACS who made a big fuss over him. Although they plied him with questions, he told them nothing about his job except the obvious thing that he thought a hangman's lot was rather a good one. He was definitely not an after-dinner speaker.

In the evening, uncorked by some schnapps and Armagnac from the enlisted men's bar, he told some gory talks which will make chills run up and down my spine long after I am tired of the usual run ghost or combat stories. He described what it was like to walk into a man's cell the day before he was scheduled to be executed, to measure and feel the texture of his neck so he could decide exactly how tight the noose should be tied and where the knot should be placed to break the neck most easily. He pointed out that the placing of the knot is very important, for only if the knot is placed between the ear and spinal column will the neck break immediately. In most Army hangings, they use a rubber suction cup on the inside of the knot to make sure it doesn't slip. Even the man without nerves admitted he was ill at ease when he walked into the condemned men's cells. Although they sometimes tried to talk to him and ask him questions, he never said a word to them. He also told us how men reacted when they walked their last steps up the gallows. Without emotion or apparent feeling, he told us how big men would cry as they were about to drop through the gallows trap, and how weak men would flinch and shy away at the very end.

In a more-or-less drunken moment, one of the men in our little group asked Woods whether he would prefer to die in the electric chair, the gas chamber, or the gallows, and, knowing what he did about judicial executions, did he consider it a relatively pleasant way to die? It seemed like such a foolish question that I was embarrassed. But Woods looked directly at all of us and said, "You know, I think it's a damn good way to die; as a matter of fact, I'll probably die that well myself." Before I could say anything, somebody else at the table had said, "Aw, for Christ's sake, be serious, that's nothing to kid about!" Woods paused and said, "I'm damn serious. It's clean and it's painless, and it's traditional."

That it was clean and painless I understood, but when he said it was traditional, I didn't know whether he was joking or serious. However, before I had much time to think about the question, he continued, "It's traditional with hangmen to hang themselves when they get old. The Limie who was the hangman at Shepton Mallet before I got there was a third-generation hangman, and both his father and grandfather had taken their own lives on the gallows. The present hangman told me that he expects to, and he claims he's told his wife."

We were all duly impressed, and before Woods had a chance to get another drink, someone asked him whether he expected to end his life that way. Again he didn't hesitate or evade the question, and he tried hard not to be dramatic as he answered, "I can't think of a better way to die. When the time comes I'll probably save myself a lot of grief and pain that you guys will have."

PREFACE

Just after the 9/11 terrorist attacks, as a teacher at the National War College I visited the Office of the Clerk of Court, US Army Legal Services Agency, in Arlington, Virginia. Anticipating that the US military would sooner or later catch some of the terrorists involved in the plot, my question to them was quite simple, "What did we do in past conflicts when we captured someone roughly equivalent to a modern terrorist?" We subsequently discussed German saboteurs who reached our shores in World War II via U-boats, and other fascinating historical anecdotes.

After several hours, I began to leave, when one of the marvelous staff of the Clerk of Court's Office asked me in passing, "Would you like to see the death book?" Not wanting to wonder the rest of my days what I had missed seeing, should I decline, and sensing that whatever it was it must be interesting, I sputtered: "Yes." What was handed to me was an old, green, oversized ledger book with neat handwritten entries—in fountain pen ink—concerning dozens of capital crimes cases involving Army personnel in World War II. All of them ended with a death penalty, either by hanging or "by musketry." Over multiple visits— the professors at the National War College are not an overworked lot—I spent hours poring over the entries; while I had recalled reading about the Eddie Slovik case, I had no idea that there were dozens more cases in Europe ending in execution.

It was more than dozens. The United States Army executed ninety-six soldiers—American soldiers—in the European, Mediterranean, and North African theaters of operation alone. Many more executions occurred in the United States and in the Pacific. After what I surmised was my last visit, I returned the ledger, at which time the lady who had handed it to me on each occasion asked, "Would you like to see the case files?" Once again, I jumped at the opportunity, amazed to find that many files were in a walk-in closet at the office. Picking the first file at random, I found a heavy envelope in which was a knife—with blood residue still on it—used in a murder. I was hooked, and the clerk of court's office kept the files ready for me whenever I called.

Over the next dozen years, I put the story together and wrote *The Fifth Field*. Three revelations occurred during this process: First, I realized that the hangman, or assistant hangman, for half of the executions was a MSgt. John C. Woods, and just from the official accounts, it was clear that Woods was the most fascinating character in the story. Second, I met two individuals—whom you will meet later—who personally knew and worked with Woods during the war or shortly after it. Their recollections were far more important than any description of Woods, in part because in the seventy years since his death, no one had bothered to publish a biography of the man. Certainly, magazines had a field day with MSgt. Woods, who could never pass up the opportunity to talk with anyone who had a pencil and notebook, or a news camera; after all, he was newsworthy.

John Woods certainly was a complex character. His rapid-fire drawl and claim of birthplace gave rise to the conclusion that he was a hard-bitten Texan, when in truth he was born and raised in Kansas, the product of a broken home.[1] Woods was fond of dogs and enjoyed doing magic tricks for his young nieces and nephews. On the other hand, given the outrageous numbers of what most observers would describe as botched executions, one might wonder if Woods's performances on the gallows might not suggest that he was more sadistic than inept. Given the magnitude of the horrendous acts of the Nazis that Woods executed—culminating in his hanging ten of the top Nazis of Germany as the final act of the International Military Tribunal at Nürnberg on October 16, 1946—others may conclude that the American hangman should be remembered for administering justice for millions of victims of the Nazis Holocaust.

The final revelation was a stunner: for years, rumors had circulated that in July 1950 Woods had died at Eniwetok Atoll, in the Pacific, of electrocution, when something went horribly wrong as he was testing an electric chair that the US Army had decided might be required for military executions during the Korean War. Those rumors turned out to be completely false. Woods had been electrocuted, but no electric chair was ever involved.

What was far more interesting was an assertion by one of the men who personally knew Woods just after World War II ended in Europe. This individual, an accomplished publisher, writer, and close friend of a former chief justice of the United States Supreme Court, believed—after years of detailed study and archive combing—that it was no accident that killed John Woods. It was murder.

ACKNOWLEDGMENTS

Marilyn Bogle and Hazel Russell, Greenwood County Historical Society and Museum, Eureka, Kansas

T. G. Bolen, Decatur, Illinois

Col. (Ret). Fred L. Borch, regimental historian and archivist, the Judge Advocate General's Corps, Charlottesville, Virginia, and former chief prosecutor, Office of Military Commissions, US Department of Defense

Matthew E. Braun and Kevin Burford, University of Iowa Law Library, Iowa City, Iowa

Brig. Gen. (Ret). David Carey, Col. (Ret). Malcolm II. Squires Jr., and Mary Chapman, Office of the Clerk of Court, US Army Judiciary, Ballston, Virginia

Beth Ann Chilcott, Linda Clark, Carol Stock, and Anna Dale Chilcott Cole, nieces of Hazel Woods, Kansas

Rich Closs and John Closs, co-owners of Closs Electric, Decatur, Illinois

Kaitlyn Crain Enriquez and Dr. Tim Nenninger, National Archives and Records Administration (NARA), College Park, Maryland

Dean Gall, Susan Nash, Eric Ki lgore, Karen Schwarm, Donna Noelken, Theresa Fitzgerald, Kayla A. Hays, and Chris Secrest, National Personnel Records Center (NPRC) St. Louis, Missouri

Heather Hale, Dynagraphics Inc. / Fast Impressions, Decatur, Illinois

Brig. Gen. (Ret). Steve Hawkins, Jeffrey Aarnio, David Atkinson, Geoffrey Fournier, James Woolsey, Nathalie Le Barbier, and Michael G. Conley, American Battle Monuments Commission, Washington, DC

Janice Leitch, Alvin Morris Administration Center, and Gwen Leivian, Wichita East High School, Wichita, Kansas

Paul Oberg, McCormick School Museum, Wichita, Kansas

Herman "Obe" Obermayer, Arlington, Virginia

Kassandra LaPrade Seuthe, US Holocaust Memorial Museum, Photography Research Section, Washington, DC

Ashley Robinson Skala, grandniece of Thomas F. Robinson, Gainesville, Georgia

Manfred Sommer, Rohrbach, Germany

Robert Tucker, Special Collections Department, Wichita Public Library, Wichita, Kansas

Dr. Thomas D. Veve, Cohutta, Georgia

Sgt. Tom Ward, Harrisburg, Pennsylvania

Florian Waitl, command historian, US Army Engineer School, Ft. Leonard Woods, Missouri

Kathy West, James Rogers, Staff Sergeant Andrew W. Peppers, and Bob Gunnarsson, US Military Police School, Ft. Leonard Wood, Missouri

INTRODUCTION

It was a scene that happened all too often when MSgt. John C. Woods was lurking in the background on a gallows. On October 31, 1944, Woods was serving as the assistant hangman in the execution of an American soldier: General Prisoner Paul M. Kluxdal at the Seine Disciplinary Training Center (Seine DTC) in Paris, France. Kluxdal had killed his first sergeant, Loyce M. "Robbie" Robertson, saying it had been an accident, but the court-martial didn't buy it. Since this was early in Woods's career, Maj. Mortimer H. Christian performed the duties of the hangman. MSgt. Woods, perhaps helped by his assistant, Technician Third Grade Thomas F. Robinson, had simple duties: adjust the black hood over the head of the condemned man and, most critically, slip the noose around Paul Kluxdal's neck and tighten the knot. Maj. Christian then promptly faced about and at 10:03 p.m. cut a light rope that released a heavy weight, which actuated the trapdoors to open. Paul Kluxdal's body silently hurtled through the square opening to eternity.

Then, all hell broke loose.

Paul Kluxdal's shoes hit the ground. At six feet tall, Kluxdal was several inches taller than most of the other soldiers Woods would hang over the next two years. Perhaps Woods had not measured the height of the condemned man before the execution. Perhaps he had not prestretched the rope the day before by suspending a sand-filled duffel bag from it—two imperatives that John Woods certainly had been taught years before, when he had served as an assistant hangman in Texas and Oklahoma, as he had claimed. That was another lie; he had not hanged anyone before joining the Army. In any case, the official Army report of execution minimized the impact of the ghastly event with classic understatement: "The toes of the shoes barely touched the floor, did not support any weight, but prevented the body from swaying."

That may have been the observation written in the report—which became the official version of the events. However, when the medical officer entered the lower portion of the scaffold—screened with canvas to prevent official observers from "seeing how the sausage is made"—to examine the condemned man's body at 10:15 p.m., the officer found that Paul Kluxdal was still alive. The doctor then waited six additional minutes—a total of eighteen minutes that a man dangled alive at the end of the rope—before he determined that Paul Kluxdal finally was dead.

We will find that this was not the only example where written reports were at odds with what actually transpired concerning John C. Woods, one of the most enigmatic figures in American history.

Chapter 1
LINEAGE

James Baldwin, American novelist, essayist, playwright, poet, and social critic, is reported to have once said, "If you know whence you came, there are absolutely no limitations to where you can go." While his assertion may be accurate, there is no evidence that John Woods was especially interested in his family history, or that he ever researched his ancestors. Had he done so, he would have found his roots going back to England some three hundred years.

On his mother's side of the family, great-great-great-great-great-great-great-grandfather John Wooters was born in 1651 in Coventry, England. He married a woman named Martha, and among their children was Phillip Wooters, who was born on April 25, 1686, in the same city. Phillip, in turn, married Priscilla Satchwell; the couple had a son, Richard Wooters, who was born in 1710 in Coventry. The Wooters family apparently decided that their future lay in the colonies, and they arrived in Maryland in 1716. Richard Wooters would die in August 1754, but not before marrying a woman named Elizabeth (last name possibly Shadrack) and siring a son, Ezekial Shadrack Wooters, who was born in 1730 in Queen Anne's County, Maryland. Ezekial remained in Maryland most of his life, passing away on December 5, 1771, in Caroline, Maryland.[1]

It would appear that Ezekial married Hannah Dunbar in what would become North Carolina; the couple had a son, John Wooters, born in 1761 in Guilford, North Carolina. John, who later married Courtney Lewis, fathered a son, Levin, in 1787, in Maryland. Levin, in turn, married Sarah Richardson in 1807. Sarah had been born in 1790 in Maryland. However, now the family was on the move westward—specifically to what would become Raccoon Township, Marion County, Illinois; Sarah would die in this southern Illinois

location in 1870, at the ripe old age of eighty.[2]

John C. Woods's great-grandfather, Nathan L. Wooters, was born in December 1826 in Raccoon Township, Marion County, Illinois, the son of Levin Wooters and Sarah Richardson; he married Sarah C. Ray on October 2, 1845, in Marion County, Illinois, and died in Central City, Bond County, Illinois, on March 28, 1881, a year after his wife had passed away in 1880.[3] Sarah Richardson's family had come west from North Carolina. The couple appeared to have had several children and to have also changed their last name to Wootrus: John M. Wootrus (born 1860), Mary H. Wootrus (born 1862), and Jackson Wootrus (born 1864).[4]

John M. Wootrus married a woman by the name of Mary S., nicknamed "Susie"; they had a daughter, Susie E. Wootrus, born in July 1879. John and his young family lived next to Nathan, his father, in Centralia, Marion County, Illinois, until about 1884.[5] Mary S. had been born about 1866 in Illinois. The family left Illinois in 1884 on their own journey westward, similar to millions of other European-descended Americans. In 1885, the Wootrus family lived in Harvey, Sedgwick County, Kansas, where John worked as a farmer.[6] John C. Woods's mother, Martha "Mattie" A. Wootrus, was born in Kansas in February 1890, the daughter of John M. and Mary S. "Susie" Wootrus. It was by then a large family. Mattie had five sisters (Annie J., Bertha E., Emma I., Teasa A., Eva E.) and one brother (Christian Wootrus). In 1900, the Wootrus family lived in Hutchinson, Reno County, Kansas.[7]

John C. Woods's father's side of the family was almost certainly from England, although traces of the Woods family go back only as far as 1753 in New Jersey. Here, John's great-great-great-grandfather Samuel D. Woods was born in 1753.

Samuel was married twice; from his second wife, Mary Ann McCoy, a son was born on March 16, 1803, in Washington County, Pennsylvania, and he would be named Samuel D. Woods Jr. Samuel D. Woods Jr. married Leah Divers in 1827 in Greene County, Pennsylvania. She was born in 1806 in Maryland, and her parents were John Divers and Anna Ford (who married in Fayette County, Pennsylvania, on December 31, 1799). The couple had nine children, including a son, James W. Woods, who was born in 1838, in Greene County. Unlike his parents—who died in Fayette County, Pennsylvania, in 1887 and 1885, respectively—James W. Woods headed west and married Mary Elizabeth Ashkettle on May 5, 1864, in Bellevue, Jackson County, Iowa; her family was also from Pennsylvania. James and Elizabeth had had three sons and three daughters, one of whom, Clarence E. Woods, was born in 1866 in the town of Clay, Wayne County, Iowa.[8]

Clarence E. Woods married a woman named Annie A. in 1887. Lee Roy Woods, who would become John C. Woods's father, was born November 23, 1888, in Kansas, the son and first child of Clarence E. Woods and Annie A. Often known as Roy while employed by the Wichita Construction Company, Lee Roy married Martha A. "Mattie" Wootrus at her home on 619 East Kellogg Street on December 23, 1905, in Wichita, Kansas. Reverend John R. Wilkie officiated at the ceremony. The *Wichita Daily Eagle* reported the event the following day.[9]

As with so much concerning John C. Woods, existing information of his heritage does not tell us much. Both sides of his family very likely—his mother's, certainly—emigrated from England. It is probable that his ancestors were Protestant and had strong backgrounds in farming. These characteristics did not put John C. Woods outside a large number of Americans in the early 1900s.

What John C. Woods did later in life would put him outside the mainstream of America. In fact, it would put him in a category of just one.

Chapter 2
HARDSCRABBLE YOUTH

John Clarence Woods was born in Wichita, Kansas, on June 5, 1911, the third child of Lee Roy Woods and Mattie A. Wootrus. Woods had two sisters (Jennie Woods and June M. Woods, born 1907) and one brother (James M. Woods, born July 2, 1908). A year later, the Woods family resided at 1229 South Market in Wichita; at the time, Lee Roy's occupation was listed as a foreman.[1]

The Woods family lived at 429 East Lewis in Wichita in 1913; Lee Roy Woods was a foreman with the Wichita Construction Company. During this year, Lee Roy and Mattie separated. The Wichita directory for 1914 indicated that Mattie Woods resided at 825 South St. Francis Avenue. Lee Roy was not listed in the directory for this year; he may have left Wichita. Mattie's parents, John M. and Susie, lived at 527 South Washington Avenue.[2] By 1915, Mattie was living at 300 West 2nd Avenue, a few doors from her parents. Lee Roy Woods was still not shown as residing in Wichita.[3] Mattie Woods, still separated from her husband, subsequently moved next to her parents with her four children. Her address in 1916 was 444 North Washington Avenue.[4]

By 1918, Mattie's parents had moved to 703 South St. Francis Avenue; there was no mention of Mattie or Lee Roy in Wichita for that year.[5] There was also no mention of Mattie or Lee Roy in 1919 or 1920 in the Wichita city directory.

On September 8, 1921, the District Court of Wichita, Sedgwick County, Kansas, issued divorce papers for Lee Roy Woods and Mattie Wootrus. As part of the decree, Clarence E. Woods was awarded sole custody of John C. Woods, just ten years old, and he moved in with his grandparents at 1837 South Main.[6] In 1922, there was a Mattie Woods listed as the widow of Lee Roy Woods; she was serving as a domestic servant at 1409 South Hydraulic Avenue.[7] She later married George H. Cooper, a carpenter, and resided at 836 North Market. In 1924, John was still with his grandparents; his grandfather Clarence Woods was listed as a carpenter. John made some extra money for the family as a newspaper delivery boy for the *Wichita Beacon*.[8]

Probably in 1925 or 1926, John Woods entered Wichita High School at 2301 Douglas Avenue.[9] The facility, first established in 1878, was a traditional high school—noted for a high academic program and numerous state championships in sports. In 1925, the boys' basketball team, the "Bulldogs," won the National Interscholastic Basketball Tournament in Chicago, an early attempt by Amos Alonzo Stagg to create a national high-school champion, defeating El Reno High School 27–6 in the final. While Woods was in attendance, the boy's outdoor track and field team won the Kansas state championship in 1926. With Wichita growing, additional schools were created, and in 1929 the school was renamed Wichita High School East.

However, John Woods was not there to see the name change. He dropped out after his first year; since high school in Wichita at that time began with tenth grade, this made John a sophomore when he departed.[10] The city directory of 1928 lists John C. Woods as a student living at 1837 South Main Street, but Woods was not likely still in school. The same source shows a Martha Woods as a housekeeper at 2305 North Lawrence.[11] The following year, 1929, John Woods's address was listed as 1837 South Main Street, Wichita, Kansas (still the same as his grandmother Annie A. Woods's).[12]

John tried some on-and-off construction work, but the trade did not pan out. With no schooling to speak of, no job, and no foreseeable future in Wichita, maybe it was time for John Woods to get out of Kansas and see the world.

Chapter 3

IN THE NAVY,
YOU CAN SAIL THE SEVEN SEAS

With minimal prospects in his early life, John C. Woods, now eighteen, decided to join the United States Navy, applying to enlist on October 24, 1929, in Wichita, Kansas. Stating that he was a cook and also wanted to be a cook in the Navy, John attested that he had never been arrested, nor had he ever been in a reform school, jail, or penitentiary. He wrote that he was a Protestant and that he had previously had the measles, but not the mumps. Finally, the applicant listed ninth grade as his education level. He convinced three men in Wichita to submit statements attesting to his trustworthiness, general intelligence, and ability. Two of the signees stated that Woods's trustworthiness was "good"; the third wrote it was "average." All three individuals, who stated they had known Woods from between four months to four years, rated his general intelligence as "good." Two men marked "fair" concerning John's ability, while the third rated that as "average."[1]

Ironically, the same day that John Woods expressed his desire to join the Navy, the Wall Street stock market crashed; known as "Black Thursday," the market lost 11 percent of its value at the opening bell. Panic and chaos reigned supreme on the trading floor, and the crash signaled the beginning of the Great Depression that would devastate the nation and the world.

At the recruiting station in Kansas City, Missouri, on December 3, 1929, enlisting for a period of four years, Woods stated that his reason for enlisting was to learn a trade. With that, Lt. (j.g.). J. B. Stuart signed the enlistment form, certifying, "no promise of any kind concerning assignment to duty or promotion during this enlistment has been made." A quick initial medical examination by the physician on duty, Lt. G. F. Cooper, showed that Woods was five feet, three and a half inches tall, weighed 116 pounds, and had a ruddy complexion with blue eyes and brown hair.[2]

Anna B. Woods provided her consent as guardian on the Consent, Declaration, and Oath of Parent or Guardian form for John to enlist in the US Navy as an apprentice seaman. She wrote that she was his guardian and lived at 1837 South Main Street in Wichita, Kansas. Her husband, Clarence E. Woods—John's grandfather—signed the form.[3]

The same day, December 3, 1929, Woods received orders to transfer to San Diego, California, for training. He arrived there on December 6, 1929, undoubtedly traveling by train. Woods's file shows that on February 5, 1930, he signed his application for United States Government Life Insurance at the US Navy Training Station at San Diego. Chief Gunner J. S. Conover witnessed the signing. John listed Mrs. Anna B. Woods, his grandmother, as his full beneficiary.[4]

Apprentice Seaman John Woods then began tests and initial training. He achieved the following marks on his entrance test: General Classification, 74; Mechanical Aptitude, 70; Arithmetic, 70; English, 59; Spelling, 80; and Handwriting, 50.[5]

After initial training, Woods received an assignment to the USS *Saratoga* on February 12, 1930. It was originally conceived as one of six large battle cruisers, but the Five-Power Naval Arms Limitation Treaty at the Washington Disarmament Conference in 1922 led to its conversion to a new type of vessel—the aircraft carrier. Launched in 1925, the "Sara" reported for duty off Long Beach, California, in 1927; the following year, the flattop would begin participating in the Navy's annual "Fleet Problem" war game in the Pacific and would thus train many of the US Navy's aircraft carrier tacticians who would gain distinction in World War II.

However, John Woods would not be part of that journey. Woods became ill the same day as his assignment to the USS *Saratoga*, and he was admitted to the US Navy Hospital at San Diego. Woods was released from the hospital on February 21, 1930, and sent to duty on the USS *Melville*, a 7,265-ton destroyer tender, for later reassignment to the USS *Hovey*, a 1,190-ton *Clemson*-class destroyer. After serving around the world for four years, the *Hovey* had been decommissioned in 1923 at San Diego but was recommissioned on February 20, 1930, at San Diego under Cmdr. Stuart O. Greig. Her initial mission would be a shakedown cruise out of port.

Woods requested a one-day pass before the assignment and went on authorized leave on February 23. He did not return. The Navy declared him a straggler at 7:50 a.m. on February 24 for not reporting to the USS *Hovey*, and offered a reward of $25 for his apprehension, although no one seemed to know his location. On March 6, 1930, naval authorities declared Woods a deserter in accordance with Article 1692 of Navy Regulations, stating that Woods showed: "manifest intent to desert by not communicating with Commanding Officer." Supply authorities then sold Woods's effects at San Diego. Unknown to the Navy, Woods was long gone from California.[6]

He had nowhere to go but home to Wichita. We do not know his plan, but given his lack of money—and the state of transportation in the United States in 1930—John Woods likely decided to "ride the rails" [illegally hopping on freight trains] eastward. It was dangerous work; many railroad hoboes fell under the moving trains and were crushed to death as they attempted to board. Railroad guards, known as "bulls," brutally beat—and sometimes killed—illegal riders they found in the freight cars. Because of the guards, would-be riders usually could not walk into a railroad yard and climb on a stationary freight train. Instead, they would hide along the side of the tracks outside town and then jump on a slow-moving train before it gained speed. Then, as the

train slowed down outside the next town, riders would jump off before the "bulls" could spot and chase them. Additionally, while Woods may have had a small amount of food at the start of his journey, he had to figure out how to eat along the route—perhaps begging for food at farmhouses.

Fortunately for John Woods, the Atchison, Topeka & Santa Fe Railway ran the 1,420 miles from San Francisco, California, through Wichita to Chicago, and given where Woods would finally be apprehended at an important junction of the railroad, it seems likely that he rode the rails with the AT & SF. John likely headed east from Mare Island to Lathrop, California, where he caught a freight train heading south. Passing through Modesto, Fresno, and Tulare, the line curved east, taking Woods through Mojave and Barstow. Crossing Arizona, the deserter would have passed through Flagstaff and Winslow. The freight that Woods was on would have crossed into New Mexico and Albuquerque. Here the railroad turned northeast, passing through Las Vegas and Springer before entering Colorado and a major stop at La Junta in the southeastern part of the state. La Junta was a small town, but an important railroad junction, where the AT & SF line coming east from California merged with the line coming southeast from Utah. Now only 75 miles from Kansas, John could smell the way home from here.

He didn't make it. La Junta was crawling with "bulls" and law enforcement officers. In a way, John was lucky, and the civilian law enforcement authorities—rather than "bulls"—apprehended the diminutive Woods. They drove their prisoner 175 miles to the US Navy Recruiting Station at Denver at 11:30 a.m. on March 8, 1930. A naval official paid the La Junta police $50 for the apprehension and delivery of a deserter; Denver police then agreed to hold Woods in the Denver city jail for safekeeping until he could be transferred west. Three days later, the Navy took custody of John Woods and transported him to a receiving ship at San Francisco, California, where on March 13 he arrived onboard for a second time on the USS *Hovey*.[7]

Navy medical personnel gave Woods a quick examination that showed that he stood 62¼ inches tall and had a small lateral scar on his forehead and another one on his left wrist. He also had a smallpox vaccination mark on his left bicep. Lt. Cmdr. J. E. Potter signed the report. He was perfectly healthy for his next encounter with naval tradition—a summary court-martial. This proceeding met on March 31, 1930, to try Seaman Second Class John C. Woods for "Absent over Leave" for a period from February 24 to March 8. The court was short but not sweet for Woods; he received a sentence of solitary confinement on the USS *Hovey* on bread and water for thirty days (with full rations every third day).[8]

John Woods was on a downward spiral, but his commanding officer tried to halt his decline. Capt. Greig wrote a letter to the Bureau of Navigation, stating that he had removed the "mark of desertion" and had ordered that Woods's pay account would be recredited with any amounts that were due and unpaid beginning February 24.[9] And the word of Stuart O. Greig carried a great deal of weight in the Navy; as a lieutenant commander, and commanding officer of the US submarine K-6, he had been awarded the Navy Cross for patrolling the waters near the Azores, after the US entered the First World War.

However, a Navy physician was not so sure that Woods could become a good sailor. Upon the recommendation of the medical officer, the Navy transferred Woods on April 16, 1930, to the US Naval Hospital at Mare Island (San Francisco Bay) for observation. A Board of Medical Survey convened on April 23, 1930, at the US Naval Hospital at Mare Island. The report, submitted by Cmdr. W. M. Kerr, Lt. Cmdr. L. J. Roberts, and Lt. (j.g.) B. L. Roberson, reads: "This patient, though not intellectually inferior, gives a history of repeatedly running counter to authority both before and since enlistment. Stigmata of degeneration [moral degeneration] are present

and the patient frequently bites his fingernails. He has a benign tumor of the soft palate for which he refuses operation. His commanding officer and division officers state that he shows inaptitude and does not respond to instruction. He is obviously poor service material. This man has had less than five months service. His disability is considered to be an inherent defect for which the service is in no way responsible. [He] is not considered a menace to himself or others."[10]

The report also provided a diagnosis for John Woods—Constitutional Psychopathic Inferiority without Psychosis (#1501). The narrative added that the disability was not the result of the service member's own misconduct, but that the patient was unfit for the service, since the probable future duration of the condition was permanent. The report concluded that Woods "be discharged from the US Naval Service."[11]

The commanding officer at the Naval Hospital, Mare Island, RAdm. Ammen Ferenholt, approved the recommendation on April 25, 1930. The same day, Lt. Cmdr. C. F. Greene, in the Commandant's Office of the Navy Yard at Mare Island, forwarded the findings to the Bureau of Navigation, which approved the conclusions and sent a letter on May 6, 1930, to the US Naval Hospital at Mare Island to execute discharge proceedings.[12]

On May 15, 1930, the United States Navy granted Woods an ordinary discharge for reasons of physical disability in the line of duty and not the result of his own misconduct; the Navy chain of command had the option to issue the sailor an honorable discharge, but they chose the lesser-quality termination. The sailor was declared to be discharged for the convenience of the government; Woods was not recommended for any future reenlistment. With that, John C. Woods was discharged from the Navy and given $75.89 for his transportation home to Wichita from North Vallejo Wharf, near Mare Island. This time, he could pay for a ticket.[13]

Chapter 4

IT WAS THE BEST OF TIMES . . .
IT WAS THE WORST OF TIMES

Almost immediately after he returned to Wichita—probably along the same Atchison, Topeka & Santa Fe Railway except now on a passenger train—John Woods attempted to obtain an upgraded military discharge. On May 17, 1931, he wrote a short letter to the Bureau of Navigation in Washington, requesting a duplicate discharge. In his letter, John erroneously wrote that he had received an honorable disability discharge (it had been, in fact, an ordinary discharge). Woods ended the letter stating that he had been discharged on May 14, 1931, which appears to be an honest mistake in that he was discharged one year earlier. The envelope had the return address of 238½ North Main St. in Wichita. The Navy sent a blank application form to Woods to begin the process on May 20, 1931.[1]

On May 25, 1931, John Woods took the application and applied for a certificate in lieu of a discharge by going through Frances B. Wood, a notary public in Sedgwick County. Woods listed that he had served on the USS *Saratoga* and USS *Hovey* and listed Capt. "Graig" [Stuart O. Greig] as one of the officers with whom he served. Although Woods mentioned the hospital on Mare Island, he provided no additional information. He mentioned that his profession was now that of a farmer and that the original discharge had been destroyed in a fire on March 1, 1931, in Wichita. The bottom of the form found in the US Navy personnel file for John Woods has a pencil annotation stating that a replacement discharge was issued on Form #62 on June 8, 1931.[2]

Over the next several years, the Great Depression grew worse. Soil erosion and weather had caused massive, unrelenting clouds of black dust over Kansas wheat fields, while the statewide unemployment rate hit 26 percent in 1932.[3] In March 1933, the new president, Franklin D. Roosevelt, established the Civilian Conservation Corps (CCC) as one of the first New Deal programs. The CCC was actually a huge public-works project designed to promote environmental conservation and build good citizens through outdoor labor that was healthful, vigorous, and disciplined. Because of the intended massive magnitude of the program, President Roosevelt decided that the CCC would operate under the control of the US Army. Work camp commanders had disciplinary powers, and corpsmen were required to address superiors as "sir."

John Woods had been out of work since January 1932. Perhaps the CCC could assist the young, single man. On June 4, 1933, John Woods traveled to Ft. Leavenworth, Kansas, and enrolled in the corps, signing an oath of enrollment that ended with "I understand further that any infraction of the rules or regulations of the Civilian Conservation Corps renders me liable to expulsion therefrom." After Woods passed a perfunctory Army physical examination, Capt. Paul M. Robinett, of the Cavalry branch, signed him up for a stint in the corps.[4]

Woods, who had told the authorities that he was experienced in mechanical work and whose previous trade had included a mechanic and bridge builder, now learned another lesson when dealing with the military—the work camp commandant designated him as a cook, and he began serving in that capacity at the CCC camp at Ft. Leavenworth (the Headquarters Company for the Missouri District of the CCC) through June 23, 1933, where he performed in a satisfactory manner. The next day, the CCC transferred Woods to another work camp at Toronto, Kansas, and he began work at this small town 60 miles east of Wichita.[5] CCC Company 1715 was located at this camp, with a mission designated Project

S-204. The venture, one of the first three CCC developments in the state, was to build a lake, initially named Lake Fegan (now called Woodson County Lake), named after the landowner, Ben Fegan. An average of two hundred men worked each day over the course of thirty months, initially using shovels and transporting the dirt in mule-drawn wagons. Later, bulldozers did the bulk of the heavy work. The local populace welcomed the new project. On June 15, 1933, the *Toronto Republican* happily reported: "The streets here were the scene of some celebration this noon when the word came through that all was well, and rightly there should have been for this project is a big one and one that has been worked for very hard by local men and sportsmen."[6]

• • •

Now a mess sergeant in the CCC, John met Hazel Chilcott in nearby Toronto.[7] Hazel Marie Chilcott was born near Toronto on April 19, 1913, daughter of Harvey Rae Chilcott and Adeline Moon. Both parents had been born in Kansas. Her father's family had come from Pennsylvania and Illinois, while her mother's family hailed from Illinois. Hazel had an older brother, Kenneth, and four younger brothers, Enloe, John William, Dale, and Max; she also had a younger sister, Helen. Harvey Rae Chilcott was a farm laborer, and his wife tended house; he also worked for the railroad.[8] Hazel, a cute girl by all accounts, was fairly religious, hard-working, and about 5'6" tall, at least 2 inches taller than John.[9] Graduating from Toronto High School in 1931, she worked at the small Toronto Café, which was frequently visited on the weekends by CCC work crews.[10]

John Woods was getting serious about Hazel Chilcott, but once again he did not think things through and went absent without leave (AWOL) from the CCC on September 21, 1933, but not before being insubordinate to his work detail leader and refusing to work. These were grounds for expulsion, and on September 27, 1933, the

Civilian Conservation Corps dishonorably discharged John C. Woods from the program.[11]

Three days later, on Saturday evening, September 30, 1933, John Woods and Hazel Chilcott were married in Eureka, Greenwood County, Kansas, some 20 miles west of Toronto. We have incomplete knowledge of the event. We do not know if John had informed Hazel of his CCC termination. We know that he got cold feet just prior to the event, and while Hazel waited, a search party from her family scoured Eureka for the young man; her younger brother Dale and Leon Wilhite, Hazel's brother-in-law (the husband of Hazel's sister, Helen), finally found Woods at one of Eureka's "watering holes" and escorted him to the ceremony. We know that Probate Judge Roy L. Hamlin signed the marriage license.[12] In attendance were Hazel, her mother, and her sister, Helen; neither her father nor her brothers were present. Although John was obviously present, we do not know just how intoxicated he was on the fateful day. Mr. Victor Thomas, probably a witness for John, also attended, although none of his family in Wichita (62 miles west of Eureka) was present.[13] We do know that several members of the bride's family maintained ongoing misgivings of the match.[14]

The announcement of the marriage in the *Toronto Republican* (which reported that Woods was still with the CCC) stated that the couple departed for Wichita the day after the wedding; the first governmental indicator that they were in the larger city is in the 1935 Wichita city directory and lists their residence as 1449 North Topeka Ave., with John's occupation listed as a laborer.[15]

The US Navy replacement discharge may not have been what Woods desired. On July 1, 1936, John Woods, who was now living at 303 East Ohio, back in Eureka, Kansas, sent a second letter to the Bureau of Navigation, along with another application for a certificate in lieu of a military discharge. In the explanation, Woods said that he had lost his original discharge about September 1, 1935, during the process of moving. Woods stated in his letter that the lost document was an honorable disability discharge; once again, that was incorrect—the discharge had been the lesser-quality ordinary discharge. He also erroneously wrote on this application that he had never before applied for a replacement, which was untrue.[16]

There is no evidence that John and Hazel lived in Wichita between 1937 and 1941. Mattie Woods is also missing during this time, although Lee Roy Woods and his second wife, Mildred Luella Martin, lived in the city in 1940 at 2736 South Seneca.[17] John and Hazel can be found residing in Eureka on March 1, 1938.[18]

John must have had business in Wichita in 1939, however, because he ran into trouble there. According to family members, John was a serious gambler, but not a successful one, and Hazel frequently had to sell or pawn various possessions—such as her hand-crocheted items—to pay off his gambling debts.[19] In December 1939, John went too far and wrote a fraudulent $50 check. Wichita detective Floyd R. Gunsaullus apprehended Woods, and Grey Dresie, deputy Sedgwick County attorney, brought charges before Judge Grover Pierpont on December 22, 1939. Woods pled guilty; Pierpont ordered him to make the $50 restitution to the victim, pay a fine of $500—as well as the trial costs—and placed John on parole for two years.[20]

In the US census dated April 8, 1940, John Woods was still living at 303 East Ohio, in Eureka, Kansas, working as a laborer at a feedstore for twenty-six weeks of the previous year, while Hazel was a nurse, most likely for Dr. John Basham at the Greenwood Community Hospital on Main Street. The previous week John had worked thirty-one hours, while Hazel worked seventy-two hours.[21] County records show that John and Hazel lived in Eureka on March 1, 1941.[22]

Later that year, the United States Army "came a-callin.'" Greenwood County received a draft call requiring that nine men report to Fort Leavenworth, Kansas, on July 8, 1941. The group, including

John C. Woods, departed Eureka on July 7. Once at Ft. Leavenworth, Woods was not accepted; while no evidence has been found regarding the reason, it is likely that it had to do with his parole, which was still in effect from December 1939.[23] That rejection did not stop John Woods's brush with Army service later that year. Again, Greenwood County had a quota and John Woods was on the list, due to travel to Ft. Leavenworth on August 27 for induction the following day. Once again, John Woods was not accepted, likely due to his legal status.[24]

In 1942, John and Hazel moved to Wichita and took up residence at 541 North Topeka Ave. That year, John found a job as a driver for the Wichita Casket Company. The firm, headed by Mrs. Abigail W. Eaton, was located at 129 North Rock Island Ave.[25] The Wichita Casket Company was established in Wichita in 1903 as a branch of the Des Moines Casket Company; it was incorporated as a Wichita institution in 1915 and was the only firm of its kind in the state, and the only manufacturer of funeral clothes west of the Mississippi River. In 1916, the company constructed its four-story factory and warehouse at 129 North Rock Island Ave. The building, in which were manufactured caskets, funeral supplies, and funeral clothes, contained 23,000 square feet of space. Abigail Eaton took over duties as president after the death of her husband, James S. Eaton, after an appendicitis operation in June 1934.

In 1943, John still lived with Hazel at 514 North Topeka in Wichita. Hazel worked at the Nifty Nut House in Wichita in 1943 and continued in this work for several years.[26] John's employment now was listed at the Boeing Company, as a tool and die maker.[27] The huge Boeing facility in Wichita had plenty of jobs. In early 1941, the factory was building PT-13D and N2S-5 "Kaydet" biplane trainers for the US Army Air Corps and the US Navy.[28] However, bigger objectives were on the horizon; the facility would become one of the main assembly plants for "Project 345"—the B-29 Superfortress. On May 11, 1940, Boeing submitted its proposal for a massive strategic bomber; this Model 345 was designated XB-29. On May 17, 1941, the War Department ordered 250 B-29s on a provisional contract, whose conditions included the expansion of the Wichita facility to meet production goals of twenty-five B-29s per month by February 1, 1943. To accomplish this, the plant needed massive expansion to build the new bomber. On June 25, 1941, new ground was broken for what was to become "Plant II," which was to be completed in January 1943. On April 15, 1943, the first production model Boeing B-29 rolled out of the plant.[29]

It may have been the first B-29 to leave the factory, but John Woods would not see many others. The US Army had other plans for him.

Chapter 5
YOU'LL FIND A HOME IN THE ARMY

John Woods and fifteen other men from Greenwood County departed Eureka, Kansas, on August 26, 1943, for Ft. Leavenworth for possible induction into military service.[1] He was past his two-year probation, and by mid-1943 the US military had already faced heavy losses at Bataan, Guadalcanal, Kasserine Pass, Sicily, and New Guinea. Men who had been rejected in mid-1941 were now seen in a new light. And so, on August 30, 1943, John C. Woods was inducted into the United States Army, receiving Army Service Number 37540591. John listed his mother, Mattie Martha Green, as his next of kin and listed her residence as 1561 South Mosely St. in Wichita.

Immediately after his induction, Woods was granted furlough to return home to finish personal business.[2] On September 19, 1943, Woods reported to Ft. Leavenworth, Kansas, to begin training. He was now thirty-two years of age, an "old man" compared to the nineteen-year-olds in the combat units of the infantry and engineers. After basic training, Woods began training as a combat engineer. Had he known the purpose of such training, he might have deserted service again, since he and his buddies had a secret destination in their future: the deadly beaches of Normandy, France.

In January 1944, John returned to Wichita for a short furlough before deploying to England. Anna Dale Chilcott, a niece, confirmed the visit; she lived with Hazel for about a year after John departed.[3] On March 30, 1944, John C. Woods was assigned to Company B of the 37th Engineer Combat Battalion in the 5th Engineer Special Brigade, near Swansea in South Wales.[4] The brigade had been organized in the United Kingdom on November 12, 1943, from the 1119th Engineer Combat Group, along with three attached engineer combat battalions (37th, 336th, and 348th).

The brigade was divided into three battalion beach groups, each consisting of an engineer combat battalion, a naval beach company, a quartermaster service company, and a DUKW company (equipped with what was colloquially known as "Ducks," six-wheel-drive amphibious modification of the 2½-ton truck). The brigade also fielded a quartermaster railhead company, a medical collection company, a platoon of a quartermaster gasoline supply company, a platoon of an ordnance medium automotive maintenance company, and a platoon of an ordnance ammunition company. Military police, joint assault signal and chemical-decontamination platoons, and two auxiliary surgical teams rounded out the organization.

The 5th Engineer Special Brigade was "expected" to do two things: first, to clear the beaches of Normandy of German obstacles so the assault infantry could get ashore, and second—unfortunately—to sustain high casualties, thanks to the diabolical defensive plan of the enemy. Along the Atlantic Wall (*Atlantikwall*), the German name for their coastal defenses in France, German officers considered a low-tide landing impossible because of the lengthy exposed area in front of their artillery and machine guns. Leaving nothing to chance, however, *Wehrmacht* engineers, supported by 260,000 laborers, littered the tidal flats on the beaches with obstacles to snare enemy landing craft coming ashore at high tide. About 250 yards from the shingle line (the area of the beach covered with pebbles and small rocks, as opposed to fine sand) stood a row of complicated structures called Element C, nicknamed "Belgian Gates" because they resembled ornamental ironwork typical of European chateaus.

Swathed with waterproofed mines, Element C covered the ends of the beach but not the centers of them—the deadly concept being to funnel the landing infantry into kill zones in the middle. Behind the Belgian Gates were irregular rows of upright, V-shaped, channeled steel rails that would rip the bottom out of a landing craft. German engineers fixed a Teller mine (an antitank mine with 12 pounds of TNT) atop every third one. In selected areas, the Germans emplaced mined logs and mined ramps to cause a landing craft to expose its vulnerable belly to direct fire—if the mine didn't destroy it first. Finally, closest to the high-water mark was a row of hedgehogs, three or more channeled rails connected at their centers so as to project impaling spokes.

The 5th Engineer Special Brigade units received further training on the south coast of Wales, and by early January 1944 they were receiving training in landing operations at nearby Oxwich Beach. However, individual and small-unit training would not be sufficient, and Allied planners developed two major rehearsals for the invasion. The second rehearsal occurred at Slapton Sands on April 28, 1944. It did not go well. As American landing craft carrying troops from the 1st Engineer Special Brigade, US 4th Infantry Division, and VII Corps Headquarters moved to their training-assault areas in the middle of the night, German *Kriegsmarine* E-boats from the 5th and 9th S-boat (*Schnellboot*, fast boat) flotillas attacked. When the carnage had ended, US Army casualties were 749 killed and over 300 wounded.

The actual landings at Normandy on June 6, 1944, were even bloodier. Groups from the 5th and 6th Engineer Special Brigades were to support the landings of the US 1st Infantry Division, the "Big Red One," on Omaha Beach. The 37th Engineer Battalion Beach Group (the battalion to which Pvt. John Woods was assigned) had the mission to support the division's 16th Regimental Combat Team in the first wave against the Easy Red sector of Omaha.[5] But Easy Red sector wasn't easy; the battalion suffered twenty-four killed in action, including the battalion commander, Lt. Col. Lionel F. Smith, killed by an enemy mortar shell along with

two staff officers; 1Lt. Charles Peckham, commander of Company B, survived, winning the Bronze Star. At 7:30 a.m. on June 6, a Landing Craft Infantry (LCI) put Company B, 37th Engineer Combat Battalion, ashore safely at Exit E-1, leading to St. Laurent; its mission was to open the exit for the 2nd Battalion of the 16th Infantry Regiment.[6]

The 5th Engineer Special Brigade marked naval hazards near the beach, then determined the best landing areas, and finally marked the beach limits and debarkation points—much of this done under heavy enemy fire. Combat engineers helped remove beach obstacles and controlled boat traffic near the beach; they also helped unload all craft beaching within their sector. Brigade troops developed beach exits to permit the flow of vehicles inland; they also directed traffic and maintained a naval pontoon causeway. Most importantly for many soldiers, the engineers provided first aid to beach casualties before evacuating them to ships offshore.

This study found no official documents placing Pvt. John Woods away from his unit when it participated in the landings on Omaha Beach on June 6. Additionally, members of the battalion present at Normandy on June 6 were later authorized to wear unit awards of the Presidential Unit Citation and the French Croix de Guerre with Palm. Woods's personnel file in 1950 authorizes a Distinguished Unit Badge, and the Presidential Unit Citation is clearly in that category. Woods also wore two official Army patches on his uniform associated with combat units on D-day. Given those observations, this study believes that John Woods was on Omaha Beach at Normandy on D-day, slugging it out with the rest of his buddies.

We know that he was not wounded; nor was he cited for bravery in combat. However, Woods saw the consequences of war and contemplated that should he remain in the combat engineers, he would experience these brutal effects again after the Army advanced across France to penetrate the vaunted Siegfried Line at Germany's frontier. It was not a pleasant thought.

Chapter 6
MY KINGDOM FOR A HANGMAN

Gen. Dwight D. Eisenhower, the European theater of operations (ETO) commander, had a problem. As long as his command remained in Great Britain, a Status of Forces Agreement (SOFA) allowed for British hangmen to be used for executions of US Army personnel who received a punishment of death by asphyxiation for capital crimes committed on British soil. The US Army would conduct the court-martial; for the punishments, the Army would supervise the execution, but the British would hang the condemned man. For the relatively rare death by musketry, it was an all-American show.

Once in France, ETO officials were in a conundrum. The US Army in France had hundreds of thousands of soldiers but did not have even one trained hangman. Thomas Pierrepoint, one of the British hangmen at Shepton Mallet Prison where hangings of US military personnel occurred in Britain—flew from England to Normandy on August 14, 1944, to hang Pvt. Clarence Whitfield at Canisy, France; the SOFA was now stretched to the breaking point. On July 8, 1943, the War Department in Washington had sent a pamphlet titled "Execution of Death Sentences" to Army commands around the globe. Buried in the lengthy pamphlet was this phrase: "The trap will be actuated personally by the officer charged with the execution of the sentence."[1] That role of a hangman was not sitting well in the ETO. Despite Washington's directive, many commanders in the field believed that it was not a fitting job for a commissioned officer.

So the Army began to look for an enlisted man. The ETO queried the War Department on the availability of civilian hangmen in the United States. Perhaps the Army could transfer the man to Europe. That did not work either. Then the Army undoubtedly turned to a time-honored method to get results; unit first sergeants asked in formation if any soldiers had experience in actual legal hangings as a civilian. The 4237th Quartermaster Sterilization Company identified a corporal who stated that he had witnessed hangings and felt qualified to perform the duties of a hangman. The Army did not select him; it was not interested in lynchings.

Then the Army got lucky. On September 10, 1944, the Normandy Base Section informed the commanding general of the Communications Zone that a soldier had been found with experience as a hangman. The message, dated September 10, 1944, reads, "John C. Woods, 37540591, Company B, 37th Engineer Combat Battalion, 5th Engineer Special Brigade, is reported as having been assistant hangman twice in the state of Texas and twice in the state of Oklahoma."[2]

A few days later, the judge advocate recommended to the ETO provost marshal, Maj. Gen. Milton Reckord, that a full investigation determine if Woods was sufficiently experienced.[3] No evidence exists that this inquiry ever occurred. Had one been conducted, it would have found that Woods had never served as an assistant hangman in either state. Only one man in Oklahoma, Arthur Gooch, had been hanged (the others executed had been electrocuted), on June 19, 1936, which was the same time that John Woods was in Eureka, Kansas, not Oklahoma. Concerning Texas, in 1923 the state ordered that all future executions be carried out in Huntsville, *by means of the electric chair* [emphasis added].

The ball kept rolling. On September 21, 1944, the ETO designated that at some future disciplinary training center (DTC) in Paris, engineers would construct a portable gallows. The Seine Disciplinary Training Center duly opened two days later. On September 28, 1944, Maj. Gen. Reckord notified

Brig. Gen. R. B. Lord, ETO chief of staff, that the search to find a hangman was successful and that "G-1 has promised to provide the grade recommended by me for the hangman in order to compensate him in a small measure for the work he is to perform. I am recommending the hangman be made a Master Sergeant and the assistant hangman a T/3 (Staff Sergeant)."

On October 2, 1944, the Normandy Base Section notified the provost marshal of the European theater that Pvt. John C. Woods and Pvt. First Class Thomas F. Robinson (554th Quartermaster Depot) would volunteer as hangmen. The issue made its way up to Gen. Eisenhower. A note from the G-1 to the provost marshal, through the judge advocate, on October 12, 1944, summarized: "Subsequent to the dispatch of the cable mentioned above [October 11, 1944] the Commanding General expressed a wish to use the soldiers whom we had located. Consequently, a cable was sent to the US cancelling the initial request for this purpose. Seine Section has been allotted the necessary grades. Request you take the necessary action to coordinate with the Adjutant General on the procurement and assignment of the hangmen to Seine Section."

Eisenhower finally had his hangman.[4]

Chapter 7

IKE'S HANGMAN

Death penalty cases were stacking up. Orders came down through channels promoting Pvt. John C. Woods directly to master sergeant and assigning him to the 2913th Disciplinary Training Center. As the leaves fell that October 1944 in Paris, it was finally show time. The place would be the Seine DTC, located at the French Caserne Mortier at 128 Boulevard Mortier. Long associated with mystery, the location would later become the home to the French Foreign Intelligence Service. Now, it would become part of the mystery surrounding John Woods. Part of the mystery was linked to the concept of discipline. From past experience, the US Army understood that in an environment that rewarded violent behavior in combat, it was nearly impossible for every soldier to turn the switch off, when not fighting the enemy. Soldiers would commit crimes—the problem was what to do with them. If they were sent home, that would serve as an incentive for more bad behavior. So the Army established a system of stockades and disciplinary training centers to incarcerate those who would not accept discipline.

Seine Disciplinary Training Center

Günther Ohletz, Saturday, October 9, 1944

It has long been accepted that MSgt. John Woods began his career as a hangman at the Seine DTC in Paris, with the executions of two American soldiers, James B. Sanders and Roy W. Anderson, on October 25, 1944.

However, Sanders and Anderson were not the first men that the US Army hanged at Caserne Mortier. According to an official US Army Report of Proceedings in the Death Chamber, dated October 9, 1944, on October 7 at 10:02 p.m., a procession of thirteen personnel entered the death chamber of the DTC. Led by Brig. Gen. Pleas B. Rogers, commanding general of the Seine Section of the Communications Zone, three colonels and two lieutenant colonels were also present, including Lt. Col. Sidney Morgan of the US Embassy in London—whose presence was an oddity. Despite the fact that Maj. Mortimer H. Christian, commander of the Seine DTC, would serve as the officer in charge, this was no routine execution in other respects, since the man to be hanged was not an American soldier, but instead *SS-Rottenführer* Günther Ohletz of the 21st *SS Panzer-Grenadier Regiment* in the 10th *SS Panzer Division Frundsberg*. Born on April 26, 1924, in Oberhausen, Germany, he had been apprehended as a spy, tried by a military commission, and sentenced to death. That the execution would occur in Paris indicated that the entire process was far more than the local execution of an enemy soldier clad in civilian clothes.[1]

At the foot of the scaffold, the prisoner was stopped and someone placed the man's hands behind him and snapped on a pair of handcuffs. Ohletz climbed the steps, as did the German-fluent chaplain Richard F. Grady and two military policemen, TSgt. Charles F. Edwards and Sgt. Richard A. Mosely; the report also states that two assistants were on the scaffold, but these men were not named. Ohletz stepped on the center of the trap at 10:03 p.m. According to the chaplain, the condemned man's last words were "Only that I thank the chaplain, and I was not a spy." Someone bound the prisoner's ankles with a web strap and placed a black cloth hood over Ohletz's head; the hood reached down to his shoulders. "The noose was adjusted by an assistant who signaled to the Commanding Officer." Maj. Christian then faced about and cut the rope that released the weight and sprung the trap at 10:05 p.m. "The fall of the weight, and the trap, and the snap of the rope were the only sounds heard." After eleven minutes of silence, at 10:16 p.m., Capt. Edward M. Sullivan, the DTC surgeon, entered the lower portion of the scaffold, examined the prisoner, and at 10:18 p.m. declared that Ohletz was dead. Then the execution recorder wrote the most significant sentence of the report. "*The assistants were unable to remove the handcuffs due to faulty locking mechanisms*"[2] [emphasis added].

In November 1946, Woods granted an interview to *True: The Man's Magazine* at Ft. Dix, New Jersey. Deep into the article, Woods said: "*The first man I hanged in Paris, France, was an SS trooper. We used handcuffs to fasten his hands behind his back. When I dropped him, his wrists swelled so bad we couldn't get the handcuffs off* [emphasis added]. *We finally had to cut 'em off. I didn't want anything like that to happen on this big job* [Nürnberg]."[3]

This study concludes that Woods participated in the hanging of *SS-Rottenführer* Günther Ohletz. Since he did not actuate the trapdoor, he was not the hangman of record but more correctly would be termed an assistant. On the basis of Army correspondence previously examined, he probably was still a private and not yet a master sergeant. Thus, Woods actually began his enigmatic career as a hangman on October 9, 1944, rather than October 25.

• • •

James B. Sanders and Roy W. Anderson, Wednesday, October 25, 1944

Technician Fifth Grade James Buck Sanders was born on June 9, 1917, at Lockhart, South Carolina. Inducted on May 26, 1942, at Ft. Jackson, South Carolina, Sanders lived in Pacolet, near Spartanburg. Three summary courts-martial had convicted him of absent without leave (AWOL), urinating on the floor of the squad tent, and being drunk in uniform in public, wearing unauthorized

staff sergeant chevrons to boot.[4] Pvt. Roy W. Anderson was born on September 22, 1917, in Jeffersonville, Indiana; he was inducted on June 22, 1942 at Columbus, Ohio. Anderson had a traumatic youth. At age six, he was in a car accident that fractured his skull. In 1937, someone shot him in the back. Communication linemen, he and Sanders were assigned to Company B of the 29th Signal Construction Battalion. He had two summary court-martial convictions. The two black soldiers arrived in France on June 17, 1944.[5] Two days later, Sanders and Anderson were walking through the countryside with some other soldiers when they arrived at Neuville-au-Plain, a few miles north of Sainte-Mère-Église. In the early morning hours of June 6, 1944, Sainte-Mère-Église had been the scene of great heroism as units of the US 82nd Airborne Division and 101st Airborne Division jumped into and occupied the town, giving it the claim to be one of the first towns liberated in the invasion. On June 22, the area would be the scene of despair and dishonor. Authorities later determined that the pair raped two women and fired a weapon at a nearby Frenchman. American authorities apprehended the men; both rape victims identified Sanders as one of the assailants, while Anderson admitted the act but said it had been consensual.[6]

An advance section of the Communications Zone general court-martial convicted both men of rape on June 22, 1944. Gen. Dwight Eisenhower confirmed the sentence on August 30, 1944, but withheld the order directing the actual execution, in part because of the shortage then of a hangman.[7] On October 25, 1944, Woods served as the assistant hangman in the execution of General Prisoner James B. Sanders at the Seine DTC in Paris, France; Maj. Mortimer H. Christian, commander of the disciplinary center, performed the duties of the hangman, as well as the officer in charge. At 10:01 p.m. on October 25, 1944, Maj. Christian led a procession into the death chamber. Chaplain Harry S. Williams and James Sanders followed him, flanked by guards TSgt. Charles F. Edwards and Sgt. Edward P. McHugh. Following in the column were the medical officer, Capt. Edward M. Sullivan, and Capt. Albert M. Summerfield, serving as the execution recorder. Col. Robert Chard, Lt. Col. Charles Day, Lt. Col. Harry L. Gustafson, Maj. Paul Hitler, and Maj. Benjamin Lehman served as witnesses.[8]

Halting at the steps of the scaffold, guards bound Sanders's hands behind his back and assisted him up the steps and onto the trapdoor. They then bound his ankles, while Maj. Christian asked Sanders if he had any last statement to make. Sanders made no reply but began to pray. The chaplain asked if the condemned had a statement to make, but the hooded Sanders continued to pray as Williams began a prayer. The report mentioned that the hood and noose were adjusted—this was probably done by Woods. At 10:05 p.m., Maj. Christian faced about and cut a rope, releasing a weight that caused the trapdoor to open.[9]

Sanders dropped through the opening; his body swayed slightly, but there were no "jerks, tremors or visible convulsions." At 10:12 p.m., Dr. Sullivan moved to his position at the lower screened portion of the gallows and made his examination, but he indicated that "life was not extinct" by shaking his head. Sullivan checked again at 10:15 p.m. and Sanders was still alive. Finally, at 10:19 p.m., Capt. Sullivan made a third inspection and pronounced Sanders dead.[10] Fourteen minutes until death was not a good start to the evening.

At 10:31 p.m., the second procession entered the death chamber. The condemned man was General Prisoner Roy W. Anderson; his guards were Sgt. Earl E. Mendenhall and Sgt. Richard A. Mosley. The procedure was the same; when asked if he desired to make a statement, Anderson said, "I thank you and the chaplain for what you have done for me. I thank the lieutenants and all the guards for the candy and stuff they brought me."[11]

Anderson thanked the chaplain, and Williams began to pray aloud. At 10:33 p.m., Maj. Christian faced about and cut the rope, resulting in the release of the trapdoor. Capt. Sullivan waited a little longer this time; after ten minutes, he began his examination and pronounced Roy Anderson dead one minute later.[12]

Paul M. Kluxdal, Tuesday, October 31, 1944

John Woods remained in Paris; his next hanging would be among his most unusual—and ostensibly the worst—of his career. Born on July 17, 1907, in Merrill, Wisconsin, PFC Paul M. Kluxdal had been a radio operator in Headquarters Battery of the 200th Field Artillery Battalion. Kluxdal had served for two years in the Wisconsin National Guard and had attended the University of Wisconsin for two years. Married, Kluxdal lived in Oak Park, Illinois, working as a construction foreman. On August 12, 1944, the white soldier shot and killed his first sergeant. Maj. Gen. Leonard T. Gerow, the V Corps commander, ordered a general court-martial to convene at Moussy le Vieux, France, on September 4, 1944; it convicted Kluxdal of murder and sentenced him to death.[13]

Gen. Eisenhower confirmed the sentence on September 30, 1944, but withheld issuing a date and location at which the execution would take place.[14] That date came on October 31, 1944. MSgt. John Woods served as the assistant hangman in the execution of General Prisoner Paul M. Kluxdal at the Seine DTC; once again Maj. Mortimer H. Christian performed the duties of the hangman, as well as the officer in charge. At 10:01 p.m., Maj. Christian entered the death chamber at the Caserne Mortier, closely followed by Chaplain Harry S. Williams, Paul Kluxdal, and two guards—TSgt. Charles F. Edwards and Sgt. Richard A. Mosley. The two military policemen bound Kluxdal's arms behind his back and helped him up the stairs.

Woods, perhaps aided by his assistant, Technician Third Grade Thomas F. Robinson, adjusted the black hood over the head of the condemned man and finally slipped the noose around Kluxdal's neck. Maj. Christian then faced about and cut the rope that released the weight, which actuated the trapdoor at 10:03 p.m. Kluxdal's body hurtled through the opening, and then all hell broke loose.[15]

Kluxdal's shoes hit the ground—actually hit the ground—before the rope went completely taut, an aberration of all execution protocol and probably an event that Maj. Christian, to say nothing of John Woods, had ever trained for or had a plan to remedy. At 6 feet tall, Kluxdal was several inches taller than most of the other soldiers Woods would hang, and perhaps neither Christian nor Woods had measured the height of the condemned man so they could determine the correct drop, and thus the correct rope length, before the execution; perhaps Christian assumed Woods knew what he was doing, on the basis of his claimed experience as an assistant hangman as a civilian. Or maybe Maj. Christian had instructed him to do so, and Woods had simply not complied. The report of execution minimized the impact of the event: "The toes of the shoes barely touched the floor, did not support any weight, but prevented the body from swaying."[16]

That may have been the observation in the report, but when the medical officer entered the lowered screened portion of the scaffold to examine the Kluxdal's body at 10:15 p.m., he found Kluxdal was still alive. The doctor, probably Capt. Edward M. Sullivan, who undoubtedly was sweating concerning what his duties should be now, waited an additional six minutes—for Kluxdal, a total of eighteen minutes barely alive at the end of the rope—before the physician determined that Paul Kluxdal finally was dead.[17]

Willie Wimberly Jr. and Joseph Watson, Thursday, November 9, 1944

A week went by, and John Woods got the call to report to the Seine DTC for a double hanging of two soldiers, who were assigned to the 257th

Signal Construction Company, an all-black organization. Technician Fifth Grade Willie Wimberly Jr., one of a dozen children, was born in Macon, Georgia, on September 21, 1912; he later moved to Chicago. Wimberly quit school in the fifth grade; he was employed as a machine operator at a tire company. He was inducted on July 8, 1942, and arrived with his unit in Liverpool, England, on December 15, 1943. Pvt. Joseph Watson, twenty-five years old, was from Texarkana, Texas. Single, he dropped out of school during the fourth grade. He was inducted on August 15, 1942.[18] On August 19, 1944, a US 3rd Army general court-martial found both men guilty of rape and other charges and sentenced them to hang. It was an open and shut case; in fact, a US 3rd Army full colonel, twenty-six-year veteran Thomas H. Nixon of the Ordnance Department, a 1918 graduate of West Point and the recipient of a Bronze Star, who had been found by the father of the victim, decided not only to report the attack, but also to grab two lieutenants and head straight to the scene of the crime, where he found one of the assailants passed out.[19]

On November 6, 1944, the Headquarters, European theater of operations, published *General Court-Martial Order Number 95*. Brig. Gen. R. B. Lord—by command of Gen. Eisenhower—directed that the two executions would be carried out on November 9, 1944. At 10:02 p.m. on that date, Maj. Mortimer H. Christian led a procession into the death chamber of the Seine DTC. He had several options, since, according to Francis MacDonald, a military policeman in the 709th Military Police Battalion, the Seine DTC had two permanent gallows, while a third scaffold was on a flatbed trailer for use elsewhere; Maj. Christian decided that one gallows would be enough tonight; Wimberly would go first.[20]

Chaplain Harry S. Williams and General Prisoner Willie Wimberly Jr. followed Christian into the chamber; TSgt. Charles F. Edwards and Sgt. Edward P. McHugh served as guards. In the rear were Capt. Edward M. Sullivan and Capt.

Albert M. Summerfield. Halting at the foot of the gallows, the two guards bound Wimberly's hands behind him, helped him climb the steps, and positioned him on the trapdoor.[21]

The guards then bound the ankles of the prisoner, while Maj. Christian asked if Wimberly had any last statement to make. Wimberly said, "No sir," which he repeated when asked the same question by the chaplain. Woods adjusted the noose and black hood; the chaplain began to pray. At 10:05 p.m., Maj. Christian faced about and cut the rope that released a weight and released the trapdoor. Wimberly dropped through the opening; his body swayed slightly. At 10:15 p.m., Dr. Sullivan moved to the lower screened portion of the scaffold and made his first examination, but Wimberly was still alive. Sullivan made a second examination at 10:20 p.m., and still Wimberly was not dead. At 10:29 p.m., Sullivan made a third and final inspection and pronounced Willie Wimberly dead. Twenty-four minutes until death; it was possible that the knot in the noose was incorrectly aligned, but nothing in the reports stated this.[22] By 10:31 p.m., Capt. Walter B. Bradley of the Graves Registration Section had removed Wimberly's body from the death chamber.

At 10:37 p.m., a second procession entered the room. The aforementioned personnel were present except that the condemned was General Prisoner Joseph Watson. A gawker, dressed as a captain, attempted to ease his way in, but officials ushered him out. The procession halted and the same procedure was followed as before. When asked if he desired to make a statement, Watson said, "Well, yes sir. I am glad to leave this world in the condition I'm in. I think I am fit to go. And I certainly appreciate your kindness."[23]

Moments later, Joseph Watson thanked the chaplain and Capt. Albert M. Summerfield in his statement, which was "No more than to say I hope to meet you in heaven and you too." Chaplain Williams began to read from the Bible. At 10:40 p.m., Maj. Christian faced about and cut the rope, which dropped the trapdoor. Dr. Sullivan began

his examination at 10:47 p.m. and pronounced death one minute later.[24] Capt. Bradley removed the body by 10:51 p.m. The bodies of both men were buried at the Solers American Military Cemetery Number 1.

Fort du Roule, Cherbourg, France

Richard Bunney Scott and William D. Pennyfeather, Saturday, November 18, 1944

The wheels of justice continued to grind as executions proceeded. It was time to take the show on the road to Fort du Roule in Cherbourg, France, for two hangings. Official files do not show that Woods was present at these two executions, nor do they say he was absent. Given that Woods had assisted Maj. Christian in so many hangings over the last month, this study has concluded that Woods was present at Fort du Roule on November 18, 1944, and was still in an assistant hangman role. Mortimer H. Christian, a graduate of the Virginia Military Institute, who had served in the 17th Cavalry and 8th Cavalry Regiments before entering the military police, may have been experiencing misgivings over just whom they had hired and exactly what experience did he really have, and those feelings may well have led the officer to conclude that he needed more time with the new master sergeant.

Richard B. Scott was born on August 23, 1917, in Carrolton, Texas, and lived there all of his civilian life until he was inducted into the Army at Dallas on March 7, 1941. Scott was married in 1935, but two years later, police arrested him for drunkenness and he spent thirty days in jail. Scott had a problem with telling the truth, so events in his life remain unclear. He stated that he had been struck by a car in 1939 and had suffered serious head injuries, which continued to give him problems; he also stated that he had dropped out of school after sixth grade and that his wife was unfaithful. This problem with honesty would have been serious enough for Scott, but he had another attribute that would prove more lethal; a board of officers at the 289th General Hospital concluded that the soldier had had the mental capacity of a six-year-old child.[25]

On September 7, 1944, a general court-martial at Cherbourg, France, convicted Scott, who was assigned to the 229th Quartermaster Salvage Collecting Company, of rape and sentenced him to be hanged. *General Court-Martial Order Number 106*, dated November 15, 1944, designated that General Prisoner Scott would be hanged in three days at Cherbourg, France.[26]

The weather was fair on the morning of November 18, 1944. Carpenters had erected a gallows in a flat area immediately behind the buildings at Fort du Roule, overlooking the harbor. Eight official witnesses stood on the east side of the scaffold at a distance of 22 feet. All were commissioned officers, ranking from second lieutenant to lieutenant colonel. Twenty men under the command of Capt. William E. Boyden, assisted by 1Lt. Cecil N. Hughes, of the 707th MP Battalion guarded the site. A command car brought Scott and two guards, Sgt. Earl F. Mendenhall and Sergeant Richard Mosley, within 90 yards of the gallows. Exiting the vehicle, they joined a small procession that started marching at 10:01 a.m. Maj. Mortimer H. Christian led; Capt. Melvin C. Swann of African Methodist Episcopal Church, one of the Army's few black chaplains, immediately followed. Scott walked next, flanked on either side by Mendenhall and Mosley. Capt. Julius C. Rivellese, a surgeon who would determine when the prisoner was deceased, marched at the rear.[27]

Reaching the scaffold, guards bound Scott's hands behind him and assisted him up the steps. Maj. Christian asked Scott if he had a last statement—he did not, and so guards guided the prisoner to the trapdoor and bound his ankles. The chaplain asked if Scott had any last statement, to which he replied: "I know my soul is going to heaven; my trust is in the Lord."[28]

The assistant hangman adjusted the noose and black hood, the chaplain started to pray aloud, and the commandant faced about and cut the rope. The trapdoor dropped at 10:04 a.m. and Richard Scott met his fate. Eleven minutes later, Christian directed the doctor to enter the lower screened-in portion of the gallows, where Capt. Rivellese confirmed that Scott had died at 10:17 a.m.: "The cause of death was Judicial Asphyxia." First Lt. Harold A. Myers, Graves Registration Section, took custody of the body. The Army buried Richard B. Scott at the US Military Cemetery at Marigny, France, in Plot Z (also known as Field GP [General Prisoner]), a separate area apart from the graves of the soldiers honorably killed in action) in grave 1-2.[29]

In a separate case, on September 2, 1944, another general court-martial at Cherbourg, France, convicted William D. Pennyfeather, of the 3868th Quartermaster Truck Company, on similar charges and sentenced him to be hanged. In fact, it was the same jury. Pennyfeather had been born in New York on July 21, 1920; he was arrested for felonious assault in 1937, but the charge was dismissed. The following year, police arrested him for a strong-arm robbery, and a court sentenced him from one to thirty years' incarceration. Serving twenty-one months in the Elmira Reformatory before being released, he subsequently violated parole and returned to Elmira for another year being finally being released on October 6, 1942. Pennyfeather never knew his mother; he was raised by his grandmother.[30] His Army career was checkered as well; a previous court-martial convicted him in September 1943 for AWOL, and in December 1943 a special court-martial convicted him of escape from restriction, breach of restriction, entering a restricted area, and absence without leave for a period of four days; it then sentenced him to six months hard labor. On September 2, 1944, a general court-martial at Cherbourg, France, convicted Pennyfeather, who was assigned to the 3868th Quartermaster Truck Company, of raping a woman in Cherbourg on August 1, 1944, and unanimously sentenced him to hang.[31] *General Court-Martial Order Number 103*, dated November 15, 1944, designated that General Prisoner Pennyfeather would be hanged on November 18, 1944, at Fort du Roule in Cherbourg, France.

A command car brought Pennyfeather and his guards, Sgt. Earl F. Mendenhall and Sgt. Richard Mosley, to 90 yards from the scaffold at 10:29 a.m. The men exited the vehicle and joined a small formation. Leading the procession, which started at 10:30 a.m., was Maj. Mortimer H. Christian, followed by Chaplain Melvin C. Swann. The condemned walked next, with a guard on either side. At the rear was Capt. Julius C. Rivellese. The group reached the gallows; the guards bound the prisoner's hands behind him and assisted him up the steps. Christian asked Pennyfeather if he had a last statement to make, and the prisoner replied, "The Lord is with me; that's about all." The guards placed the prisoner on the trapdoor and bound his ankles, and the chaplain asked if Pennyfeather had any last statement, he did and said, "Take the ring off my finger, chaplain, please. Send it home to my wife."[32]

The chaplain attempted to comply but could not remove the ring; perhaps Pennyfeather's bound hands were starting to swell, but Maj. Christian assured Pennyfeather that Chaplain Swann would later send the ring home. Woods and Robinson adjusted the noose and black hood, the chaplain started to pray aloud, and Christian faced about to cut the rope at 10:33 a.m. Pennyfeather dropped through the trapdoor. All was silent except for the chaplain, who continued praying another minute. At 10:48 a.m., Christian directed the surgeon to enter the lower screened-in portion of the scaffold; he then reported that Pennyfeather was dead. Once again, 1Lt. Harold A. Myers, Graves Registration Section, took custody of the body from Maj. Christian. The Army buried the remains at the US Military Cemetery at Marigny, France, in Plot Z, grave 1-3.[33]

Saint Lô, France

Theron W. McGann, Monday, November 20, 1944

According to one study, 4,441 men went directly from American penal institutions into military service in World War II.[34] While Theron McGann was not one of those prison-to-platoon felons, the soldier was characteristic of those personnel with prior significant criminal records who were of little value to the Army. Born in Portland, Oregon, on June 25, 1921, he had served in the 162nd Infantry Regiment of the Oregon National Guard, but a civil court conviction led to his discharge. Inducted into the service on May 21, 1943, at Portland, he later had two summary court-martial convictions: one for AWOL, and a second for loitering on his post.[35] The white soldier, assigned to Company A in the 32nd Signal Construction Battalion of the US 1st Army, entered the home of two French women, threatened them with a pistol, and raped one on August 5, 1944, at Quibou, France, 4 miles from Saint Lô. Three weeks after he was arrested, a general court-martial, lasting 145 minutes, tried McGann on August 28, 1944, at Fougerolles du Plessis, France, convicted him, and sentenced him to death.[36]

On November 15, 1944, the headquarters of the European theater of operations published *General Court-Martial Order Number 104*. Brig. Gen. R. B. Lord—by command of Gen. Eisenhower—directed that the execution would be carried out on November 20, 1944, under the direction of the commanding officer, Seine DTC.[37]

On November 20, 1944, Saint Lô, France, was cloudy with intermittent light rain. Maj. Mortimer H. Christian had previously selected a location for the execution in the northern section of the city, in a courtyard off the main highway. The building adjacent to the gallows had been heavily shelled, and only the walls remained standing. A hedge screened the northern side of the gallows; a stone wall enclosed the rear. Ten official witnesses stood 18 feet from the scaffold. Twenty-eight authorized spectators were present as well, including eleven officers, seven enlisted men, and ten French officials. Eight soldiers from Company B of the 793rd MP Battalion guarded the area.[38]

At 9:59 a.m., a command car eased down the main highway to the courtyard. General Prisoner Theron W. McGann dismounted with two guards, Sgt. Earl F. Mendenhall and Sgt. Richard Mosley. Maj. Christian formed the group into a column and marched to the gallows. Catholic chaplain Anthony R. Feeherry followed; to his rear, McGann walked with two guards. Following them was Capt. Julius C. Rivellese. Capt. Albert M. Summerfield joined the procession along the march.[39]

At 10:00 p.m., the formation reached the bottom of the scaffold steps; Mendenhall and Mosley bound the condemned man's hands behind him and assisted him up the steps. The condemned stood on the trapdoor while his ankles were firmly bound; Maj. Christian asked McGann if he had any last words, but McGann did not. The chaplain then asked the prisoner if he had any last statements, and McGann replied simply, "Pray for my soul." Chaplain Feeherry began to pray the Last Rights at 10:02 a.m., and, after the black hood and noose were adjusted, the commandant faced about at 10:03 a.m. and cut the rope, which released the weight that actuated the trapdoor. At 10:16 a.m., the medical officer and the recorder entered the lower screened portion of the gallows. One minute later, Capt. Rivellese announced: "I pronounce . . ." At that precise moment, a wall of the damaged building south of the gallows began to collapse with a roar. As spectators shouted a warning, personnel scurried to avoid the falling rubble. Rivellese, quite shaken, composed himself and announced: "I pronounce this man dead." Chaplain Feeherry entered the area and performed the last rites. First Lt. Louis B. Weiss of the 3047th Quartermaster Graves Registration Company signed for the remains, which were interred at the US Military Cemetery at Marigny, France, in Plot Z, grave 1-4.[40] Once again, official records do not show the names of any assistant hangmen. This study concludes that Woods was present and likely assisted Maj. Christian, as he had many times before.

Montours, Ille-et-Vilaine, France

Charles H. Jordan and Arthur E. Davis, Wednesday, November 22, 1944

On August 10, 1944, at La Rouennerie en Montour, France, Pvt. Charles H. Jordan, 3327th Quartermaster Truck Company, and Pvt. Arthur E. Davis, 3326th Quartermaster Truck Company, violently assaulted and raped a French woman at her farm. Charges were preferred against the pair on August 13; at the end of the same day that the investigation was completed, the US 3rd Army judge advocate had reviewed the charges and passed them to his boss. Lt. Gen. George S. Patton, never a man to dawdle, made the decision that evening to refer the matter to a general court-martial.

Charles Jordan, age twenty-four, enlisted on January 6, 1942, at Ft. McPherson, Georgia, his home state; he had nine years of education. Jordan had a summary court-martial conviction for AWOL and another summary court-martial conviction for breach of restriction; a third summary court-martial convicted him of breach of restriction, using an unauthorized alias, and unlawfully carrying a concealed weapon. Adding to his misery, a special court-martial convicted him for taking and using a second lieutenant's vehicle and for breach of restriction. Born in Cleveland, Ohio, on August 8, 1919, Arthur Davis was inducted on November 8, 1943, in Chicago. Davis had finished eighth grade; he stood 5'7½" tall, weighed 132 pounds, and had previously been a bread delivery truck driver, making $35 per week.[41]

The joint offense general court-martial convened at 1:15 p.m. on August 16, 1944, at Poilley, France; the defense made no motion to sever the trials to try each man separately. Jordan and Davis pled not guilty to carnal knowledge, a violation of the 92nd Article of War; attempted murder, a violation of the 93rd Article of War; and assault, a violation of the 96th Article of War. Defense counsels introduced no evidence, and both defendants elected to remain silent at the trial, although statements they had previously made about being in the area were admitted at trial; more damning, the victims identified the defendants as the two perpetrators. The jury found both soldiers guilty of all three charges (but struck murder from the charge due to a doubt concerning intent) and then unanimously sentenced both men to be hanged.[42]

Gen. Eisenhower signed the order confirming the death sentences of Pvt. Davis and Pvt. Jordan. The Headquarters, European theater of operations, published *General Court-Martial Order Number 105* on November 15, 1944. By command of Gen. Eisenhower, Brig. Gen. R. B. Lord directed that the commanding officer, Seine DTC, would carry the sentence into execution on November 22, 1944, at Montours, Ille-et-Vilaine, France.[43]

Execution records for both are fragmentary. On the basis of previous double executions, we can make several solid assumptions. The short report indicates that ten French gendarmes attended the executions as witnesses; five French civilians also attended. Given Brig. Gen. Lord's direction, Maj. Mortimer H. Christian was responsible for conducting the execution, and he cut the rope to spring the trap. Therefore, Woods would have been his assistant. General Prisoner Charles H. Jordan would have gone first, with that proceeding commencing at 10:00 a.m. Therefore, the trapdoor probably dropped at about 10:05 a.m., with his death pronounced about 10:20 a.m. General Prisoner Davis was led up the stairs of the gallows and guided to the trapdoor at 10:31 a.m. The chaplain began to pray one minute later, and at 10:33 a.m. the executioner activated the trapdoor. At 10:45 a.m., a physician examined the body of Arthur Davis; one minute later he pronounced Davis dead. The executioner

cut the body down at 10:48 a.m., and it was removed from the area by graves registration personnel two minutes later.

Both men's remains were interred at the US Military Cemetery at Marigny, France, in Plot Z (in graves 1-5 and 1-6) on November 24, 1944.

Plumaudan, Côtes-du-Nord, France

James E. Hendricks, Friday, November 24, 1944

PFC James E. Hendricks, born in Drewry, North Carolina, on April 29, 1923, had a tough early life; his mother died in childbirth and he experienced "violent temper tantrums." He was drafted in February 1943, inducted at Ft. Meyer, Virginia, and sent to Camp Van Dorn, Mississippi. Assigned to the 272nd Quartermaster Battalion, in February 1944 Hendricks and his unit shipped to England.[44]

At 10:00 p.m. on August 21, 1944, a black American soldier wearing a helmet and raincoat and carrying a rifle went to the Bouton home in Plumaudan, France. After entering, he attempted to kiss a French woman there and followed her around. Departing, he went across the road to the home of Victor Bignon and knocked on the door, and when no one answered, he fired a shot through the door, which brought Victor and his wife, Noémie, to the inside of the door, where they held it shut. The soldier fired a second shot through the door, which blew a fatal hole in Victor's head. Entering the home, the soldier grabbed the Bignons' eighteen-year-old daughter. The soldier and the three surviving members of the Bignon family then walked across the street to the Bouton home, where he attempted to rape a woman but was unsuccessful.[45]

Then a hero walked onto the stage—or rather, ran. First Lt. Donald Tucker, a black officer in command of the 3326th Quartermaster Truck Company, heard two shots and ensuing screams.

He dressed, assembled a group of soldiers, and ran down the road a quarter of a mile to a farmhouse that had the lights on. Just outside, Tucker heard a noise in a hedge and fired warning shots. Out of the hedge, 10 yards from the Bignon home, stepped a soldier whom 1Lt. Tucker recognized—James Hendricks, who had been in the 3326th eleven days.[46]

Over the next three hours, Hendricks changed his story four times. An investigation took one day, and two days later the results went to the VIII Corps headquarters. Col. Cyrus H. Searcy, the corps chief of staff, verbally approved a general court-martial. It convened at Morlaix, Finistère, France, at 9:05 a.m. on September 6, 1944. Hendricks pled not guilty to murder, a violation of the 92nd Article of War, and to breaking and entering and assault—both violations of the 93rd Article of War.[47]

A statement by Hendricks was admitted as evidence, although the defense counsel fought the process, stating that the accused was under duress when talking to his commander. None of the French civilians could positively identify Hendricks; they could say only that the soldier who visited both houses was the same man. Hendricks did not take the witness stand. The jury concluded that Hendricks had shot and killed Victor Bignon while in the process of looking for a French woman to rape. By a unanimous vote on September 7, 1944, the court members found James Hendricks guilty and, by another unanimous vote, sentenced him to be hanged by the neck until dead.[48]

Gen. Eisenhower confirmed the sentence for PFC James E. Hendricks on October 27, 1944, but withheld the order directing the execution. On November 15, 1944, the headquarters of the European theater of operations published *General Court-Martial Order Number 109*. Brig. Gen. R. B. Lord directed that the execution be carried out on November 24, 1944, at Plumaudan, Côtes-du-Nord, France, under the direction of the commanding officer, Seine Disciplinary Training Center.[49]

The weather on that day in Plumaudan was wretched, with a continuous cold rain. Château La Vallée, a fourteenth-century manor house, stood down the road from the small village church. The deserted chateau's stone walls appeared unstable and the windows were long gone, but it did have a sizable courtyard where early that day, American soldiers had shattered the serene ambiance with the noise from constructing a scaffold. Nine officers stood as official witnesses; seventeen authorized spectators were present as well, including eight officers, four enlisted men, and five French officials. The murder victim's family declined to attend. Soldiers from the 795th Military Police Battalion guarded the area to prevent unauthorized spectators.[50]

At 10:58 a.m., a cargo truck rolled up to the entrance of the chateau and backed into the yard. General Prisoner James E. Hendricks dismounted with his two guards, Sgt. Earl F. Mendenhall and Sgt. Richard A. Mosley. Maj. Mortimer H. Christian, the commandant of the Seine DTC, formed the official party into a column and began marching to the gallows. He was followed by Capt. Robert J. Sanders, who was a black Baptist minister, and then by the condemned and the two guards. Following were Capt. Norman Duren, a medical officer, and Capt. Albert M. Summerfield, the recorder.

The procession reached the bottom of the scaffold steps at 10:59 a.m. Maj. Christian and Chaplain Sanders ascended the steps to the scaffold. Mendenhall and Mosley bound Hendricks's hands behind him and then assisted him up the thirteen steps. Capt. Duren took his position in front of the witnesses, about a dozen feet from the scaffold. While Hendricks stood on the trapdoor, John Woods and Thomas Robinson bound his ankles. Maj. Christian asked James Hendricks if he had any last words; the condemned replied that he did not. The chaplain then asked the prisoner if he had any last statements, and Hendricks finally admitted his crime, replying, "Thank you for what you've did for me. Tell all the boys not to do what I did."

Chaplain Sanders began to pray aloud; after Woods placed the black hood and noose over Hendricks's head and shoulders, the commandant faced about at 11:04 a.m. and cut the rope, which released the weight that sprang the trapdoor. Dropping through, Hendricks's body showed no muscular movement, swaying slightly. A few French civilians, watching from a distance, could be heard talking. At 11:14 a.m., Duren and Summerfield entered the lower screened portion of the scaffold to examine the prisoner. One minute later, Capt. Summerfield announced: "I pronounce this man dead."[51]

Maj. Christian dismissed the official witnesses and spectators. Woods and Technician Third Grade Robinson cut the rope, lowered the body to the ground under the scaffold, removed the hood, and unbound Hendricks's hands. Capt. Poole Rogers, 610th Quartermaster Graves Registration Company, received the remains, which were interred at the US Military Cemetery at Marigny, France, in Plot Z, grave 1-7.[52]

Beaunay, Marne, France

Leo Valentine Jr. and Oscar N. Newman, Wednesday, November 29, 1944

On September 18, 1944, three soldiers lured a seventeen-year-old French girl into a military vehicle and raped her in the back of the truck. She escaped, but they recaptured her and assaulted her again. The sergeant cooperated with investigators; Technician Fifth Grade Leo Valentine Sr., of the 396th Quartermaster Truck Company, and Technician Fifth Grade Oscar N. Newman, of the 712th Railway Operating Battalion, did not.[53]

Leo Valentine Sr. had been an assistant to the unit supply sergeant. Twenty-four years old, hailing from Gastonia, North Carolina, the black soldier had been inducted into the Army at Ft. Dix, New Jersey, on July 16, 1943.[54] Oscar Newman, white, was born in Macon, Ohio, on July 19, 1918; he was inducted at Columbus, Ohio, on August

13, 1943. Newman had arrived in France on August 16, 1944.[55]

A general court-martial from the Advance Section of the Communications Zone met at Reims, France, on October 3, 1944, convicted both men, and sentenced them to death by hanging. Gen. Dwight Eisenhower confirmed the sentences on November 5, 1944, but initially withheld designating when or where the sentence would occur. On November 25, 1944, the European theater of operations published *General Court-Martial Order Number 114* (for General Prisoner Leo Valentine Sr.) and *General Court-Martial Order Number 115* (for General Prisoner Oscar N. Newman). Brig. Gen. R. B. Lord, by command of Gen. Eisenhower, directed that both executions would occur on November 29, 1944, at the village of Beaunay in the Marne District of France.[56]

The weather that day at Beaunay—in the heart of champagne country—was fair, but engineers constructed the gallows inside a large barn on the edge of the village just in case conditions worsened. Two large, open doors of the barn, facing north and south, permitted a dozen officials and twenty-five authorized spectators to see both hangings. On the north side of the barn, 35 feet from the gallows, stood the spectators, including ten French citizens. Two were members of the victim's family. Official witnesses stood on the opposite side, about 20 feet away. Company C of the 391st Military Police Battalion guarded the roads nearby.[57]

At 2:55 p.m., a weapons carrier approached the barn and stopped 100 yards away. General Prisoner Leo Valentine Sr. dismounted with two guards, Sgt. Alfonso "Big Al" Girvalo and Sgt. Robert V. Childers. Sgt. Thorrolf P. Dyro carried a collapse board; should Valentine faint or offer resistance, the sergeants would strap him to the board and carry him to the scaffold and even up the steps to the trapdoor if necessary. Lt. Col. Henry Peck, commanding officer of the 2913th Disciplinary Training Center, formed the official party into a column. Behind him was 1Lt. Sanford N. Peak—a black, Baptist chaplain—then Valentine and the guards. Following them were Capt. Ernest J. Haberle, serving as the recorder, and three medical officers, Maj. Lenpha P. Hart, 1Lt. Paul B. Jarrett, and 1Lt. Jack E. Keefe.[58] The 2913th, formed two years earlier at Shepton Mallet Prison in England, had now deployed to France and taken over many of the executions from the Seine DTC.

The procession reached the gallows at 2:58 p.m.; guards bound Valentine's hands behind him and then assisted him up the steps. Valentine stood on the trapdoor; Lt. Col. Peck asked him for any last words. General Prisoner Valentine replied simply, "See that my wife and children are taken care of." Chaplain Peak then asked Valentine if he had any last statement; although Valentine nodded in the affirmative, he said nothing, as the chaplain began to pray aloud. Woods placed the hood over Valentine's head, followed by the noose, adjusting them snugly. Meanwhile, Technician Third Grade Thomas Robinson bound Valentine's ankles. At 3:00 p.m., Lt. Col. Peck faced about and cut the rope, which released the weight that actuated the trapdoors. Ten minutes later, the medical officers entered the lower portion of the gallows and pronounced Leo Valentine Sr. dead of judicial asphyxia at 3:11 p.m.[59]

The same procedure applied to General Prisoner Oscar N. Newman, who arrived at the scaffold at 3:36 p.m. When asked for a final statement, Newman replied, "I am awful sorry for everything I did. If I wasn't drunk, I would not have done it. God bless all you boys. God bless the Army."

Newman, now moments from death, asked if Chaplain Peak would say a prayer with him, which the chaplain did. Woods adjusted the noose and hood, and at 3:40 p.m., Peck cut the rope, releasing the trapdoor. Medical officers Hart, Jarrett, and Keefe pronounced Oscar N. Newman dead of judicial asphyxia at 3:51 p.m.[60] The remains of both men were interred at the US Military Cemetery at Solers, France.

Guiclan, Finistère, France

William E. Davis, Wednesday, December 27, 1944

December was a slow month for John Woods, although he was reassigned to the Provost Marshal Section in the headquarters of the Brittany Base Section. However, December 27, 1944, was a big day for Woods, who—for the first time—would serve as the primary hangman of an American soldier, the execution of General Prisoner William E. Davis at Guiclan, Finistère, France. Davis had been born in Richmond, Virginia, on March 8, 1915. In 1940, while farming, he suffered severe frostbite in both feet that resulted in both his big toes being amputated at the upper joints. William took a common-law wife in 1943 and was inducted on October 7, 1943, in Richmond. He stood 5'5½" tall and weighed 141 pounds.

On August 28, 1944, PFC Davis, assigned to the 3121st Quartermaster Service Company, an all-black unit assigned to the US 9th Army, and PFC J. C. Potts had gone to a farmhouse after drinking some cider alcohol. They saw a woman and tried to bribe her into having sex with them. A group of Frenchmen burst into the house, and one tried to grab Davis's weapon. Davis later stated that he then ran out of the house and started shooting at the Frenchmen. He said that he saw the woman, also running out of the house, fall, and told his companion: "I think I shot that woman."

A general court-martial convened at Morlaix, France, on September 23, 1944; Davis was convicted of assault and murder of a French woman and sentenced to death the following day. The court sentenced J. C. Potts to life imprisonment to be served at the US penitentiary at Lewisburg, Pennsylvania. The US 9th Army commander, Lt. Gen. William H. Simpson—"Big Simp"—looked over the records, approved the verdict and sentence, and then sent the case up the chain of command.[61]

On December 21, 1944, the headquarters of the European theater published *General Court-*

Martial Order Number 146. Brig. Gen. R. B. Lord—by command of Gen. Eisenhower—directed that the execution would be carried out six days later.[62] On December 26, 1944, Maj. Harry M. Campbell read the execution order to General Prisoner Davis at the Brittany Base Section Guardhouse at 10:00 a.m. At 8:45 p.m., Capt. Thomas Baer, 49th Field Hospital, examined Davis and found him in excellent physical and mental condition.

The execution site was 200 yards from the actual spot of the murder, in compliance with command guidance that when possible, executions would be carried out near the scene of the crime. Engineers constructed the scaffold in a field 25 yards from the nearest road. In addition to the official party, there were five official witnesses, eleven US spectators, and three French observers. No townspeople were present.[63]

Twenty-seven men of Company A of the 795th Military Police Battalion, under the command of Capt. William G. Fleming, guarded the site. A covered personnel carrier brought General Prisoner Davis to the edge of the field; he dismounted with his guards and joined the official procession, which started at 10:54 a.m. in the following order: Lt. Col. Henry L. Peck; Chaplain (Major) Gerald P. O'Keefe; General Prisoner William E. Davis; guards Sgt. Dino A. Cavicchioli, Sgt. Thorrolf P. Dyro, and Sgt. Alfonso Girvalo; Capt. Milton Asbell, the recorder; and medical officers Capt. Walter V. Edwards, Capt. Chapin Hawley, and Capt. Thomas B. Baer. Up on the scaffold were Woods and Technician Third Grade Thomas F. Robinson.[64]

Lt. Col. Henry L. Peck, as the officer in charge, read *General Court-Martial Order Number 146* in its entirety. Davis made no statements; at 11:00 a.m., Woods, aided by Robinson, adjusted the black hood over Davis's head and then the rope noose around his neck. At 11:01 a.m., Peck signaled Woods, who cut the rope that released the weight and sprung the trap. At 11:13 a.m., the medical officers pronounced William Davis dead. Woods

then cut the execution rope and removed the body from under the scaffold.[65] Capt. Poole Rogers of the 610th Graves Registration Company signed for the body and removed it.[66] The Army interred the remains at the US Military Cemetery at Marigny, France, in Plot Z, grave 1-8.

Lérouville, Meuse, France

John David Cooper, Tuesday, January 9, 1945

John David Cooper and J. P. Wilson committed one of the worst crime sprees of the war, a two-night assault violently raping two fourteen-year-old girls, one eighteen-year-old girl, and one forty-year-old woman. Two of the rapes took place on September 19, 1944, at Lérouville, France; the second two rapes happened two days later at Ferme de Marville, France. The men also assaulted and wrongfully imprisoned several Frenchmen in a cellar. Born in Dover, Georgia, on June 11, 1922, John David Cooper was inducted at Ft. Benning, Georgia, on December 26, 1942. As a civilian, he was a coal truck driver, earning $25 a week. The US 3rd Army convened a general court-martial at Nancy, France, on October 25, 1944. The two men, assigned to the 3966th Quartermaster Truck Company, were tried together; they pled not guilty, but the court convicted them and sentenced them to death by hanging. General Prisoner J. P. Wilson subsequently escaped from the stockade.[67]

The Army proceeded with Cooper's execution, which occurred at a rock quarry southwest of Lérouville during a drizzling snow as the sun tried to peep through the clouds. The previous night, military police had guarded Cooper at Commercy, 3 miles southeast of the scaffold. Two of the rape victims were in attendance as spectators. Lt. Col. Henry Peck supervised the event; Sgt. Alfonso Girvalo, Sgt. Dino Cavicchioli, and Sgt. Thorrolf Dyro served as guards. John David Cooper had no final words, and everything went according to plan; Woods dropped the trapdoor at 11:07 a.m.[68] Cooper's body was interred at the US Military Cemetery Number 1, Limay, in Meurthe-et-Moselle, France.

Beaufay, Sarthe, France

Walter J. Baldwin, Wednesday, January 17, 1945

It was a cool morning with a steady drizzle of rain on January 17, 1945, in the village of Beaufay in the Sarthe region of France. Snow blanketed a 100-by-60-yard, rectangular, hedgerowed field on the farm of Monsieur Adolpha Drouin, but Adolpha was not present; an American soldier had murdered him the previous August. Now that soldier, Walter J. Baldwin, was going to die.[69]

Baldwin, a black soldier born August 20, 1923, in Shellmound, Mississippi, was the oldest of four children. Baldwin worked in a furniture store; he was inducted into the service in March 1941 at Camp Shelby, Mississippi, becoming an ammunition hauler.[70] Pvt. Baldwin and his unit were assigned in the Communications Zone in the European theater of operations. Baldwin went AWOL on August 18, 1944. Five days later, on August 23, he entered a barnyard at about 3:30 p.m. There was a struggle just outside the Drouin home; Adolpha was fatally shot, and his wife, Madame Louise Drouin, was wounded in the thigh. Later that day, Baldwin walked in to an American unit bivouacked nearby and admitted that he had just shot a Frenchman.[71]

A general court-martial convened on October 6, 1944, at the Palais de Justice, Le Mans, France. Baldwin pled not guilty to all charges and did not testify in his own defense, but Madame Drouin and her daughter testified for the prosecution. The court convicted Baldwin of one count of murder, a violation of the 92nd Article of War; one count of absenting himself from his unit, a violation of the 61st Article of War; and one count of assault, a violation of the 93rd Article of War. The court then sentenced Pvt. Walter Baldwin

to death by hanging.[72] Brig. Gen. Leroy P. Collins, Loire Section commander, approved the verdict and sentence. On January 10, 1945, the headquarters, European theater of operations, issued an order directing that the execution be carried out.

Shortly before 11:00 a.m., a ½-ton, 4x4 command-and-reconnaissance car drove to the edge of the field, and from it guards assisted the condemned man from the vehicle. At 10:57 a.m., the official procession, headed by Lt. Col. Henry L. Peck and including a chaplain, General Prisoner Baldwin, three guards (Sgt. Russell E. Boyle, Sgt. Kenneth L. Breitenstein, and Sgt. David E. Miller), and four official witnesses, marched in column to the scaffold, a crisp pace lasting but thirty seconds. The procession halted and the guards tied Baldwin's hands behind him, while Peck and the chaplain ascended the steps. Less than one minute later, Baldwin—assisted by the guards— climbed the steps, stood on the trapdoor, and had his ankles bound. The time was 10:59 a.m.; thirty seconds later, Peck read the general court-martial order and asked Baldwin if he had a statement to make. The prisoner replied, "No, I have nothing to say to you, Colonel."[73]

Baldwin had nothing to say to the chaplain either, and at that point the hangman adjusted the hood and noose. The time was 11:03 a.m.; the chaplain started intoning a prayer. Seconds later, Peck silently signaled Woods, who cut the rope that released the weight and sprung the trap. The trap mechanism operated without fault, and the prisoner dropped cleanly through the trapdoor, remaining motionless. Witnesses heard no sounds and saw no swaying or muscular movement. Ten minutes later, Peck signaled medical officers to examine the body; they entered the lower screened understructure of the scaffold. At 11:19 a.m., the senior medical officer, Lt. Col. D. H. Waltrip, emerged and reported: "Sir, I pronounce this man officially dead."[74] The Army buried Baldwin's remains at the US Military Cemetery at Marigny, France, in Plot Z, grave 1-9.

St. Sulpice de la Forét, Ille-et-Vilaine, France

Arthur J. Farrell, Friday, January 19, 1945

On September 24, 1944, in Brittany, Pvt. Arthur J. Farrell, 17th Cavalry Reconnaissance Squadron, and Cpl. Wilford Teton raped a fifty-seven-year-old French woman. Ferrell, who was tall and white, and Teton, a Shoshone Indian who was short, were identified by the victim and two other French civilians with whom she lived. Almost immediately 1Lt. Maurice C. Reeves of the 1391st Engineer Forestry Battalion—who had received a report of a disturbance and arrived with an interpreter—apprehended Farrell just 75 yards from the scene of the crime. Teton escaped for the time being but was later apprehended.[75]

Arthur J. Farrell had been born in Jersey City, New Jersey, on November 20, 1906. He dropped out of high school after sophomore year and held a variety of trades. In one job as a Standard Oil truck driver, he accidentally backed over a woman and killed her. In 1944, he was convicted twice by summary courts-martial for AWOL.[76]

Brig. Gen. Roy W. Grower, the commander of the Brittany Base Section in the Communications Zone, ordered that a general court-martial convene at Rennes, France, on October 16, 1944; the two accused would be tried jointly. The panel sentenced Farrell to death by hanging and Teton to life imprisonment at the US penitentiary at Lewisburg, Pennsylvania. On January 10, 1945, in *General Court-Martial Order Number 11*, Brig. Gen. R. B. Lord—by command of Gen. Eisenhower—directed that the execution occur on January 19, 1945, at St. Sulpice de la Forét, France.[77]

Engineers constructed a scaffold in the rear courtyard of a school in that village. The tiny square was bordered on its southern side by a stone and wooden fence; on the northern side was a thick hedge. The schoolhouse formed a third side of the square, which may have served at one time as a playground. On the remaining side stood a small shed. A frigid blanket of slush covered the ground. Although the sun was shining, the weather was cool and a northerly winter wind made it seem even colder. The little square, no bigger than a high-school basketball court, was packed with about thirty-five officials, witnesses, and authorized spectators.[78]

The three medical officers were ninety minutes late, and since no military hanging could proceed without them, the officials and witnesses were standing around in the cold, which did nothing to improve the mood. The doctors finally arrived and at 12:08 p.m. a covered personnel carrier brought Arthur Farrell to an alley next to the schoolyard. He descended and joined a procession for the death march. Leading was Lt. Col. Henry Peck, Chaplain Gerald P. O'Keefe walked to Peck's left, and then walked Farrell and three guards: Sgt. Russell E. Boyle, Sgt. Kenneth L. Breitenstein, and Sgt. David E. Miller. Capt. Milton B. Asbell, the recorder, followed.[79]

One of the MPs carried a brace board in case the prisoner grew violent or fainted. In that case, the condemned would be placed on the 6'6" long by 7" wide hardwood board, and three leather straps would be buckled to pinion him to the frame. Farrell halted at 12:09 p.m.; the guards tied his hands behind his back, while Lt. Col. Peck read *General Court-Martial Order Number 11*. Guards assisted Farrell up the stairs; he stood on the trapdoor as his ankles were bound. He had no last statement as Woods adjusted the black hood and the noose around Farrell's neck and head. Peck gave the silent signal to Woods, who cut the rope that released a weight, springing the trapdoor at 12:13 p.m. The three tardy medical officials, Capt. Isadore G. Manstein, Capt. Charles E. Cassady, and Capt. Charles E. Thompson, pronounced Farrell dead at 12:26 p.m. His remains were interred at the US Military Cemetery at Marigny, France, in Plot Z, grave 1-10, on January 22, 1945.[80] Wilford Teton was released from prison in June 1955.

Loire Disciplinary Training Center, Le Mans, France

James W. Twiggs, Monday, January 22, 1945

Arguments between soldiers have occurred since armies were created, and World War II was no different. Pvt. James W. Twiggs of Company F, 1323rd Engineer General Service Regiment, shot and killed Pvt. William Adams after a discussion in which his mother was mentioned. Maj. Gen. Lucius D. Clay, commander, Normandy Base Section, Communications Zone, determined that the soldier be tried by a general court-martial, and one met on October 25, 1944, at 9:00 a.m. at the Omaha Beach Section in Laurent, France. Twiggs pled not guilty to one charge of murder; the court ruled that Twiggs had lain in wait for Adams and that it had been a premeditated ambush. The court convicted him and sentenced him to death. The staff judge advocate of the Normandy Base Section reviewed the case file for sufficiency on November 18, 1944. Maj. Gen. Clay approved the sentence on November 21, 1944. Gen. Eisenhower signed the confirmation order, confirming the sentence of death but stating no place or date of execution. On January 13, 1945, in *General Court-Martial Order Number 16*, Brig. Gen. R. B. Lord directed that the execution be carried out on January 22, 1945, at the Loire DTC in Le Mans.[81]

Born in Topeka, Kansas, on January 4, 1920, James W. Twiggs later moved to Grand Lake, Arkansas, and also lived in Leland, Mississippi. The black soldier was inducted into the Army on December 3, 1942, at Camp Wolters, Texas; he later served at Camp Swift, Texas, where he was convicted by a special court-martial for AWOL, and a summary court-martial convicted him of being drunk on duty as a driver.

On January 21, Woods drove an Army flatbed truck to a ravine just outside the northwest corner of the Loire DTC. On the truck was a portable scaffold; Woods, engineers, and a prisoner detail removed the scaffold from the truck and set it up just outside the barbed-wire fence. Woods tested the trapdoor that afternoon and the following morning. At 10:45 a.m. on January 22, officials, witnesses, and spectators gathered at the site. A large crowd of sixty-seven personnel, including for the first time eight general prisoners (GPs)—four black and four white—would witness the death of General Prisoner Twiggs. The GPs stood in a single rank behind the stockade barbed wire, about 20 yards behind the other spectators. Fifty-one enlisted men of Company C, 389th Military Police Battalion, under the command of 1Lt. Roland B. Dixon, guarded the site.[82]

A command and reconnaissance car brought James Twiggs to within 25 yards of the scaffold, where he met Lt. Col. Henry L. Peck, Chaplain James M. Maudy, and guards Sgt. Russell E. Boyle, Sgt. Alfonso Girvalo, and Sgt. Robert V. Childers. Capt. Milton B. Asbell, the recorder, stood in the rear. No one else was allowed within 25 yards of the prisoner. Twiggs halted at the base of the scaffold at 10:58 a.m. The guards tied his hands behind his back and assisted him up the steps, while Peck read *General Court-Martial Order Number 16*. Standing on the trapdoor, Twiggs was asked if he had any last statements; he said nothing. Woods adjusted the noose and hood at 11:02 a.m., and Chaplain Maudy began to recite a prayer.[83]

Seconds later, Lt. Col. Peck nodded to Woods, who then cut the rope that released the weight and sprung the trapdoor. Ten minutes later, three medical officers entered the lower section of the scaffold, which was screened by green canvas to prevent view of the deceased by the spectators, and examined the condemned, but he was not yet dead. Eight minutes later they checked again, and Lt. Col. Harry Butler of the 166th General Hospital pronounced James Twiggs dead at 11:22 a.m. Peck dismissed the witnesses; Woods and Robinson cut the rope, releasing the body.[84] Capt. Poole Rogers, 610th Graves Registration Company, signed for the remains, which were buried the following day at the US Army Cemetery at Marigny, France, in Plot Z, grave 1-11. Twenty minutes to die was rough on the GPs in attendance—and even rougher on James Twiggs.

• • •

This was the first of many executions at the Loire Disciplinary Training Center. Known to many GIs as the "Continental Stockade," the center—which officially opened on December 5, 1944—was a rough place because it had rough inmates, over 1,600 in January 1945. The Army believed that anything less strict would invite many GIs to "ride out the war" behind the front in comparative safety, rather than face combat. The stockade administration ensured that each prisoner worked eight hours per weekday, including three hours of hard labor. Incarcerated soldiers participated in thirty minutes of physical training and thirty additional minutes of close-order drill every weekday. Soldiers lived in two-man pup tents, administration personnel were located in red brick buildings. The "Continental Stockade" had ominous trappings: soldiers condemned to death wore distinctive black uniforms.[85]

Fort d'Orange, Citadel, Namur, Belgium

Mervin Holden and Elwood J. Spencer, Tuesday, January 30, 1945

At about 11:00 p.m. on October 24, 1944 two soldiers—one described as a "tall Negro" and the other as a "small mulatto," rang the doorbell at the home of a Belgian couple and stated that they were police. The soldiers, who had been drinking, entered. A neighbor heard a cry for help. The next day the couple went to American authorities; a US Army physician examined the fifty-one-year-old woman but could not determine if she had been raped. The victim and her husband identified Pvt. Elwood J. Spencer and Pvt. Mervin

Holden, 646th Quartermaster Truck Company, as the perpetrators at a lineup of soldiers at an MP headquarters the next day.[86]

Mervin Holden, born on October 1, 1920, in Robeline, Louisiana, completed the fourth grade at age twelve. Before the war he had been in several knife fights and had four jagged scars to prove it. Holden was inducted on September 24, 1942, at Shreveport, Louisiana. He had one previous special court-martial conviction for failure to obey a lawful order by a superior. He weighed 210 pounds and was 6'1" tall. Elwood Spencer was born in Gastonia, North Carolina, on December 4, 1924. He completed seventh grade, leaving at age fifteen to go to work. He had one previous special court-martial conviction for disobeying an order; his punishment was a reduction from technician fifth grade.[87]

A general court-martial met on November 14, 1944, at 9:00 a.m. The men were charged separately but were tried together by the same jury. Spencer was charged with one count of carnal knowledge, a violation of the 92nd Article of War, and a charge of sodomy and a charge of assault, both violations of the 96th Article of War. Holden was not charged with sodomy but was charged with the other violations. Both men pled not guilty, took the stand, and stated that all actions with the woman were consensual. The victim testified that both men had held a knife to her. The panel convicted both men on charges and sentenced them to death by hanging.[88] Gen. Eisenhower confirmed the sentences of death on December 23, 1944. Brig. Gen. R. B. Lord directed that the executions would occur on January 30, 1945, at Fort d'Orange, the Citadel of Namur, in Namur, Belgium.[89]

The fort, known as "The Devil's Castle," sat atop a hill 2 miles southwest of Namur, overlooking the Meuse and the Sambre Rivers; surrounding the stronghold was a dry moat 50 feet deep. A long wooden bridge spanned the moat and led to the fort's entrance. Inside was an irregular hexagon courtyard measuring 40 by 20 yards. Dreary gray stone walls stretched to a height of 20 to 50 feet. A wooden scaffold stood in the center; 3 inches of snow blanketed the entire area, and a slight but "crisp" wind propelled snow flurries. Present were 108 officers and men, perhaps the biggest execution gathering of the war.[90]

At 11:00 a.m., a ¼-ton, 4x4 vehicle halted 10 yards from the bridge, and from it guards assisted General Prisoner Mervin Holden from the vehicle. At 11:01 a.m., the official procession, headed by Lt. Col. Henry L. Peck and including Chaplain Lorenzo Q. Brown—a black, Methodist minister—General Prisoner Holden, three guards (Sgt. Russell E. Boyle, Sgt. Kenneth L. Breitenstein, and Sgt. Alfonso Girvalo), Capt. Milton B. Asbell (the recorder), and six official witnesses, marched over the bridge, passed through the arched entrance, executed a column half left and halted at the foot of the scaffold. The march took two minutes, finishing at 11:03 a.m. Technician Third Grade Thomas Robinson bound Holden's hands behind his back and assisted him up the wooden steps. Standing on the trapdoor, Holden's feet were bound while he listened to Lt. Col. Peck read *General Court-Martial Order Number 20*. Peck then asked if Holden had a statement to make, and the condemned man asked a question instead: "May I see the rope?" Lt. Col. Peck replied, "It is forbidden." Woods took over and adjusted the hood and noose; Chaplain Brown started intoning a prayer. Thirty seconds later, Peck silently signaled Woods, who cut the rope that released the weight and sprung the trap at 11:05 a.m. Everything functioned smoothly.[91]

Numbingly cold, time seemed to creep by excruciatingly slowly before the second execution. At 11:53 a.m., the same vehicle returned with Elwood Spencer. At 11:54 a.m., the official procession marched over the bridge and ended at the foot of the scaffold at 11:56 a.m. Thomas Robinson bound Spencer's hands behind his back and assisted him up the wooden stairs. Standing on the trapdoor, Spencer's feet were bound while he listened to Lt. Col. Peck read *General Court-*

Martial Order Number 21. The prisoner made no statement; to Chaplain Brown he simply said, "Explain it to my mother, that's all."[92]

Woods adjusted the hood and noose. The time was half a minute before high noon; Chaplain Brown started praying. Again, some thirty seconds later, Peck silently signaled Woods, who cut the rope that released the weight and sprung the trap. The trap mechanism operated without fault, and Spencer dropped cleanly through the trapdoor, remaining motionless—no sounds or muscular movement were heard or seen; the body swayed slightly in the frigid breeze. No witnesses showed visible or audible reaction. Ten minutes later, Peck signaled three medical officers, Maj. John S. Wilson, Capt. Thomas C. Hankins, and Capt. Charles J. Tommasello, to examine the body; entering the lower screened understructure of the scaffold, at 12:13 a.m. Maj. Wilson emerged and reported: "Sir, I pronounce this man officially dead."[93] The remains of both men were buried at the US Military Cemetery at Andilly, France.

Lérouville, Meuse, France

J. P. Wilson, Friday, February 2, 1945

The Cooper-Wilson case, in which the two soldiers had raped four women in September 1944, had been on temporary hold after General Prisoner J. P. Wilson escaped from the stockade and John David Cooper had been hanged on January 9, 1945. Wilson had been born in Columbus, Mississippi, on January 24, 1918; his religion was listed as Protestant. Standing 5'11" tall, he weighed 185 pounds. Wilson was married and had an eighteen-month-old son. Entering the Army on December 26, 1942, at Ft. Dix, New Jersey, he had been convicted in three previous courts-martial for AWOL.

As John Woods would find, sometimes hanging equipment just didn't work quite the way the Army manual had intended, and there was no better example of that than one cold Friday morning of

February 2, 1945, at a rock quarry southwest of Lérouville, France. A shear 80-foot-high cliff behind the scaffold jutted upward to the blue sky. The gray rock wall had been scarred by heavy sledgehammers and sharp steel chisels until there were gaping fissures throughout its face.[94]

Maybe it was the cold that caused the malfunction; the quarry was covered with a 2-inch blanket of snow and ice, and slush was slippery throughout the area. Although the weather was now clear with a slight breeze, the temperature was dropping. The seventy-one witnesses, officials, and spectators made for a large crowd—all present to see General Prisoner J. P. Wilson hang, but that almost did not happen, although the previous evening at 8:30 p.m., a medical officer in Commercy had declared that Wilson was in excellent physical and mental condition.[95]

A ¾-ton, command-and-reconnaissance vehicle brought Wilson and his guards at 10:50 a.m. to a position 100 yards from the scaffold; he would walk to the gallows from there. Lt. Col. Henry L. Peck led the way at a brisk pace. They arrived at the scaffold; MP guards Sgt. Russell E. Boyle, Sgt. Kenneth L. Breitenstein, and Sgt. Alfonso Girvalo tied Wilson's hands behind him at 10:52 a.m. and assisted him up the thirteen steps. Peck read *General Court-Martial Order Number 30*; the prisoner made no last statement. At 10:59 a.m., Woods, assisted by Technician Third Grade Thomas Robinson, adjusted the hood and noose over Wilson's head and neck, and Peck gave the nod to spring the trapdoor. The recorder described what happened next:[96] "The trap mechanism did not function properly due to faulty construction. The quick action and ingenuity of the executioner and his assistant in overcoming the mechanical failure of the trap brought the suspense and delay to a very minimum. However, the body was catapulted to the lower portion of the scaffold clearly and hung suspended with a slight swaying due to the mild breeze, but, with no sounds or muscular movement."

We probably will never know exactly what happened up on the scaffold in the vicious cold, but it is likely that Woods, Robinson, or both precariously held on to the railing and jumped on the frozen trapdoor to free it, all the while trying not to fall into the opening, when the door did finally give way. All's well that ends well—although not for J. P. Wilson—and the duo finally forced the trapdoor to drop. Three medical officers, Maj. Andrew J. McAdams, Capt. Ralph S. Blasiele, and Capt. William H. Devinelli, pronounced the prisoner dead at 11:19 a.m.[97] For the spectators, it was an event they would never forget; for John Woods it was just another day at the office.

Bricquebec, Manche, France

Waiters Yancy and Robert L. Skinner, Saturday, February 10, 1945

On the night of August 1, 1944, at 10:30 p.m., two soldiers assigned to the 1511th Engineer Water Supply Company strolled into the tiny three house hamlet of Hameau-Pigeon, France, looking for cider. They ended up murdering one man, shooting two others, and assaulting a nineteen-year-old girl.[98] Waiters Yancy, born in 1923, considered Chicago his home; in civilian life he had been charged with statutory rape and in another case had assaulted an older woman by hitting her in the head with a rock. Robert Skinner, born on May 20, 1924, in Paris, Tennessee, lived with his mother in Chicago and Dayton, Ohio, after his father died. He graduated from high school in Murphysboro, Illinois, and later attended a trade school in Chicago. Just after his fifteenth birthday, Skinner received probation for two years for petty larceny. Three years later he was arrested at a crap game and given the all-too-frequent ultimatum of "jail or the Army." Skinner picked the latter and was inducted on May 21, 1943, at Fort Thomas, Kentucky; he later went to Ft. Leonard Wood, Missouri, for engineer training.[99]

Both men were black and were tried separately. The general court-martial of Pvt. Waiters Yancy met at 9:00 a.m. on November 7, 1944, at Cherbourg, France. Yancy pled not guilty to all charges, including rape and murder; the panel unanimously found him guilty on all charges, and on November 9, 1944, the court sentenced Waiters Yancy to death by hanging. On November 8, 1944, Robert L. Skinner's trial began at the same location at 9:05 a.m. Five of the jurors had previously been members of general courts-martial that convicted and sentenced to death Richard Scott and William Pennyfeather; the jury unanimously found Skinner guilty of carnal knowledge. The court adjourned at 11:15 a.m., the entire trial taking just 130 minutes. Gen. Eisenhower signed the order confirming the death sentence for Pvt. Skinner on December 14, 1944; he signed the order confirming the death sentence for Private Yancy on December 23, 1944.[100]

On the cold, rainy morning of February 10, 1945, at Bricquebec, France, twenty-eight authorized spectators stood near a wooden scaffold located in an orchard off the Avenue Matignon. At approximately 9:58 a.m. a covered 2½-ton truck approached the field and halted 50 yards from the single entrance. A procession then formed and marched from the vehicle to the scaffold. In the lead was Lt. Col. Henry L. Peck. To his left was Chaplain Kilian R. Bowler. Next walked General Prisoner Yancy, who was flanked by two guards and trailed by a third guard, who carried the brace board: Sgt. Clyde R. Perkins, Cpl. Albin S. Paprocki, and PFC George B. Weber. Capt. Milton B. Asbell and five official witnesses brought up the rear.[101]

The party halted at the foot of the scaffold; the guards bound the arms of the condemned behind him and escorted him up the steps. At 10:04 a.m., Lt. Col. Peck read *General Court-Martial Number 33* while the guards bound the prisoner's ankles, and then asked the prisoner if he had any final words. Yancy replied, "Thank you for everything." Chaplain Bowler then asked

the same question, to which the prisoner replied, "Thank you for all that you've done." Woods adjusted the hood and rope at 10:07 a.m. and the chaplain began to pray. Thirty seconds later, Peck gave a silent signal and Woods cut the rope that released the weight and sprung the trapdoor. Everything functioned smoothly, and at 10:18 a.m. Peck ordered the three medical officers to examine the prisoner. Capt. Louis J. Baronberg, Capt. Bernard S. Betherick, and Capt. Louis J. Guardino walked into the lower scaffold and reported at 10:20 a.m.: "Sir, we do not find this man dead." Peck ordered that the medical officers wait five more minutes. They did so, examined the body, and pronounced Yancy dead at 10:27 a.m., almost twenty minutes after the trapdoor opened. Woods then cut the rope and removed the body from beneath the scaffold.[102]

The witnesses remained in the cold rain for another twenty-five minutes for the second execution. Once again a vehicle pulled up to the entrance of the field; General Prisoner Robert Skinner dismounted. Everything occurred in the same sequence, with Lt. Col. Peck reading *General Court-Martial Order Number 32* at 10:58 a.m. He then asked Skinner for his last words, which were "Thanks very much." Then Chaplain Bowler spoke to the condemned man, who answered, "Thank you very much, chaplain." Again the trapdoor slammed open, and by 11:17 a.m. the three medical officers pronounced Robert L. Skinner dead.[103] The Army buried both bodies at the US Military Cemetery at Marigny, France, in Plot Z (Yancy in grave 1-12 and Skinner in grave 1-13) on February 12, 1945.

• • •

On February 12, 1945, MSgt. Woods was formally assigned to the 2913th DTC. The next day, perhaps to tie up loose ends, the center commandant wrote a letter to the Army adjutant general, Maj. Gen. J. A. Ulio, requesting confirmation concerning Woods's previous service in the US

Navy. The letter finally made its way to the Records Division of the Navy, and a Lt. (j.g). Harrison Fiddesof sent a letter to Gen. Ulio confirming that Woods had indeed enlisted on December 3, 1929, that he had been AWOL from February 24, 1930, to March 7, 1930, and that he had been discharged—with an ordinary discharge, under honorable conditions—on May 15, 1930.[104]

Plabennec, Finistère, France

William Mack, Thursday, February 15, 1945

Five days after the previous execution, Woods had more work to do. Pvt. William Mack was a cook in Battery A of the 578th Field Artillery Battalion. A black soldier, he had been born in St. George, South Carolina, on September 21, 1910. He lived with his family until his father died when William was fourteen; he then lived on his own until 1937, finishing the sixth grade at age eighteen. He later worked for a steel company in Brooklyn, New York, and also was employed by the Peoria Paper Box Company and the Burr Metal Company. Mack was inducted into the Army on November 7, 1942, at Ft. Dix, New Jersey.[105]

In France on August 20, 1944, Mack had the day off. At about 8:00 p.m., armed with his M1 carbine, he told his fellow soldiers he was leaving the battery area. Three hours later he entered the home of Eugene Tournellec, 1.5 miles from the battery area. Mack demanded cognac, wine, and cider and initially tried to kiss Tournellec's oldest daughter, Catherine. Eugene left the house to get help, during which time Mack fired a round through the door and then fired outside five or six times. One of the shots slammed into Eugene Tournellec's forehead, blowing a large hole in the top of his head, which proved mortal. Authorities arrested Mack, who told six versions of an alibi before admitting that he had shot the victim.[106]

A general court-martial convened at Morlaix, Brittany, France, at 10:30 a.m. on November 23, 1944. The charges against Mack included murder and assault; Mack pled not guilty to all charges and specifications and elected not to take the stand. The defense counsel introduced that Mack had been drinking heavily, inferring that he was not responsible for his actions. The court did not agree, voted unanimously to convict Mack of all charges, and sentenced him to hang.[107]

The Board of Review Number 1, consisting of Judge Advocates B. Franklin Riter, Ellwood W. Sargent, and Edward L. Stevens of the Branch Office of the Judge Advocate General with the European theater of operations, reviewed the case on January 30, 1945, and found that there were no serious problems with the trial. On February 9, 1945, the headquarters of the European theater of operations published *General Court-Martial Order Number 40*. Brig. Gen. R. B. Lord—by command of Gen. Eisenhower—directed that the execution of Private William Mack would be carried out at Plabennec, Finistère, France, on February 15, 1945.[108]

The site of the execution was an athletic field just outside the village of Plabennec, 8 miles north of Brest. First Lt. Allan H. Toole, with fifteen enlisted men of the 795th Military Police Battalion, guarded the perimeter of the field. A bright sun was shining, with mild and clear weather, and a slight wind was blowing that February 15, 1945. At 12:58 p.m. a covered 1½-ton truck halted 60 yards from the scaffold. Out stepped General Prisoner William Mack, joining Lt. Col. Henry Peck and Chaplain John E. Sjanken. Flanking Mack were two guards, SSgt. Charles R. Brinker and Sgt. John R. Hands. Behind, carrying a brace board, was Pvt. Jay D. Pease. The recorder, 1Lt. Lawrence Slon, came next, followed by six official witnesses.[109]

The procession stopped at the scaffold, and the two guards bound Mack's hands behind his back. The MPs then assisted him up the wooden steps, positioned him on the center of the trapdoor, and bound his ankles. Lt. Col. Peck read *General Court-Martial Order Number 40* and asked Mack if he had any final words. Mack responded: "I'm proud to say that I've made my peace with the

Lord. I've nothing to fear because I am on my way to peace and glory. I hope that the war will soon be over and everyone will return home to the ones that we love. Good Lord, take care of my family. Lead them and keep them on the straight and narrow path to glory. This is thy faithful servant talking."[110]

Chaplain Sjanken asked Mack if he had anything to say; the prisoner replied, "See that those pictures are kept together and are sent home with those letters I wrote." The chaplain then began to pray, while Woods first adjusted the black hood and then the rope. At 1:07 p.m. Peck gave a silent signal to Woods, who cut the rope that released a weight springing the trapdoor. At 1:17 p.m., Peck directed Capt. Frederick W. Hall, Capt. George G. Lenk, and Capt. Thomas B. Baer to examine the body of William Mack. They did but reported that he was not dead. Five minutes later, the three medical officers reentered the scaffold understructure, examined the prisoner, and pronounced Mack officially deceased, signing a certificate stating that at 1:25 p.m. on February 15, 1945, William Mack died of judicial asphyxis (execution by hanging).[111] The Army interred the remains of William Mack on February 19, 1945, at the US Military Cemetery at Marigny, France, in Plot Z, grave 1-14.

Étienville, Manche, France

William C. Downes, Wednesday, February 28, 1945

On July 12, 1944, three black soldiers in the 597th Ordnance Ammunition Company, Pvt. James R. Parrott, Pvt. Grant U. Smith, and Pvt. William C. Downes, broke into a home in Étienville, France, and raped a sixty-two-year-old woman and her fifteen-year-old daughter. Two weeks later, the three soldiers went on the prowl again, broke into a home in the village of Renouf, 2 miles from Étienville, and raped a middle-aged widow. Notified of the attack, 1Lt. Michael Sorbello of the 795th

Anti-Aircraft Artillery Automatic Weapons Battalion rushed to the scene and found the three men near the location of the Renouf attack.[112]

A general court-martial met at Cherbourg, France, on November 22, 1944. All three soldiers pled not guilty to three counts of carnal knowledge, and two counts of breaking and entering. The jury found William C. Downes guilty of all charges but determined that James R. Parrott and Grant U. Smith were guilty only of the charges related to the July 26, 1944, attack. The jury sentenced all three men to death by hanging.[113]

Gen. Eisenhower confirmed the sentences but then cited "special circumstances" and commuted the sentences of Parrott and Smith to dishonorable discharges from the service, forfeiture of all pay and allowances, and confinement at hard labor for life at the US penitentiary at Lewisburg, Pennsylvania. On January 14, 1945, Eisenhower signed the order confirming the sentence of death for Pvt. Downes.[114] On February 23, 1945, the headquarters of the European theater of operations published *General Court-Martial Order Number 50*. Brig. Gen. R. B. Lord—by command of Gen. Eisenhower—directed that the execution of Downes would be carried out at Étienville, Finistère, France, on February 28, 1945.[115] William Clifton Downes had been born on January 27, 1915, in Copeland, Virginia. He had been inducted into the Army on December 17, 1942, at Norfolk, Virginia. In May 1944, a special court-martial convicted him of AWOL.[116]

A set of orders from the headquarters of the Loire DTC directed that Woods, Technician Third Grade Thomas F. Robinson, and Technician Fifth Grade Herbert A. Kleinbeck Jr. proceed to Étienville two days before the execution.[117] At 9:45 a.m. on February 28, 1945, twenty-two observers—including one of the rape victims—met at a scaffold constructed in an open field 300 yards south of Étienville, France. An intermittent rain fell, and the sky was slightly overcast. Low hedgerows surrounded the field; the scaffold faced south. First Lt. David J. Duff and a detail from Company A of the 384th Military Police Battalion guarded the site. At 9:58 a.m. a closed, 2½-ton, 6x6 truck slowly approached the field and halted 50 yards from the scaffold. William Downes climbed down and took his place in a column of men, led by Lt. Col. Henry L. Peck, who was followed by the prisoner and Chaplain Augustus G. Spears. Surrounding the prisoner were three MP guards: Sgt. Russell E. Boyle, Sgt. Kenneth L. Breitenstein, and Sgt. Alfonso Girvalo. Recorder 1Lt. Lawrence Slon and five officials brought up the rear.[118]

The procession marched to the foot of the steps and halted at 10:00 a.m. The MPs bound Downes's arms behind his back and assisted him to climb the scaffold steps. After Technician Fifth Grade Herbert Kleinbeck Jr. bound the prisoner's ankles, Lt. Col. Peck read the general court-martial order. The prisoner made no final statement, nor did he make a statement to Chaplain Spears. After Woods adjusted the black hood and rope, the prisoner prayed aloud for one minute. Peck nodded to Woods, who cut the rope that released the weight and sprung the trapdoor at 10:05 a.m. The body dropped. After reaching its lowest point, it swung in a slight motion, but that was not visible to anyone not on the platform. At 10:19 a.m., Peck ordered Capt. Robert L. Kasha, Capt. Louis J. Baronberg, and Capt. Louis J. Guardino to examine the body of the condemned; they entered the lower screened understructure of the scaffold and pronounced that Downes was dead.[119] The Army interred Downes at the US Military Cemetery at Marigny, Manche, France, the same day as his death. He was buried in grave 1-15 of the General Prisoner section; to his left was William Mack. The grave was marked with a wooden cross and an embossed identification tag.

•••

Herbert A. Kleinbeck Jr. (Army Service Number 16100440), a technician fifth grade and assistant hangman to MSgt. Woods for this execution, was born on August 9, 1920, in Chicago. He was single, had one year of college at the University of Illinois, and was also trained as an apprentice tool and die maker. Kleinbeck, who listed his residence as Elmhurst, Illinois, was inducted in Chicago on August 14, 1942. He stood 5'10" tall and weighed 164 pounds. After basic training, he attended military police school, where he trained as a clerk, light-truck driver, and motor dispatcher. Discharged from the Army at Ft. Sheridan, Illinois, on December 24, 1945, for his service, he was awarded the European–African–Middle Eastern Campaign Medal and the Good Conduct Medal.[120]

La Saussaye, Commune de Bure, Orne, France

Amos Agee, John C. Smith, and Frank Watson, Saturday, March 3, 1945

Privates Amos Agee, John C. Smith, and Frank Watson, 644th Quartermaster Troop Transport Company, arrived in France on August 30, 1944. Within four days they had raped a French woman and robbed two French men. Shortly afterward, the victims identified all three. On October 18, 1944, a general court-martial began at Rambouillet, outside Paris. All three accused submitted sworn statements in which they admitted going to the house that afternoon, but all three stated they had nothing to do with the events of later in the evening. All three were convicted of the more serious charge of carnal knowledge. The next day, the jury sentenced the defendants to death by hanging. The commanding general of the Advance Section, Communications Zone, Brig. Gen. Ewart G. Plank, approved the sentences on December 4, 1944. On January 14, 1945, Gen. Eisenhower signed a letter confirming all three sentences but withheld the order directing the executions.[121]

Amos Agee was born in 1916 in Alabama; he attended high school for three years. Agee was inducted into the Army on November 19, 1941, at Ft. McClellan, Alabama; he stood 5'8" tall and weighed 174 pounds. He had been convicted three times before at a court-martial, once for failure to obey the order of a superior officer and twice for AWOL. John C. Smith was born on September 20, 1917, in Bedford County, Virginia, one of ten children. He left school after four years and became a farmer. Smith was inducted on October 14, 1942, at Roanoke, Virginia; he stood 5'2" tall and weighed 127 pounds. Frank Watson, born in Florida in 1923, was inducted at Camp Blanding, Florida, on September 29, 1943.[122]

On Saturday, March 3, 1945, Lt. Col. Henry L. Peck assembled twenty-six observers at a temporary gallows in a hedgerowed orchard in the village of La Saussaye, France. The weather was cool, clear, and sunny. First Lt. William Malkenson and twenty men from Company B, 389th Military Police Battalion, provided the guard force. At 11:00 a.m. a ½-ton, command-and-reconnaissance vehicle approached and drove to the entrance to the field; from it, guards assisted Amos Agee. At 11:02 a.m., Lt. Col. Peck led the execution procession, consisting of himself, a chaplain, the prisoner, three guards (Sgt. Russell E. Boyle, Sgt. Alfonso Girvalo, and Sgt. Kenneth L. Breitenstein), and recorder Capt. Milton B. Asbell. During the half-minute march, Agee repeated: "Lord Jesus have mercy . . . through the Valley of Death . . . Lord have mercy . . . thy rod and thy staff . . . O Lord have mercy." The group reached the foot of the gallows, at which point Peck and the chaplain ascended the stairs.[123]

Guards bound Agee's hands behind his back at 11:03 a.m. and led him up the steps and to the trapdoor. Thirty seconds later, Peck read *General Court-Martial Order Number 53*, directing the execution. Thomas Robinson bound Agee's feet at 11:04 a.m. Peck and then the chaplain asked Agee if he had any last words. Agee replied to Peck: "Thank you for everything." To the chaplain he replied, "Father, I thank you for everything." After a moment, the chaplain began the Lord's Prayer, and Woods adjusted the hood and noose.

The time was 11:07 a.m. The prisoner then asked: "Let me pray a little."[124]

After ninety seconds, Lt. Col. Peck silently signaled Woods, who cut the rope that released the weight and sprung the trap. The trap mechanism operated without a hitch, and the prisoner dropped cleanly through the trapdoor and hung suspended in the lower screened recess of the scaffold. The witnesses stood silent without reaction as the chaplain performed the last rites; the time was 11:09 a.m. At 11:20 a.m., Peck ordered the three medical officers to examine the body. The men made their examination and returned to their original positions. The senior medical officer, Lt. Col. Herman F. DeFeo, then reported: "Sir, we pronounce this man officially dead." The time was 11:23 a.m.[125]

Pvt. John C. Smith was the next to meet Woods. At 11:40 a.m., the ½-ton, command-and-reconnaissance vehicle approached and returned to the entrance to the field, this time carrying Smith. The proceedings followed the same sequence as before until 11:45 a.m., when Lt. Col. Peck asked the condemned if he had anything to say. Smith replied, "I want to shake hands with you." Lt. Col. Peck complied and said, "Good luck, son." The prisoner replied, "See you all somewhere." Peck asked if Pvt. Smith had anything to say to the chaplain. Smith answered, "Write to my mother; see that she gets everything." The trapdoor opened at 11:47:30 a.m. That's when something went wrong. Smith's body dropped, but the fall apparently did not break his neck; possibly it was that Smith weighed 51 pounds less than Agee. When medical officers entered the lower understructure of the scaffold at noon, Lt. Col. DeFeo examined Smith for two minutes and announced, "Sir, this man is not dead." Peck ordered the doctors to wait five minutes. They did, and at 12:10 p.m. the medical officer reported, "Sir, I pronounce this man officially dead." Thomas F. Robinson cut the rope and removed the body. Graves registration personnel signed for the remains in just one minute, half the time the two procedures took in the first execution—the reason for this promptness was that Woods was scheduled to hang three men—and three it would be.[126]

That third man was Pvt. Frank Watson. At 12:35 p.m., the ½-ton, command-and-reconnaissance vehicle returned to the entrance to the field with Watson. Again, the same procedures were followed; Watson made no statement to the Peck, but to the chaplain he said, "All I want you to do is pray for me." At 12:44:30 p.m. the trapdoor opened; this time there were no problems, and by 1:00 p.m. the senior medical officer pronounced Watson dead. All three bodies were interred on March 5, 1945, at the US Military Cemetery at Marigny, France, in Plot Z, graves 1-16, 1-17, and 1-18. The recorder prepared three separate reports of the proceedings, all ending with "Each official performed his task in a highly efficient manner. The proceedings were conducted with dignity, solemnity, and military precision."[127]

Le Chene Daniel, Manche, France

Olin W. Williams, Thursday, March 29, 1945

Woods was on the clock on March 29, 1945; he had to hang two men that day in two different locations, but if anyone could get the job done, John would. Pvt. Olin W. Williams, 4194th Quartermaster Service Company, had been convicted of rape and murder, which had occurred on September 23, 1944, at the village of Le Chene Daniel, near Chérence-le-Héron, France. Per General Eisenhower's wishes, when possible, if a soldier committed a capital crime in a small French village, the execution would occur close to the scene so that the French people would see that the Americans would not tolerate such behavior. Olin Williams, a black soldier, had been born in Columbia, South Carolina, in 1923. He was inducted into the service on March 20, 1943, at Ft. Jackson.[128]

Unlike most capital crimes discussed in this study, which were quickly adjudicated, the investigation continued forty-seven days, until October 10; a few days later the commander of the Normandy Base Section decided a general court-martial was appropriate to handle the matter. However, by this time the unit had moved eastward to Belgium, and in the confusion of the front, it was not possible to begin the trial until December 15, 1944, when the witnesses were brought back to Granville, France. The court convened at 1:30 p.m. that day. Williams pled not guilty to one count of murder and one count of carnal knowledge, both violations of the 92nd Article of War. The panel convicted him of both and sentenced him to death. However, the next day, the German *Wehrmacht* launched a massive attack that would become known as the Battle of the Bulge. Not only did it disrupt tactical operations but it interrupted judicial proceedings as well, and the appropriate judicial reviews did not begin until late January.[129]

Gen. Eisenhower signed the order confirming the sentence of Pvt. Williams on March 4, 1945, but did not state when and where the execution would take place. On March 24, 1945, *General Court-Martial Order Number 85* directed that the execution would be carried out on March 29, 1945, near Le Chene Daniel, France.[130]

At 9:48 a.m. on March 29, 1945, the commanding officer, Loire DTC, assembled twenty-five personnel in a field along Route N 799, only 500 yards from the scene of the murder and rape.

The sky was sunless, the weather was cool, and the ground was soggy. Six enlisted men of the 387th Military Police Battalion and five enlisted men of the Beach District Guardhouse guarded the area. At 10:00 a.m. a 1½-ton, 6x6 covered personnel carrier arrived at the field, and General Prisoner Olin Williams dismounted. He joined a procession led by Lt. Col. Henry L. Peck, Chaplain Raymond W. Parker—a black, Presbyterian minister—and three MP guards: Sgt. Russell E. Boyle, Sgt. Alfonso Girvalo, and Sgt. Jack D. Briscoe (who carried a brace board). Behind the

MPs walked Capt. Milton B. Asbell, the recorder, and five official witnesses. The group arrived at the scaffold at 10:02 a.m. The MPs bound Williams's hands behind his back and led him up the thirteen steps and onto the trapdoor. At 10:03 a.m., Technician Third Grade Thomas Robinson bound Williams's ankles.[131]

Williams had no statements to make. At 10:05 a.m., Woods placed the black hood over Williams's head and then put the noose around the prisoner's neck and tightened it. Thirty seconds later Lt. Col. Peck gave a silent signal to Woods, who then cut the rope that released the weight and sprung the trap. Everything functioned as planned; about 10:19 a.m., Capt. Lawrence B. Kuhlmann, Capt. Robert S. Randall, and 1Lt. Carlos B. Brewer pronounced Williams dead. Peck dismissed the witnesses and spectators. Thomas Robinson cut the rope, and 1Lt. Milliard R. Jones, 3059th Quartermaster Graves Registration Company, took possession of the body, as Woods and Robinson readied to race to the next execution.[132] The Army buried the remains at the US Military Cemetery at Marigny, France, in Plot Z, grave 2-21.

Prise Guinment, Manche, France

Tommie Davison, Thursday, March 29, 1945

In midafternoon on August 23, 1944, a black American soldier came to a farm in the hamlet of Prise Guinment, asking for a chicken; he received one and promptly paid for it. Three other "colored" soldiers were with him; one of them warned the French farmer Henri Duqueroux that the soldier was dangerous, and almost on cue, Private Tommie Davison began yelling, made suggestive gestures, and asked Duqueroux for a mademoiselle, showing him 500 francs. The family quickly locked themselves inside the farmhouse. Davison departed but later returned about 5:00 p.m., waved a pistol, and raped one of the French women.[133]

One of the Frenchmen reported the incident to American authorities, and the 427th Quartermaster Troop Transport Company formed up; observing the formation, the Frenchman spotted Davison and informed Chief Warrant Officer (CWO) Earl E. Lane Jr., the unit personnel officer. Lane approached Davison, who suddenly started to withdraw a pistol, pointing it at the officer. A scuffle ensued, with CWO Lane and the company first sergeant trying to subdue Davison.[134] Davison's actions at the formation would undoubtedly have triggered serious repercussions, but he was in a lot more trouble than that. Born on August 10, 1914, in West Point, Mississippi, he was older than most of the other soldiers. Davison had no formal education and could neither read nor write. Inducted at Camp Shelby, Mississippi, on December 2, 1942, he had three previous court-martial convictions before this latest arrest.[135]

The Normandy Base Section commander decided to convene a general court-martial, which met at 1:30 p.m. on December 9, 1944, at Granville, France. Pvt. Davison pled not guilty to all charges, including assault, attempted assault against an official, and rape. The court found Tommie Davison guilty of all three charges—making a few minor changes to the lesser charges concerning wording—and sentenced him to be hanged by the neck until dead.[136] On March 24, 1945, the headquarters of the European theater of operations published *General Court-Martial Order Number 86*, which directed that the execution would be carried out on March 29, 1945, near Prise Guinment, Manche, France.

At 2:45 p.m. on March 29, 1945, Lt. Col. Henry L. Peck assembled the spectators at the gallows near the village of Prise Guinment. The weather was cool and clear. The ground was soggy, covered with a blanket of grass punctuated by a few trees. In the southeast corner of the field stood the scaffold; six enlisted men of the 387th Military Police Battalion and five enlisted men of the Beach District Guardhouse guarded the area. Lt. Col. Peck read aloud *General Court-Martial Order Number 86* and instructed everyone on proper conduct.[137]

At 2:59 p.m. a 1½-ton, 6x6, covered personnel carrier arrived at the entrance to the field, and General Prisoner Tommie Davison dismounted, joining a procession led by Lt. Col. Peck, Chaplain William B. Crocker—a minister in the Negro Baptist Church, and three guards, Sgt. Russell E. Boyle, Sgt. Alfonso Girvalo, and Sgt. Jack D. Briscoe, the last of whom carried a brace board. Capt. Milton B. Asbell walked behind the guards. The procession soon arrived at the scaffold, where the MPs bound Davison's hands behind his back, led him up the steps, and guided him to the center of the trapdoor. At 3:01 p.m., Technician Third Grade Thomas Robinson bound Davison's ankles. Lt. Col. Peck asked Davison if he had any last words; Davison was ready and answered: "I want you to understand, sir, I am innocent. I had nobody to talk to . . . if I could get out of the stockade. I went from the cell to the mess hall. I never had a chance. I had five non-coms to prove it."[138]

Lt. Col. Peck made no reply. Chaplain Crocker asked the prisoner if he had any last statements to make; Davison remained silent. At 3:02 p.m., Woods placed the black hood over Davison's head, put the noose around Davison's neck, and adjusted both. Thirty seconds later, Peck gave a silent signal. Woods cut the rope that released the weight and sprung the trap. At about 3:14 p.m., Capt. Lawrence B. Kuhlmann, Capt. Robert S. Randall, and 1Lt. Carlos B. Brewer marched to the understructure of the scaffold and examined the body. Returning to their positions, the senior officer reported, "Sir, there is still some evidence of life." Peck directed the physicians to wait until 3:21 p.m., when they made a second evaluation; this time they found that the prisoner was officially dead. Peck dismissed the spectators and Woods cut the rope.[139] First Lt. Milliard R. Jones of the 3059th Graves Registration Company signed a hand receipt and took possession of the body at 3:25 p.m. The remains were buried in Plot Z, grave 2-22, at the US Military Cemetery at Marigny, France.

• • •

Another soldier had taken too long to die. By this time, there had been too many SNAFUs—Situation Normal, All Fouled Up—concerning hangings throughout the Army. Too many procedures were being botched, and the War Department was none too pleased. Because the European theater of operations hanged more soldiers than any other during the war, those hangings carried out by MSgt. Woods must have been part of the perceived problems. On April 9, 1945, Maj. Gen. J. A. Ulio signed a letter transmitting an order from Secretary of War Henry L. Stimson, which read: "The attention of the War Department has been invited to the practical difficulties of carrying out a court-martial sentence of death by hanging. In many cases, the facilities and the experienced personnel necessary for carrying into effect such a sentence are unavailable. Paragraph 103, *Manual for Courts-Martial, 1928*, makes it optional with the court to prescribe, in the case of a death sentence, whether the method of execution thereof shall be by hanging or shooting. All officers exercising general court-martial jurisdiction will advise courts-martial entertaining charges for which the death sentence can be adjudged that, in the absence of paramount considerations to the contrary, the method of execution should be by shooting."[140]

The letter was sent to every officer exercising general court-martial jurisdiction, in effect every division, corps, army, and army group commander, as well as to the Judge Advocate General section of every theater commander, such as Gen. Dwight Eisenhower for Europe. However, those officers had not been elevated to senior command positions because they were dumb. They knew three things: the war was almost over and after the war the crime rate would go down, military justice was working just fine now, and general good order and discipline were being maintained under the current system. Finally, the letter did not order them to stop the hangings, only to advise commanders to evaluate each situation, and the word "paramount" was a large enough loophole to drive a deuce-and-a-half truck through.

Loire Disciplinary Training Center, Le Mans, France

Benjamin Hopper, Wednesday, April 11, 1945

After the March 29 roadshow it was time to return to Le Mans, because back on October 28, 1944, just after midnight, Pvt. Benjamin Hopper and four other soldiers were in the Maison des Huiets Heures Café in Welkenraedt, Belgium, when an event happened that ultimately would involve John Woods. Hopper and Pvt. Randolph Jackson Jr. began to argue. Hopper took a weapon and shot Jackson to death, firing multiple rounds. He was arrested the same day. His general court-martial convened at 10:00 a.m. on November 23, 1944, at Soumagne, Belgium, the location of the US 1st Army headquarters. Hopper pled not guilty and elected not to testify, and his defense presented no evidence. The jury found him guilty of murder, a violation of the 92nd Article of War, and sentenced him to be hanged by the neck until dead.[141]

Hopper had been born on August 20, 1920, in Hickory, North Carolina, one of eight children. He and his siblings needed a father, but his father had left the home—headed for New York City—and Benjamin was raised by his mother. Educated only through the fourth grade, the black soldier had a limited ability to read and write, relying on others to assist him. A special court-martial in Georgia had convicted him of AWOL. Earlier in 1944, a summary court-martial convicted Hopper of visiting Liege, Belgium, without a pass from his unit.[142]

A psychiatric evaluation after the murder indicated that Hopper had an IQ of 50 and that he had a mental age of just nine years. Lt. Gen. Courtney H. Hodges, US 1st Army commander, recommended clemency and a reduction of the penalty to life imprisonment, but the ETO judge advocate general, Brig. Gen. Edward C. Betts,

recommended that "Ike" let the death penalty stand. On April 7, 1945, the headquarters of the European theater of operations published *General Court-Martial Order Number 107*. Maj. Gen. R. B. Lord—by command of General Eisenhower—directed that the execution would be carried out on April 11, 1945, at the Loire DTC at Le Mans.[143]

At 10:42 a.m. on April 11, 1945, Lt. Col. Peck assembled the official spectators, including eight GPs, in a ravine in the northwestern corner of the Loire DTC. The official witnesses stood in a single rank twenty paces south of the scaffold. The weather was clear, bright, warm, and sunny, the final spring of the war. First Lt. Roland B. Dixon and twenty-five enlisted men of the 389th Military Police Battalion guarded the execution site. Peck read aloud *General Court-Martial Order Number 107*. At 10:58 a.m., a ½-ton, 4x4 covered reconnaissance car pulled up to the ravine, and General Prisoner Benjamin F. Hopper dismounted, joining a procession led by Lt. Col. Peck, Chaplain Andrew Zarek and three MP guards: Sgt. Russell E. Boyle, Sgt. Alfonso Girvalo, and Sgt. Jack D. Briscoe—who carried a brace board. Capt. Milton B. Asbell marched behind them. The group arrived at the scaffold. The MPs then bound Hopper's hands behind his back, led him up the thirteen steps, and guided him to the center of the trapdoor. At 11:00 a.m., Technician Third Grade Thomas Robinson bound the ankles of the prisoner.[144]

Lt. Col. Peck asked the prisoner for any last words and Hopper replied, "Pray for me." Peck, who seems to have made an effort to know every condemned man he was ordered to execute, replied, "God bless you, son." But Peck could not help Hopper now. Chaplain Zarek asked the prisoner if he had any last statements to make, to which Hopper replied, "Father, I would like you to write to my mother." The chaplain began praying. At 11:01 a.m., Woods expertly handled the black hood and noose. Seconds later, Peck gave a silent signal and Woods cut the rope that released the weight and sprung the trap. At about 11:13 a.m., Maj. Roy Campbell, Capt. Daniel

Thaw, and Capt. Francis O. Lamb marched to the understructure of the scaffold and examined the body. They returned to their positions, and Campbell reported, "Sir, this man is not dead." Lt. Col. Peck directed the medical officers to wait, and at 11:24 a.m. they made a second evaluation and found that Hopper was officially deceased. Peck dismissed the witnesses and spectators and Robinson cut the rope. Capt. Benjamin D. Lucas of the 3045th Graves Registration Company took possession of the body and signed a hand receipt for the same.[145]

La Pernelle, Hameau Scipion, Normandy, France

Milbert Bailey, James L. Jones, and John Williams, Thursday, April 19, 1945

By October 1944, the Nazis were long gone from the Normandy invasion area, but it was still a dangerous location. On October 11, 1944, Privates Milbert Bailey, James L. Jones, and John Williams stabbed and killed a man and then raped his nineteen-year-old daughter at the village of La Pernelle, Hameau Scipion, on the eastern tip of the Cherbourg Peninsula. The three soldiers belonged to the 434th Port Company of the 501st Port Battalion, an all-black logistical unit based at Maghull, England, before deploying to France.[146]

Milbert Bailey was born in 1914 and had attended grammar school. He was inducted at Jacksonville, Florida, on September 20, 1941. Bailey had several previous court-martial convictions. James L. Jones was born in Reform, Alabama, on December 12, 1912; he later lived in Millport, Alabama. Jones was inducted into the Army on May 6, 1942, and went overseas in May 1944. He had one previous court-martial conviction. John Williams was born in Florida in 1917; he had also attended grammar school and was married. Williams enlisted on February 6, 1943, in New York City; he also had a previous court-martial conviction.

Military police investigators apprehended the three soldiers on October 16, 1944.[147] A general court-martial on December 14, 1944, found all three soldiers guilty of murder and rape and sentenced all three to be hanged. The headquarters of the European theater of operations published *General Court-Martial Order Number 116* on April 15, 1945. It stated that Privates Milbert Bailey, James L. Jones, and John Williams would be hanged on April 19, 1945, at La Pernelle, Hameau Scipion, France.[148]

The sun was shining and the weather was clear on the morning of April 19 at the village of La Pernelle. A blanket of grass, interrupted only by an occasional tree, covered the ground of a hedgerowed meadow, the size of a football field, located 200 yards east of road GC 125. On the southwestern corner of the area, the scaffold faced east. Adjacent to the field was the house of the victim; six months after the shocking crime, justice was coming home in the form of Master Sergeant John Woods.

At 9.55 a.m., Lt. Col. Henry L. Peck gathered twenty-six witnesses, including two family members of the victims. The event would be starting late, since the military spectators were slow to arrive. Peck read *General Court-Martial Order Number 116* to the assembly and followed with instructions on proper decorum. The official witnesses moved to a position ten paces from the side of the scaffold; the medical officers had the best view just eight paces from the stair side of the scaffold. First Lt. David J. Duff, with ten men of the 387th Military Police Battalion and five soldiers from the Beach District Guardhouse, guarded the area.[149]

This study found no existing execution report for Milbert Bailey, but we can extrapolate what occurred. At about 10:05 a.m., an open ½-ton, 4x4 truck brought General Prisoner Milbert Bailey to the field and halted 20 yards from the scaffold; he stepped out of the vehicle. At 10:06 a.m., a procession began from the 4x4 to the scaffold; in the lead was Lt. Col. Peck, with

Chaplain William L. Bell (a minister of the African Methodist Episcopal Church) to his left. The officers were followed by the prisoner—flanked on each side and to the rear by MPs Sgt. Russell E. Boyle, Sgt. Alfonso Girvalo, and Sgt. George M. Harris. Harris was new to this type of mission; Boyle and Girvalo, unfortunately, were veterans.[150]

The group reached the scaffold; Lt. Col. Peck and the chaplain climbed the steps, and the MPs bound Bailey's hands behind his back and assisted him up the thirteen steps—during the climb, the recorder gave the command "Attention." Once Bailey was on the center of the trapdoor about 10:08 a.m., Technician Third Grade Robinson bound his ankles. Peck and the chaplain then each asked the condemned man if he had a statement to make; we do not know if Bailey did. Chaplain Bell then started praying as Woods adjusted the black hood and noose at 10:09 a.m. Peck then signaled Woods, who cut the rope that released the weight and sprung the trap at 10:10 a.m. The recorder then gave the command "Parade Rest," and the assembly began the seemingly endless wait until Lt. Col. Peck directed the medical officers to make their examinations. They did, and Lt. Col. Fred G. DeBusk, the senior medical officer, reported, "Sir, we pronounce this man officially dead."[151]

There was a fairly long wait until the second execution; chain-smoker John Woods probably had enough time for one or two cigarettes, and with his reputation, no one was going to complain. At 10:50 a.m., the same vehicle returned with General Prisoner James L. Jones to the same field and halted. At 10:51 a.m. the same procession began from the truck to the scaffold. The group reached the scaffold; Peck and Bell climbed the steps, while the guards bound Jones's hands behind his back and then assisted him up the stairs, as the recorder again gave the command "Attention." Once on the trapdoor, Jones had his ankles bound by Robinson at 10:53 a.m. Peck and the chaplain then each asked the condemned man if he had a statement to make, but he did

not. Chaplain Bell then started intoning a prayer, and Woods adjusted the black hood and noose at 10:54 a.m. Peck signaled Woods, who cut the rope that released the weight and sprung the trap. The prisoner "precipitated" through the open trapdoor and hung suspended in the lower recess of the scaffold. The recorder gave the command "Parade Rest," and the assembly waited until 11:09 a.m., when Peck directed the medical officers to make their examinations. They did, and Lt. Col. DeBusk reported at 11:11 a.m.: "Sir, we pronounce this man officially dead."[152]

Pvt. John Williams's report of execution was also missing. The sequence of events was quite likely the same, with the trapdoor opening at 11:30 a.m. First Lt. Milliard R. Jones of the 3055th Graves Registration Company signed for all three bodies. The three men were buried at the US Military Cemetery at Marigny, France, in Plot Z, in graves 1-20, 2-23, and 2-24. The three executions had taken a total of ninety minutes; although he did not realize it at the time, Woods would have to get even faster.

• • •

On May 7, 1945, Woods was assigned to the headquarters of the Normandy Base Section but was attached back to the 2913th Disciplinary Training Center for duty. For the Army, it was a paperwork drill, but for John Woods—like soldiers worldwide—it was just another opportunity for the Army to screw up your pay.

Loire Disciplinary Training Center, Le Mans, France

George Green Jr., Tuesday, May 15, 1945

Another way not to get paid was to kill a fellow soldier. Pvt. George Green Jr., a black soldier born in New Boston, Texas, and assigned to the segregated 998th Quartermaster Salvage Collecting Company, probably did not consider those potential repercussions the morning of November 18, 1944, when he shot and killed Cpl. Tommie Lee Garrett, a black noncommissioned officer in the unit. The event had been so out of character; Green had been an excellent soldier prior to that morning.[153]

George Green was born in Steven, Arkansas, on May 10, 1924, and later moved to East Texas, where he completed the tenth grade. He then took on the job of a house mover, earning three dollars a day before getting a job as a janitor at the Red River Ordnance Plant in Texarkana, Texas, at $65 a month. Green entered active duty on April 19, 1943; he joined the 998th Quartermaster Salvage Company on January 8, 1944. He previously had one summary court-martial for being drunk and disorderly.[154]

A general court-martial convened at 3:30 p.m. on December 9, 1944, at Nancy, France. Green pled not guilty to the charge of murder and elected not to take the stand, despite overwhelming evidence that he had killed Cpl. Garrett. The jury voted unanimously to convict Green and sentenced him to be hanged by the neck until dead. Lt. Gen. George S. Patton approved the findings and sentence on January 9, 1945. The legal section at the headquarters, European theater of operations, examined the records of the trial on February 25, 1945. The reviewing officer found that the record of trial was legally sufficient to support the findings and sentence, and also recommended that no clemency be extended in the case. Gen. Eisenhower signed the order confirming the sentence for Green on the same day, but the order directing the execution of sentence was withheld.[155]

On May 1, 1945, the headquarters of the European theater of operations issued *General Court-Martial Order Number 129*. Maj. Gen. Thomas B. Larkin—by command of Eisenhower—directed that the execution be carried out at the Loire DTC on May 15, 1945.[156]

The weather that morning at 10:43 a.m. was warm, clear, bright, and sunny when Lt. Col. Henry L. Peck gathered fifty authorized witnesses

and spectators. Eight spectators were GPs—four black and four white—under guard behind the camp's barbed-wire fence. Peck briefed everyone on the proper conduct at the event and read *General Court-Martial Order Number 129* in its entirety. Capt. Roland B. Dixon and twenty-five men of Company C of the 389th Military Police Battalion guarded the area. At 10:58 a.m., a command-and-reconnaissance car, a ½-ton, 4x4 vehicle, halted in the ravine, 35 yards from the gallows. Out stepped General Prisoner George Green Jr. and three military police guards.[157]

Green joined a procession that marched toward the scaffold a minute later. Lt. Col. Peck led the way, followed by Chaplain Alfred S. Kramer, the prisoner, and MP guards Sgt. Russell E. Boyle, SSgt. Charles R. Brinker, and TSgt. Frank Landi. First Lt. Lawrence Slon, the recorder, followed in the rear. The procession reached the foot of the scaffold just after 10:59 a.m. Peck and Kramer ascended the steps, while the guards bound Green's hands behind his back, assisted him up the thirteen steps, and positioned him on the center of the trapdoor. Technician Third Grade Robinson bound Green's ankles, and Lt. Col. Peck asked Green if he had any last statements, to which Green replied: "Yes sir, I have. I don't have any hard feelings toward you for this. Pray for everyone. I hope that if you are not a Christian that you become one. I have no fear. A person has no fear of death if he is right with God. Death is an honor. Jesus died for a crime he did not commit. I really did a crime, a bad crime. I believe that the Good Lord has forgiven me for what I did. I hope that the Lord forgives all of you for what you are doing here today. I hope God blesses all of you."[158]

Lt. Col. Peck replied to the condemned: "May the Lord have mercy on you, son." Chaplain Kramer asked Green if he had any last words. Green replied, "You have been very nice to me. I wish that you would keep on being nice to people. I want to say a word of prayer." Green began a short prayer lasting about one minute. He was allowed to finish, at which point Chaplain

Kramer began praying, while Woods adjusted the black hood and noose. At 11:05 a.m., Lt. Col. Peck signaled Woods, who cut the rope that released the weight and sprung the trap. Everything "operated perfectly"; the condemned man hung motionlessly and made no sound. First Lt. Lawrence Slon then gave the command of "Parade Rest."[159]

At 11:19 a.m., Lt. Col. Peck directed that medical officers Maj. Roy Campbell, Capt. Daniel Thaw, and Capt. Robert E. Hansen examine the body. They did and promptly declared that George Green Jr. was officially dead. Peck then dismissed the formation. Robinson cut the rope and removed the body from the lower part of the scaffold. Capt. Hardy C. Derx, 3058th Quartermaster Graves Registration Company, signed for the body at 11:25 a.m. and removed it for interment at the US Military Cemetery at Marigny, France, in Plot Z, grave 2-25.[160]

Mesnil-Clinchamps, Calvados, France

Haze Heard, Monday, May 21, 1945

PFC Haze Heard, 3105th Quartermaster Service Company, shot and killed a French woman on October 13, 1944, at Mesnil-Clinchamps in the Calvados region of France. On that evening he had entered the home of a French couple and demanded two glasses of alcohol. After leaving for a short time, he returned and demanded that he be given the young woman. The family ushered Heard outside and locked the door, but the soldier fired two rounds through the window, which killed Madame Berthe Robert. He then fired two more rounds through the door.[161]

Haze Heard had been born in Toccoa, Georgia, a small town on the border with South Carolina, on June 7, 1922. He had five brothers and sisters; he was married and had a young son. Heard was inducted into the Army on December 18, 1942. Prior to this incident, he had no previous court-martial convictions.[162]

Heard was not arrested until December 13, 1944. On January 25, 1945, a general court-martial convened at Granville, Manche, France, convicted him of murder, and sentenced him to death by hanging. Gen. Eisenhower confirmed the sentence on March 18, 1945. The headquarters, European theater of operations, published *General Court-Martial Order Number 137* on May 11, 1945, stating that Haze Heard would be executed on May 21, 1945, at Mesnil-Clinchamps, Calvados, France. The day before the execution, Capt. Henry McHarg III read the general court-martial order to the condemned man.[163] This was a change in procedure, since it was felt that forcing the condemned man to listen to the lengthy order on the gallows was too stressful.

The site of the execution was one-half mile south of Mesnil-Clinchamps, in the Calvados region, some 5 miles west of Viré in an apple orchard belonging to Monsieur Eugene Roberts. A low hedgerow surrounded the grove on three sides; farm buildings completed the rectangular farmyard in the north. The scaffold, in the center, faced south. The weather was overcast and cool with a light intermittent rain. At 10:45 a.m., Lt. Col. Henry L. Peck gathered twenty-seven witnesses. He read *General Court-Martial Order 137* and gave them instructions on their expected conduct, which meant no noise and no disturbances. At 11:00 a.m., a 1½-ton, 6x6 personnel carrier arrived and halted 20 yards from the scaffold. Haze Heard descended and joined a procession to the gallows. Lt. Col. Peck led the way with Chaplain (1st Lt.). Emanuel L. Briggs. The prisoner followed, escorted by SSgt. Charles R. Brinker, Sgt. George M. Harris, and Sgt. Jack D. Briscoe, who probably carried the brace board. First Lt. Lawrence Slon, the recorder, followed in the rear.[164]

Shortly after 11:01 a.m., the procession halted at the foot of the gallows; already on the platform were Woods and Technician Third Grade Thomas Robinson. Peck and Briggs walked up the steps to join them, while the guards bound Heard's wrists and then helped him up the steps. Both Peck and Briggs took their positions and asked General Prisoner Heard if he had any last words, to which he replied, "No, sir." The chaplain then started praying, and Woods slipped the black hood over Heard's head and adjusted the noose around his neck. At 11:04 a.m. Peck nodded to Woods, who cut the rope that released a weight and sprung the trap. Everything operated smoothly, and the prisoner "precipitated through the opened trap door."[165]

Heard's body hung suspended; Woods could see a slight muscular action and a minor swaying motion. Military personnel stood silent, awaiting the pronouncement of death, but several French civilians did not. "The Commanding Officer, at 11:15 a.m. ordered Slon to instruct the French civilians, who were conversing among themselves, to maintain silence until they were dismissed." Peck ordered the medical officers to examine the body at 11:19 a.m. They did and pronounced Haze Heard "officially dead." Robinson cut the rope and removed the body from the lower part of the scaffold, and 1Lt. Milliard R. Jones, 3059th Quartermaster Graves Registration Company, removed the body; the remains were interred at the US Military Cemetery at Marigny, France.[166]

Loire Disciplinary Training Center, Le Mans, France

It was time to return to Le Mans, since although the war in Europe was over, the wheels of justice continued to roll, and John Woods soon would have three hangings over a period of four days.

William J. McCarter, Monday, May 28, 1945

On the morning of February 1, 1945, at the barracks of the 465th Quartermaster Laundry Company, an all-black unit at Thionville, France, a crap game was in session, but by 2:30 a.m. there were only three troopers left, including PFC William J. McCarter and Pvt. Charles P. "CP"

Williams. The dice turned cold for McCarter, who then accused the other men of cheating. The game broke up about 3:00 a.m. McCarter walked by the guardhouse and asked if any of his fellow soldiers were out of the company area. The guard replied that only Williams was gone. McCarter answered, "I'll get him; he got my money." Fifteen minutes later a guard heard McCarter say, "Is that you, Williams?" The guard then heard Williams reply, "Yes, it's CP," at which time a carbine fired six rounds and "CP" fell with single shots to his neck, his left buttock, and his left foot, and three to his back—all from behind. The guard recalled that PFC McCarter then stated, "I got him."[167] Williams died later that day.

William McCarter had been inducted into the Army on June 22, 1943, at Ft. Bragg, North Carolina; he had been born on October 22, 1906, in Charlotte, North Carolina. McCarter had attended school for seven years; later he worked as a waiter and cleaned clothes, and in the 465th Quartermaster Laundry Company, he was a laundry machine operator. He stood 5'2" tall and weighed 122 pounds.[168]

A general court-martial convened in Thionville, France, at the headquarters of the XX Corps at 1:30 p.m. on February 16, 1945. McCarter pled not guilty to the charge of murder, but the evidence against him was overwhelming, and the jury quickly convicted him of the crime and unanimously sentenced him to death.[169] On May 12, 1945, the headquarters, European theater of operations, issued *General Court-Martial Order Number 138*. Maj. Gen. Thomas B. Larkin—by command of General Eisenhower—directed that the execution be carried out at the Loire DTC at Le Mans on May 28, 1945.[170]

On May 27, 1945, Woods wheeled an Army flatbed truck to a ravine just outside the northwest corner of the Loire DTC. Woods directed engineers and a prisoner work detail to remove the scaffold from the truck and set it up outside the barbed-wire fence. Woods tested the trapdoor numerous times that day and the next morning.[171]

On May 28, 1945, the weather in Le Mans was warm with overcast skies. At 10:43 a.m., Lt. Col. Henry L. Peck briefed the authorized witnesses and spectators near the scaffold on the proper conduct at the event and read aloud *General Court-Martial Order Number 138*. Eight of the spectators were GPs, who were under guard behind the DTC's barbed-wire fence. Capt. Roland B. Dixon and twenty-five men of Company C of the 389th Military Police Battalion guarded the site. At 10:58 a.m., a ½-ton, 4x4 command-and-reconnaissance vehicle halted 35 yards from the scaffold. GP McCarter stepped out and promptly joined a procession that marched toward the scaffold a minute later. Lt. Col. Peck was in front, followed by Chaplain Alfred S. Kramer, McCarter, and MP guards Sgt. Russell E. Boyle, Sgt. Alfonso Girvalo, and TSgt. Frank Landi. The recorder followed in the rear. The procession reached the scaffold at 10:59 a.m. Peck and Kramer ascended the thirteen steps; the guards bound McCarter's hands behind his back.[172]

They then assisted McCarter up the steps and positioned him on the center of the trapdoor. Technician Third Grade Robinson bound McCarter's ankles. Lt. Col. Peck then asked the prisoner for any last statements. McCarter replied, "I am ready to die, sir. The chaplain and I have prayed together. I believe that Jesus listened to me. I believe that I am forgiven. I fear nothing, I am satisfied that I am forgiven." Then the chaplain asked if McCarter had any last words. The condemned man replied: "Chaplain, sir, I am glad that you were with me. You being with me gave me spirit, and you and Smith praying with me, I got more out of it. Thank you for what you have done."[173]

Woods and Robinson adjusted the hood and rope over McCarter's head and neck. Chaplain Kramer began to pray; at 11:03 a.m., Peck signaled Woods to cut the rope, which released the weight and sprung the trap. First Lt. Lawrence Slon then gave the command of "Parade Rest." Those present observed the uncomfortable scene for four minutes,

when suddenly an official witness became ill and unsteadily departed the area. At 11:18 a.m., Lt. Col. Peck directed that Maj. Ernest A. Weizer, Capt. Daniel Thaw, and Capt. Robert E. Hansen examine the body. The physicians did and promptly declared that McCarter was officially dead at 11:20 a.m. Peck then dismissed the formation. Robinson cut the rope and removed the body from the lower part of the scaffold. Capt. Hardy C. Derx, 3058th Quartermaster Graves Registration Company, removed the body for interment, which occurred at the US Military Cemetery at Marigny, France, in Plot Z, grave 2-27.[174]

Clete O. Norris and Alvin Roberts, Thursday, May 31, 1945

Sgt. Clete O. Norris, a black soldier in the segregated 3384th Quartermaster Truck Company, shot and fatally injured Capt. William E. McDonald, his company commander, on January 6, 1945. Earlier in the evening, McDonald had disarmed the soldier following a disturbance. A short while later, Norris found another pistol and proceeded to a café. As the sergeant approached the establishment, a voice from somewhere in the darkness directed the soldier to "Halt." Norris fired a round at the sound and Capt. McDonald fell mortally wounded. Military police arrested Norris the next day; the soldier confessed that he was drunk on the night of the incident and also admitted shooting at someone outside the café after the person flashed a light on him and said "Halt."

Clete Norris had been born in Palestine, Texas, on March 1, 1918. He attended elementary school for seven years and then became a waiter before moving with his mother to South Kinlock Park, Missouri. He was inducted into the Army at Jefferson Barracks, Missouri, on September 25, 1941. On June 29, 1943, a court-martial convicted Clete Norris for using an Army truck for personal work and sentenced him to six months at hard labor, although Norris was generally considered a good soldier.[175]

Capt. William McDonald died of his wound on January 9, 1945. On February 9, 1945, a general court-martial convened at Verviers, Belgium, and Norris pled not guilty to murder.[176] However, the court convicted him of murder and sentenced him to death by hanging. Brig. Gen. Ewart G. Plank, commander of the Advance Section of the Communications Zone, approved the sentence on February 25, 1945. Gen. Eisenhower confirmed the sentence on April 3, 1945, withholding the order directing the execution. That order was issued on May 26, 1945; Clete Norris would be hanged on May 31, 1945, at the Loire DTC.[177]

At 9:45 a.m. on May 31, 1945, in a ravine in the northwestern corner of the Loire DTC, a scaffold stood at a square, leveled area approximately 15 yards on each side. It was cut out of the northern embankment in a position that the stairs faced the wall of that embankment. Witnesses, who included Sgt. Tom Ward, stood in a single rank about twenty paces south of the scaffold.[178] The weather was clear, bright, warm, and sunny. Capt. Roland B. Dixon and twenty five enlisted men of Company C of the 389th Military Police Battalion guarded the execution site. Lt. Col. Peck read *General Court-Martial Order Number 174* to thirty authorized spectators and gave instructions on proper decorum. At 9:57 a.m., a command-and-reconnaissance car, a ½-ton, 4x4 vehicle, pulled up to the ravine and out stepped General Prisoner Clete Norris with MP guards Sgt. Russell E. Boyle, Sgt. Alfonso Girvalo, and TSgt. Frank Landi. One minute later, the men joined a procession led by Lt. Col. Peck with Chaplain Charles O. Dutton, then Norris and the guards, followed by 1Lt. Lawrence Slon, the official recorder.[179]

The group arrived at the scaffold at 9:58 a.m. While Peck and Dutton ascended the steps, guards bound Norris's wrists behind his back and led him up the stairs and to the trapdoor. At 10:00 a.m., Technician Third Grade Robinson bound the ankles of the prisoner. Peck asked Norris if he had any last words, but Norris did not. The

chaplain asked if he had any last statement; again Norris said nothing. Chaplain Dutton began to pray. Woods then placed the black hood over Norris's head, put the noose around his neck, and adjusted them both; the time was 10:01 a.m. Seconds later, Peck gave a silent signal to Woods, who cut the rope that released the weight and sprung the trap. First Lt. Slon then gave the command "Parade Rest."[180]

At 10:11 a.m., Lt. Col. Peck ordered medical officers Maj. Ernest A. Weizer, Capt. Daniel Thaw, and Capt. Robert E. Hansen to examine the deceased, and the three marched in a single file to the understructure of the scaffold. They returned to their positions, where Weizer reported at 10:13 a.m. that death had not yet occurred. The doctors waited five minutes and repeated the process; at 10:20 a.m. Maj. Weizer reported, "Sir, we pronounce this man officially dead."[181] Nineteen minutes had elapsed from the trapdoor dropping to the pronouncement of death.

Lt. Col. Peck dismissed the medical officers; before they departed the physicians signed a certificate stating the time of death as 10:20 a.m. and the cause of death as judicial asphyxis. Peck subsequently dismissed the witnesses and spectators, and Woods cut the rope. Capt. Hardy C. Derx, 3058th Quartermaster Graves Registration Company, signed a hand receipt for the body at 10:23 a.m. Clete Norris's remains were interred at the US Military Cemetery at Marigny on June 1, 1945, in the section for General Prisoners.[182]

Time was flying by, and there was another execution to conduct in just thirty minutes. PFC Alvin R. Rollins, of the all-black 306th Quartermaster Railhead Company, had been arrested by MPs at an off-limits café in Troyes, France, on February 23, 1945. As the group entered a jeep, Rollins pulled a German Luger and killed two MPs; a third was seriously injured. Authorities arrested Rollins on February 24, 1945, and preferred charges on March 1, 1945. After an investigation, the charges were forwarded to the convening authority on March 3, 1945. On March 4, 1945, Brig. Gen.

Charles O. Thrasher, commander of the Oise Intermediate Section of the Communications Zone, referred the case for action by a general court-martial, which convened at Reims, France, on March 13, 1945. The court unanimously voted to convict the defendant and sentenced him by another unanimous vote to be hanged.[183]

Gen. Eisenhower signed the order confirming the death sentence in the case of Rollins on April 29, 1945. On May 18, 1945, Board of Review Number 1 of the Branch Office of the Judge Advocate General with the European theater of operations reviewed the case. Judge Advocates B. Franklin Riter, William F. Burrow, and Edward L. Stevens Jr. found that the record of trial was sufficient and that no significant errors had been made.[184] Alvin Rollins had been born on December 5, 1924, in Chattanooga, Tennessee; he was inducted on June 15, 1943, at Camp Forrest, Tennessee. With no previous court-martial convictions, his chain of command said he was an excellent performer; he was entitled to wear a battle star.

At 10:45 a.m. on May 31, 1945, Lt. Col. Henry C. Peck reassembled all official personnel at the execution site and read aloud *General Court-Martial Order Number 180*. The vehicle transporting Alvin Rollins arrived at 10:57 a.m. The procedure was the same; Peck asked the prisoner if he had any last words, and Rollins replied, "I am glad to know that I have met Jesus." The chaplain asked the prisoner if he had any last statements to make, to which Rollins replied at 11:00 a.m.: "I like to say that I am glad that you were with me. You helped me to see God." Chaplain Kramer then began to pray. Woods then placed the black hood over Rollins's head, then put the noose around his neck and adjusted them both; the time was 11:01 a.m. Seconds later, Peck gave Woods a silent signal, and the executioner cut the rope that released the weight and sprung the trap. The recorder again gave the command "Parade Rest." Everything worked correctly, and at about 11:16 a.m. the same medical officers marched in a single file to the understructure of the scaffold and examined the body of Alvin R. Rollins. They returned to their positions, and the senior officer reported at 11:18 a.m.: "Sir, we pronounce this man officially dead." Capt. Hardy C. Derx, 3058th Quartermaster Graves Registration Company, took possession of the body, signing a hand receipt for the same at 11:23 a.m. Rollins's remains were interred the following day at the US Military Cemetery at Marigny, in Plot Z, grave 2-29.[185]

Fontenay-sur-Mer, Manche, France

Matthew Clay Jr., Monday, June 4, 1945

At 9:30 p.m. on October 9, 1944, PFC Matthew Clay Jr. was walking down a road a mile from where his unit, the 3236th Quartermaster Service Company, was bivouacked. He had already consumed about a quart of cider alcohol and stopped at a small bakery in the village of Fontenay-sur-Mer, France, the home of Monsieur Victor Bellery. He demanded more alcohol, and when Bellery refused, Clay stabbed him with a bayonet in the back and neck and then struck Madame Bellery three times with the lethal weapon. Clay ran away, but an hour later an officer found him with a bloody bayonet near the scene of the crime. Victor Bellery would succumb to his wounds later that night.[186]

Born July 26, 1920, in Avery, Louisiana, Clay had a tough childhood. His mother died when he was three; he finished the sixth grade, leaving to become a common laborer, working for two years on a farm and later for the Myles Salt Company. He married in 1940; his wife and three-year-old daughter lived at Galveston, Texas. Matthew Clay was inducted into the Army on December 11, 1943, at Lafayette, Louisiana, and joined the Quartermaster Corps.[187]

A general court-martial convened at 11:00 a.m. on January 20, 1945, at Cherbourg, France, to hear the case. Clay pled not guilty to all charges. Madame Bellery testified for the prosecution.

The defense team stated that Clay struck Monsieur Bellery in self-defense, after Bellery first hit him on the head with a wooden mallet. The court didn't buy the self-defense rationale, convicted Clay of murder, and then sentenced him to death by hanging. Three of the jurors had been assigned to three previous general courts-martial that ended with death sentences. The Normandy Base Section judge advocate general reviewed the case on February 19, 1945; everything was in order. The Branch Office of the Judge Advocate General with the European theater of operations reviewed the case on May 18, 1945. The three-judge panel ruled that the court was legally constituted, had jurisdiction of the person and offenses, and committed no errors injuriously affecting the substantial rights of the accused—in short that the record of trial was legally sufficient to support the findings of guilty and the sentence of death. On May 27, 1945, the headquarters, European theater of operations, issued *General Court-Martial Order Number 185*, directing that the execution be carried out.[188]

On June 2, 1945, Army carpenters under the direction of Master Sergeant John Woods constructed a temporary gallows in an orchard one-half mile southeast of Fontenay-sur-Mer, Manche, France. Two days later, the sun beamed down on a clear, warm, and bright morning. About 10:34 a.m., Lt. Col. Henry L. Peck assembled nineteen US Army officials and witnesses and one French civilian (the mayor of Fontenay-sur-Mer) and read *General Court-Martial Order Number 185*. Peck then gave instructions concerning the proper conduct at the upcoming event.[189]

That upcoming event began at 11:00 a.m., when a 1½-ton, 6x6 personnel carrier drove to within 20 yards of the scaffold; from it, guards assisted General Prisoner Matthew Clay Jr. At 11:02 a.m., Peck led the execution procession; following were a chaplain, Clay, three MP guards (Sgt. Russell E. Boyle, Sgt. Alfonso Girvalo, and Sgt. Thomas J. Doyle), and 1Lt. Lawrence Slon, the recorder, who noted, "The condemned man cried, whimpered and faltered during the march to the gallows."[190]

At 11:03 a.m. the procession reached the scaffold, at which point Peck and the chaplain ascended the steps. Clay burst into tears and wrapped his arms around his head, imploring, "Lord, have mercy on me." The three guards forcibly tied Clay's hands behind him and pushed him upward, as he haltingly climbed his final thirteen steps. The thought of having to use the dreaded brace board crossed a few minds. Upon reaching the top, the guards led Clay to the center of the trapdoor, and Technician Third Grade Robinson bound his ankles at 11:04 a.m.[191] Robinson had been with Woods as an assistant since the beginning last October; today the raw emotion of the condemned man was pushing Robinson to the edge of how much more he could take.

The commanding officer and the chaplain asked Clay if he had any last words. In both instances Clay responded in the affirmative but then said nothing. After a moment, the chaplain began intoning a prayer, and Woods adjusted the black hood and the noose at 11:05 a.m. Thirty seconds later, Peck silently signaled Woods, who cut the rope that released the weight and sprung the trap. The trap mechanism operated as designed, and Matthew Clay stopped wailing as he dropped cleanly through the trapdoor and hung suspended in the lower screened recess of the scaffold. His body swung silently in a circular motion; witnesses stood hushed without reaction. Fifteen minutes later, Lt. Col. Peck ordered the three medical officers to examine the body for life. The trio marched in single file to the understructure, made their examination, emerged, and returned to their original positions. The senior medical officer, Capt. Peter W. Chernenkoff, reported at 11:22 a.m.: "Sir, we pronounce this man officially dead."[192] Peck dismissed the gathering, while Woods cut the rope and removed the body, which was then signed for by Capt. Robert E. Berry, 3059th Quartermaster Graves Registration Company.[193] Clay's remains were buried at the US Military Cemetery at Marigny, France, in Plot Z, grave 2-30.

Loire Disciplinary Training Center, Le Mans, France

Victor Ortiz, Thursday, June 21, 1945

Witnesses in the 3269th Quartermaster Service Company near Lille, France, observed Pvt. Victor Ortiz shoot and kill his company commander in the unit orderly room over an issue concerning guard duty. A general court-martial convened at Lille, France, on March 1, 1945, at 1:30 p.m.; the trial last three days, which was unusually long. Ortiz was charged with murder, a violation of the 92nd Article of War. The defense maintained that the defendant believed that Capt. Ignacio Bonit was going for a pistol during the incident, and that Ortiz fired his M1 carbine in self-defense; that was generally what Ortiz stated when he took the witness stand. However, the jury did not buy the claim of self-defense; they voted to convict the accused and sentenced him to death.[194]

Victor Ortiz, the son of Antero Ortiz-Sanchez and Aurelia Reyes-Rentas, was born on January 6, 1914, in Puerto Rico; he had four sisters.[195] He volunteered for Army service on April 28, 1941, at Ft. Buchanan, Puerto Rico; he had served with the 3269th Quartermaster Service Company since he enlisted. His service up to the date of the crime had been characterized as excellent.[196]

The staff judge advocate concluded that the record was legally sufficient to support the findings of the court. Brig. Gen. Fenton S. Jacobs, commander of the Channel Base Section of the Communications Zone, approved the sentence and forwarded the record of trial on March 25, 1945. On May 6, 1945, Gen. Eisenhower signed a letter confirming the sentence of death for Victor Ortiz but withheld the order directing the execution of the sentence. On June 16, 1945, the headquarters, European theater of operations, issued *General Court-Martial Order Number 213*. Maj. Gen. Thomas B. Larkin—by command of Gen. Eisenhower—directed that the execution be carried out at the Loire DTC at Le Mans on June 21, 1945.[197]

On the morning of June 20, 1945, Lt. Col. Peck read *General Court-Martial Order Number 213* to General Prisoner Victor Ortiz. To ensure complete understanding, 1Lt. Robert Celaya translated the order into Spanish. The same day, Woods drove an Army flatbed truck to the ravine just outside the northwest corner of the Loire DTC. Woods, engineers, and a prisoner work detail removed the scaffold from the truck and set it up just outside the barbed-wire fence. Woods tested the trapdoor numerous times so there would be no surprises the following day.[198]

The morning of June 21 was cool and overcast; a light wind blew from the north. At 10:40 a.m., Lt. Col. Henry L. Peck gathered twenty-eight authorized witnesses and spectators at the scaffold, briefed them on the proper conduct at the event, and read *General Court-Martial Order Number 213*. At 10:58 a.m., a command-and-reconnaissance car, a ½-ton, 4x4 vehicle, halted 35 yards from the scaffold, and out stepped General Prisoner Victor Ortiz, who then joined a procession that marched toward the scaffold a minute later. Peck led the way, followed by Chaplain Kilian R. Bowler, Ortiz, and MP guards TSgt. Frank Landi, Sgt. Alfonso Girvalo, and Technician Fifth Grade Vincent J. Martino. The recorder, 1Lt. Lawrence Slon, and Pvt. Alfred Portillo, who would serve as interpreter if required, brought up the rear. The procession reached the foot of the scaffold just before 11:00 a.m. Peck and Bowler ascended the steps while the guards bound Ortiz's hands behind his back. They then assisted him up the steps and positioned him on the center of the trapdoor. Technician Third Grade Robinson then bound Ortiz's ankles.[199]

Peck then asked the prisoner if he had any last statements. Ortiz replied that he did not, at which point Peck asked if Ortiz fully understood what he had said. Ortiz replied that he did, and then Chaplain Bowler asked if he had any last words. Ortiz replied, "I ask for your prayers and the prayers of the Lord."[200]

With no need for an interpreter, Portillo departed the scaffold. Woods and Robinson adjusted the black hood and rope over Ortiz's head. Chaplain Bowler began to pray; at 11:03 a.m., Peck signaled Woods, who cut the rope that released the weight and sprung the trap. Everything worked well; the condemned man made no motion or sound. At 11:18 a.m., Lt. Col. Peck directed that medical officers Maj. Ernest A. Weizer, Capt. Daniel Thaw, and Capt. Henry H. Kalter examine the body. They did so and declared that Victor Ortiz was officially deceased. Peck dismissed the formation. Robinson cut the rope and removed Ortiz's body from the lower part of the scaffold. Capt. Hardy C. Derx, 3058th Quartermaster Graves Registration Company, signed for the body and removed it for interment at the US Military Cemetery at Marigny, France, in Plot Z, grave 2-31.[201] MP Technician Fifth Grade Vincent J. Martino would soon become Woods's assistant; it is quite likely that after the Clay execution, Thomas F. Robinson requested permission to be relieved of his duties, and bringing Vincent Martino in as a guard was the first step in the transition.

La Haye Pesnel, Manche, France

Willie Johnson, Tuesday, June 26, 1945

At 8:30 p.m. on August 23, 1944, three French women near Rennes, France, flagged down a US Army gasoline tanker truck and asked the driver if they might catch a ride. Pvt. Willie Johnson, 3984th Quartermaster Truck Company, agreed. Sometime over the next hour Johnson decide to rape one of the women. Two of the women managed to jump off the speeding truck; in doing so, one woman broke her right leg. The remaining French woman was not so fortunate; Madam Julien Fontaine was found the next morning lying in the middle of a road. She had been raped, and tire marks indicated that a heavy vehicle had run over her head and both legs. A fellow soldier talked the next day to Johnson and heard enough detail concerning the event to notify the chain of command. After his arrest, Willie Johnson made the following written confession: "I decided to keep her from telling anybody so I dragged her out and put her in front of the right rear wheel. I don't know whether she was alive when I put her there, but she was warm, I know that. I put her on the road so that her feet were near the side of the road and her head near the middle of the road. Then I drove the truck over her."[202]

Willie Johnson was a twenty-two-year-old black soldier from Idaville, Oklahoma. Born on December 25, 1921, Johnson had a history of five periods of unconsciousness following head injuries from age eleven to twenty-one. He had attended school for only six months and could not read or write. Inducted in September 1942, Johnson could not complete the dismounted road marches, nor was he able to qualify with either a rifle or a carbine.[203]

A board of medical officers convened at the 165th General Hospital prior to Johnson's general court-martial. Doctors found Willie Johnson to have a mental age of eight years and classified him as a moron but did not rule that he could not stand trial.[204] A general court-martial convened at Granville, Manche, France, at 9:20 a.m. on January 27, 1945. The defense argued that Johnson's admissions of guilt were not voluntary. The jury weighed the evidence, unanimously voted to convict Willie Johnson of murder, and sentenced him to be hanged by the neck until dead.[205]

On June 21, 1945, the headquarters, European theater of operations, issued *General Court-Martial Order Number 218*. Maj. Gen. Thomas B. Larkin directed that the execution be carried out at the village of La Haye Pesnel, France, on June 26, 1945. At 11:00 a.m. the day prior, 1Lt. David J. Duff, military police, read the GCM order to General Prisoner Willie Johnson. Later that day, a medical officer examined the prisoner and found him to be in excellent physical and mental health.[206]

La Haye Pesnel, France, on the morning of June 26 was bright, clear, sunny, and warm. Lt. Col.

Henry L. Peck gathered seventeen authorized witnesses and spectators at 10:40 a.m. at an old rock quarry one-half mile from the village. A scaffold faced south; it had not been there two days before. The personnel stood some 10 to 15 yards away. First Lt. Harry Bender and eleven men of Company B of the 387th Military Police Battalion guarded the area. Peck briefed the personnel on the proper conduct at the event, in essence to keep quiet and not move, and then read *General Court-Martial Order Number 218* in its entirety. At 10:58 a.m., a 2½-ton, 6x6 covered cargo vehicle halted 50 yards from the gallows. Out stepped General Prisoner Willie Johnson; it had been a 2½-ton truck with which he had committed murder, and it would be a 2½-ton truck, the venerable "Deuce-and-a-Half," in which he would have his last ride.[207]

Johnson joined a procession that marched toward the scaffold. Peck led the way, followed by Chaplain William L. Bell, Johnson, and MP guards Sgt. Thomas J. Boyle, Sgt. Alfonso Girvalo, and Technician Fifth Grade Vincent J. Martino. It was important that Martino get the "hang" of the job, since he would soon be Woods's assistant. First Lt. Lawrence Slon followed in the rear. The procession reached the foot of the scaffold at 11:00 a.m. Lt. Col. Peck and Capt. Bell ascended the thirteen steps, while the MPs bound Johnson's hands behind his back. They then assisted the condemned man up the steps and positioned him on the center of the trapdoor, after which Technician Third Grade Robinson bound Johnson's ankles. Peck asked the prisoner if he had any last statements. Johnson replied, "No." Chaplain Bell then asked if Willie Johnson had any last words. Johnson again replied, "No."[208]

Woods and his assistant Robinson then adjusted the hood and rope over the condemned man's head and neck. The chaplain began to pray; at 11:01 a.m., Peck signaled Woods, who cut the rope that released the weight and sprung the trap. Willie Johnson made no motion or sound after he dropped. At 11:16 a.m., Peck directed that

medical officers Capt. Nelson J. Dente, Capt. Marion F. Whitten, and Capt. Frank J. Gallagher examine the body. The physicians marched to the understructure of the scaffold, made their examinations, and promptly declared that the prisoner was officially dead; they later signed a certificate stating that the cause of death was judicial asphyxis. Peck then dismissed the formation. Woods and Robinson cut the rope and removed the body from the lower part of the scaffold. First Lt. Milliard R. Jones, 3058th Quartermaster Graves Registration Company, signed for the body and removed it for interment at the US Military Cemetery at Marigny, France, which occurred on July 12, 1945, at 3:00 p.m. Johnson was buried in Plot Z, grave 2-32.[209] A cross marked his original grave.

Loire Disciplinary Training Center, Le Mans, France

Tom Gordon, Tuesday, July 10, 1945

About 1:30 a.m. on November 12, 1944, Pvt. Tom E. Gordon, 3251st Quartermaster Service Company, walked into his barracks after a night of drinking and proceeded to create a ruckus, yelling and cursing. Witnesses later said that Gordon threatened to kill anyone who bothered him. Moments later, two shots rang out and Cpl. Laurence Broussard lay dying, while Pvt. Willie Best was grabbing his thigh that had just been shattered by a bullet. The death certificate showed that Broussard died at 7:10 a.m. on November 18, 1944; the cause of death had been the gunshot wound he received six days earlier, which fatally damaged his pancreas and left kidney.[210]

A general court-martial met at Lunéville, France, at 9:00 a.m. on February 13, 1945. Gordon pled not guilty to murder, assault, and AWOL. He elected to make an unsworn statement at the trial, saying he had received a pass, went to three bars, and could not remember anything about the night until he woke up on November 13, when he was told that he had shot someone. The jury did not buy his defense and voted to convict him of murder, and then they unanimously voted to sentence Gordon to be hanged by the neck until dead.[211]

Tom Gordon, a black soldier, was born on March 7, 1915, in Greenville, South Carolina. He dropped out of school after three years. A summary court-martial convicted him on October 1, 1943, for being off-limits in the street and for resisting arrest. Nineteen days later he was convicted at a second summary court-martial for entering an off-limits establishment in Oran, Algeria. On December 9, 1943, Gordon was convicted by a third summary court-martial for wrongfully entering a house of prostitution in Oran. A special court-martial convicted him for being AWOL from March 8 to 25, 1944.[212]

Lt. Gen. Alexander M. Patch, commander of the US 7th Army, approved the sentence on April 3, 1945, and forwarded the record of trial up the chain of command. Gen. Dwight D. Eisenhower signed the order May 6, 1945, confirming the sentence for Gordon. Days earlier, Gordon had written the supreme commander a letter, stating that he did not remember what had happened, and requested a pardon. Eisenhower withheld the order directing the time and place of execution. He also did not pardon Gordon.[213]

The morning of July 10, 1945, was overcast and cool; a light rain fell on Le Mans. At 10:45 a.m., Lt. Col. Henry L. Peck gathered twenty-one authorized witnesses and spectators at the site of the scaffold. Peck briefed them on the proper conduct at the event and read *General Court-Martial Order Number 235*; then the attendees moved ten to twenty paces from the scaffold. At 10:59 a.m., a command-and-reconnaissance car, a ½-ton, 4x4 vehicle, halted 35 yards from the scaffold, and out stepped Tom Gordon.[214]

Gordon joined a procession that marched toward the scaffold. Peck led the way, followed by Chaplain James F. Donald, Gordon, and MP guards TSgt. Frank Landi, Sgt. Alfonso Girvalo,

and Technician Fifth Grade Vincent J. Martino; Martino was now in his final preparation to be Woods's new assistant. First Lt. Lawrence Slon, the recorder, brought up the rear of the column. The procession reached the scaffold at 11:00 a.m. Lt. Col. Peck and Chaplain Donald ascended the thirteen steps while the guards bound Gordon's hands behind his back, assisted the condemned man up the steps, and positioned him at the center of the trapdoor. Technician Third Grade Robinson then bound Gordon's ankles. Lt. Col. Peck quickly asked the prisoner if he had any last statements. Gordon replied, "Thank you for everything you have done." Peck then replied, "The Lord have mercy on you." Chaplain Donald then asked Gordon the same question, to which he replied, "Will you read the 51st Psalm to me?"[215]

The chaplain started reading the psalm, and the hood and noose were adjusted at 11:02 a.m. Thirty seconds later, Lt. Col. Peck gave a nod to John Woods, who cut the rope that released the weight and sprung the trap. At 11:18 a.m., Lt. Col. Peck directed that medical officers Lt. Col. Arthur J. Gavigan, Capt. Daniel Thaw, and Capt. Henry H. Kalter examine the body. They did and promptly declared that the prisoner was officially dead; they would later write that the cause of death was judicial asphyxis. After Peck dismissed the formation, Robinson cut the rope and removed the body from the lower part of the gallows. Capt. Hardy C. Derx, 3058th Quartermaster Graves Registration Company, signed for the body and removed it for interment, which occurred two days later at 3:00 p.m. at the US Military Cemetery at Marigny, France, in Plot Z, grave 2-33.[216]

• • •

From January 31 to May 25, 1945, a special observer from the Office of the Provost Marshal General in Washington toured the European theater of operations, preparing data concerning law enforcement functions—to include executions. On July 12, 1945, Col. W. H. Maglin, director of the Military Police Division of that office, signed a letter of transmittal to all theaters, forwarding a copy of the report prepared by Col. Ralph Wilthamuth. Maglin stated that the report reflected the findings and opinions of Wilthamuth, but the observations did not necessarily adhere to established doctrine. A casual read of the report quickly explains the caveat.[217] Col. Wilthamuth began with the following statement: "If your observer were to be hanged, and many people doubtless believe that he should be, one personal favor would be asked and that is, 'Please obtain the services of a professional hangman to do the job.'"[218]

Woods is not mentioned once in the following three-page report, but since he was the only hangman in the ETO at the time, the report obviously includes Woods's performance. The observer then offers that the hangmen in the ETO and Mediterranean theater of operations (MTO) "learned the hard way in the laboratory of the United States Army." The phrase would indicate that some of the hangings had problems. Col. Wilthamuth then got into specifics and later recommended that a three-way trap was preferable, where three officers are standing under the gallows, each with a lever; the levers are pushed simultaneously, but only one actually springs the traps. This method was used in Italy; Woods never used it. Wilthamuth later recommended ¾-inch manila rope be used for hangings; Woods often used ⅝-inch manila. War Department Pamphlet No. 27-4 specified neither but called for a 1¼-inch rope! The observer also said that the rope must be suspended using a 300-pound weight for at least three days prior to its use.[219] Woods did not do that, although later he would use a 200-pound weight suspended from the rope for up to one day. Wilthamuth closed with the following observation: "In the case the subject's neck is broken; it will take from twelve to eighteen minutes for his heart to stop, depending upon the vitality of the man. There is nothing unusual about this. In case the neck is not broken, prepare for a disagreeable fifteen or twenty minutes, then check to see what you did wrong or failed to do."[220]

Wilthamuth's opinion on the length of time it took a man to die does not assist us in the study of Woods. We can compute the time duration from the drop to the time that physicians believed the condemned man was deceased for sixty-eight of Woods's hangings. Those results are as follows: eight minutes, one man; ten minutes, two men; eleven minutes, six men; twelve minutes, five men; thirteen minutes, seven men; fourteen minutes, seven men; fifteen minutes, seven men; sixteen minutes, fourteen men; seventeen minutes, five men; eighteen minutes, five men; nineteen minutes, two men; twenty minutes, three men; twenty-three minutes, two men; and twenty-four minutes, two men. These numbers give us a median time to death of fifteen minutes. We can conclude only that some of the condemned men had their neck broken in the execution and some did not, but given that no autopsies were done, we cannot be more precise than that.

Loire Disciplinary Training Center, Le Mans, France

Robert Wray, Monday, August 20, 1945

Pvt. Robert Wray, 3299th Quartermaster Service Company, shot and killed PFC Billy Betts on December 17, 1944, at the "Café Moderne" in Golbey, France—a suburb of Épinal. Although witnesses saw the event, Wray's defense team asserted that it was an act of self-defense. A general court-martial convened on March 23, 1945, at Lunéville, France. Wray pled not guilty to the charge of murder; after being advised of his rights, he elected to take the stand and admitted shooting the victim, reasserting self-defense. The jury did not buy Wray's claim and voted to convict him. The jury then unanimously sentenced him to be hanged by the neck until dead.[221]

The staff judge advocate for the European theater of operations, Brig. Gen. Edward C. Betts, reviewed the case on June 19, 1945. He came to the conclusion that the trial was complete and that the evidence justified the outcome.[222] On June 26, 1945, Gen. Omar N. Bradley, then in command of the European theater of operations, signed the order confirming the sentence against Robert Wray. Bradley withheld issuing the order directing the time and place of execution.[223]

Robert Wray was born on March 27, 1921, in Shelby, North Carolina. He was inducted into the service on November 7, 1942, at Ft. Bragg, North Carolina. In September 1943, a summary court-martial convicted Wray of violating standing orders. Another summary court-martial convicted him in December 1943 for going AWOL. In January 1944, a third summary court-martial convicted him of smuggling 5 gallons of cognac and other intoxicating liquor into the company. Finally, in July 1944, he was convicted by a fourth summary court-martial for another incident of AWOL.[224]

On August 11, 1945, the headquarters, European theater of operations, published *General Court-Martial Order Number 319*. It stated that Robert Wray would be executed on August 20, 1945, at the Loire DTC. On August 19, 1945, MSgt. Woods drove the flatbed truck to the ravine just outside the northwest corner of the Loire DTC, set up the scaffold, and tested it. August 20, 1945 was overcast and cool; a light northeasterly wind was blowing. At 10:48 a.m., Lt. Col. Henry L. Peck gathered the official spectators and read the general order.[225]

At 10:59 a.m., a command-and-reconnaissance car, a ½-ton, 4x4 vehicle, halted 35 yards from the scaffold. General Prisoner Robert Wray stepped out and joined a procession that marched toward the scaffold. Lt. Col. Peck led the way, followed by Chaplain Charles O. Dutton, Wray, and MP guards Sgt. Russell E. Boyle, Sgt. Alfonso Girvalo, and Technician Fifth Grade Vincent J. Martino. The recorder, 1Lt. Lawrence Slon, brought up the rear of the column, which reached the scaffold at 11:00 a.m. Peck, Dutton, and Martino ascended the steps to join Woods on the platform, while the MPs bound Wray's hands behind his back, assisted him up the stairs, and positioned

him on top of the trapdoor. The executioner's assistant, for the first time Vincent J. Martino, then bound Wray's ankles at 11:01 a.m. Peck asked the prisoner if he had any last statements. Robert Wray replied, "Thank you for what you have done." Peck then replied, "May the Lord have mercy on you." Chaplain Dutton then asked the condemned man the same question, but Wray said nothing. Peck then added, "Let us pray."[226]

The chaplain started praying, and Woods, perhaps assisted by Martino, adjusted the hood and noose at 11:02 a.m. Thirty seconds later, Lt. Col. Peck gave a silent signal to Master Sergeant Woods, who cut the rope that released the weight and sprung the trap. Everything worked well; as the report stated, "The body hung suspended with no sounds but a slight muscular action of the shoulders and knees and a slight swaying motion that lasted for three to four minutes."[227]

At 11:17 a.m., Lt. Col. Peck directed Capt. Daniel Thaw, Capt. Theodore E. McCabe, and Capt. Forrest R. LaFollette to examine the body. They did and two minutes later declared that the prisoner was officially dead; they later wrote that Wray died of judicial asphyxis. Lt. Col. Peck dismissed the formation. Woods or Martino cut the rope, and 1Lt. Milliard R. Jones, 3058th Quartermaster Graves Registration Company, signed for the body and removed it for interment.[228] Wray's remains were originally buried at the US Military Cemetery at Marigny, France, in Plot Z, grave 2-34.

• • •

John Woods now had almost three weeks off, although the Army kept rolling along, especially in paperwork. On September 3, 1945, Woods was released from attachment to the 2913th DTC and assigned to the headquarters of CHANOR Base Section, a new organization that had been created on July 1, 1945, by combining the Normandy and the Channel Base Sections.

Charles M. Robinson, Friday, September 28, 1945

On the evening of March 31, 1945, the French girlfriend of Pvt. Charles Robinson, assigned to the segregated, all-black 667th Quartermaster Trick Company in the US 66th Infantry Division, came to camp at Messac, France—15 miles southwest of Rennes, entered the tent in which Robinson lived, jumped into bed with another soldier named "Jimmy," and remained with him until the next morning. Later that day, Robinson appeared very angry and told her to "go and fetch Jimmy." She made it perhaps 4 or 5 feet from the accused when he shot her one time above the right ear with a .45 pistol, and she dropped dead.[229]

Charles M. Robinson had been born on April 4, 1923, in Houston, Texas. He was inducted on July 2, 1942, at San Antonio, Texas, at Fort Sam Houston. He stood 5'8" tall and weighed 150 pounds. Robinson had a previous special court-martial conviction but had later risen to Technician Fifth Grade before being busted. His company commander stated that his leadership was very poor and he had a tendency to lie.[230] A general court-martial convened at Ploërmel, France, on April 18, 1945; Robinson pled not guilty to the charge of murder. His defense counsel attacked the validity of a police lineup and presented a witness who stated that the defendant had been in a tent moments before the shooting, putting his whereabouts in doubt. Robinson took the stand and denied shooting the victim. The jury did not buy it—one witness testified that Robinson pulled the trigger, while another witness stated he saw him standing over the body, looking at it, and saw Robinson conceal the pistol under his jacket—and convicted him or murder and then sentenced him to death by hanging.[231]

On September 27, 1945, Woods transported the venerable portable scaffold from the motor pool to the ravine just outside the Loire DTC and supervised the setup of the gallows. The weather was clear, bright, warm, and sunny on Friday, September 28, 1945. At 10:43 a.m., Lt. Col. Henry L. Peck gathered seventeen authorized witnesses and six general prisoners near the gallows. Peck briefed the men on the proper conduct expected at the event, and read *General Court-Martial Order Number 416* in its entirety to them.[232]

At 10:59 a.m., a ½-ton, 4x4 command-and-reconnaissance car halted 35 yards from the scaffold. Out stepped General Prisoner Charles M. Robinson, who joined a procession that marched toward the gallows. Lt. Col. Peck led the way; following were Chaplain Charles O. Dutton, Robinson, and MP guards Sgt. Cleon Seeber, Sgt. Alfonso Girvalo, and Technician Fifth Grade Vincent J. Martino. The column arrived at the gallows at 11:00 a.m. Peck and Dutton climbed the steps while the guards bound Robinson's hands behind his back, assisted him up the steps, and positioned him on the center of the trapdoor. Technician Fifth Grade Martino bound Robinson's ankles at 11:01 a.m. Robinson had a last statement to make: "All I can say, sir, is that they are taking the life of an innocent man." He added to the chaplain: "I hope the Lord forgives and receives me." The chaplain started intoning a prayer as Master Sergeant Woods adjusted the black hood and noose a few seconds later. Peck silently signaled Woods, who cut the rope that released the weight and actuated the trap. At 11:16 a.m., Peck directed that Maj. Melvin H. Blaurock, Capt. Daniel Thaw, and Capt. Forrest R. LaFollette examine the body. They did and two minutes later declared that Robinson was officially dead. Woods cut the rope and removed the body from the lower part of the gallows. Capt. Hardy C. Derx, 3058th Quartermaster Graves Registration Company, signed for the body and removed it to Marigny—some 100 miles away. Army personnel interred Charles M. Robinson at the US Military Cemetery at Marigny in Plot Z, grave 2-35.[233]

Blake W. Mariano, Wednesday, October 10, 1945

On October 9, 1945, Woods drove the now-familiar Army execution truck to a ravine outside the Loire DTC at Le Mans—the final hanging he would do at that location, although Woods did not realize that at the time. Woods supervised a prisoner detail that removed the scaffold from the truck and set it up just outside the barbed-wire fence. The hangman would test the trapdoor of the scaffold that afternoon.

The subject of the execution was Blake W. Mariano, formerly a private first class in Company C, 191st Tank Battalion, in the US 45th Infantry Division. On April 16, 1945, near Lauf an der Pegnitz, Germany—just east of Nürnberg—an intoxicated Mariano had raped two civilian women and shot and killed a third. Blake W. Mariano, a full-blooded Navajo named Hoska-Yith-Ela-Wood, was born on April 4, 1916, near Gallup, New Mexico. He quit school after completing the third grade at the age of thirteen. Mariano had an Army General Classification Test score in the bottom quintile and scored a mental age of eleven years on the Kent Emergency Scale. A medical board classified him as a "high grade moron." But Mariano could fight; the 191st Tank Battalion fought at Anzio, where he served as a gunner on a Sherman tank. Near Épinal, France, on September 23, 1944, enemy shrapnel wounded Mariano in the left hip.[234] He was one of those fighters who Gen. George Patton had said were the "hard core of scrappers" an army needed to win a war. In another time and place, Mariano would have been considered a hero; today he was a condemned murderer.

The weather was clear, bright, and sunny on that Wednesday morning of October 10; fall was in the air at Le Mans. Lt. Col. Henry L. Peck gathered thirteen witnesses and spectators at the ravine at 10:39 a.m. Peck briefed the personnel on the proper conduct expected at the event and read *General Court-Martial Order Number 458* in its entirety.[235] At 10:59 a.m., a ½-ton, 4x4, command-and-reconnaissance car halted 35 yards from the gallows. Out stepped General Prisoner Blake W. Mariano, who joined a procession led by Lt. Col. Peck toward the scaffold. Peck was followed by Chaplain Charles O. Dutton, Mariano, and guards Sgt. Russell E. Boyle, Sgt. Alfonso Girvalo, and Sgt. Howard C. Jones. The column reached the gallows at 11:01 a.m. Peck and Dutton ascended the steps while the guards bound Mariano's hands behind his back, assisted him up the steps, and positioned him on top of the trapdoor. Technician Fifth Grade Vincent Martino then bound Mariano's ankles at 11:02 a.m. Mariano had no last statements to make.[236]

Chaplain Dutton began to pray; John Woods adjusted the black hood and noose a few seconds later. Peck gave a silent signal to Woods, who released the trapdoor. Everything worked as planned, although one general prisoner observing the event doubled over and began to vomit. At 11:19 a.m., Peck directed Maj. Melvin H. Blaurock, Capt. Theodore E. McCabe, and Capt. Forrest R. LaFollette to examine the body. Two minutes later they emerged from under the gallows, declaring that Mariano had officially died at 11:21:30 a.m.[237]

Woods cut the rope and removed the body from the lower screened part of the scaffold. Capt. Hardy C. Derx, 3058th Quartermaster Graves Registration Company, signed for the body; it was interred the next day at the US Military Cemetery at Marigny in Plot Z, grave 2-36.[238]

• • •

This was the last execution that a very significant eyewitness of John Woods observed. Sgt. Thomas J. Ward served as the supply sergeant of the Loire DTC. Born on June 9, 1925, at Harrisburg, Pennsylvania, he enlisted on September 2, 1943, and was assigned to Company I, 23rd Infantry Regiment, 2nd Infantry Division. Wounded in action four times, he fought in France, Belgium, and the Siegfried Line before transferring to the Loire DTC in February 1945.[239]

Ward subsequently witnessed twelve executions at the DTC. At Le Mans, he was John Woods's closest friend, often going downtown in the evening for a beer together. He recalled that the day before each execution, Woods would walk to the supply room to get the rope and black hood that would be used in the upcoming event; a new rope was used for each hanging, although Woods would use each black hood several times. On the first occasion before a hanging, Woods openly carried the rope from the supply room through the stockade, and the observant prisoners ascertained what was happening and began to throw rocks at the hangman; in the future, Woods wore a trench coat, rain or shine, and concealed the rope and hood under it. Ward later recalled that concerning the trapdoor, Woods had both a lever and a backup rope that could be cut to release the trapdoor. Ward remembered that many of the executions occurred just before noon, when many of the men in the stockade—not involved in the execution—were standing in line outside the mess hall for lunch, and when the trapdoor opened, the motion was so violent and unique that the loud noise could be heard throughout the DTC, and this distinctive sound spoiled many a man's appetite. At LeMans, Woods asked Ward if he would become his assistant, but Tom declined.[240]

Thomas Ward remained at the DTC until November 1945, when he returned to the States. During the war, he received the following awards: Bronze Star Medal, Purple Heart with three Oak Leaf Clusters, Combat Infantryman's Badge, European–African–Middle Eastern Campaign Medal (with four campaign stars), Good Conduct Medal, Occupation (Germany) Medal, and World War II Victory Medal. He also qualified as sharpshooter with a rifle, automatic rifle, and carbine.[241] In civilian life, he worked as a construction foreman at Miller and Norford Inc. and the New Cumberland Army Depot before retiring.

Ellsworth Williams, Saturday, January 5, 1946

As 1946 began, Woods was scheduled to report to Bruchsal Prison for more executions of Germans, but first he apparently had to serve as the hangman at the execution of another American soldier. Pvt. Ellsworth Williams, of Company E in the 1349th Engineer General Service Regiment, had shot and grievously wounded 2Lt. Eddie L. May on May 24, 1945, while Williams was on guard duty at the Army airfield at Le Havre, France. May died two days later. A general court-martial found Williams guilty of murder on June 19, 1945, and sentenced him to death by hanging. Brig. Gen. E. F. Koening, commander of the CHANOR Base Section, approved the sentence on July 28, 1945, and Gen. Eisenhower confirmed the sentence on October 8, 1945. Finally, on December 19, 1945, Lt. Gen. Walter Bedell Smith, the chief of staff for the theater, signed *General Court-Martial Order Number 626*, which stated that Williams would be executed on January 5, 1946, at the Loire DTC at Le Mans.[242]

The day before the execution, Col. Leon L. Kotzebue, the latest commanding officer of the Loire DTC, directed that five officers would serve as official witnesses; three medical officers would have the unfortunate task of certifying the death of the condemned man. At 10:55 a.m. on January 4, Kotzebue, accompanied by Chaplain William B. Crocker, met with the condemned man; it was Kotzebue's duty to read the general court-martial order in its entirety, sparing Williams the ordeal of having to hear it while on the gallows. Kotzebue departed, while the chaplain remained with Williams to provide spiritual assistance through the day. Medical officer Capt. Edwin A. Kiss examined General Prisoner Williams and "found him to be in excellent physical and mental condition."[243]

Ellsworth Williams, a black soldier, was born on March 14, 1922, in Douglas, Georgia. Single, he completed seventh grade before quitting school to become a delivery boy making $6.00 a week at the L. F. Lodge Grocery Company in Sanford,

Florida, before enlisting at Ft. Benning, Georgia, on January 24, 1942.[244]

Saturday, January 5, 1946, was foggy, overcast, and cold. The execution site at the DTC was the same as during the war. A ¾-ton command-and-reconnaissance vehicle, with side curtains attached due to the cold, brought General Prisoner Williams to the site at 10:57 a.m.; he was sitting in the back seat between the chaplain and one of the guards, to whom he was shackled. The party dismounted and Col. Kotzebue met them 35 yards from the scaffold. The colonel and the chaplain marched side by side at the front of the short column. Behind them walked Ellsworth Williams, flanked by two guards and followed by a third guard carrying a brace board—the three, Technician Fifth Grade Vincent J. Martino, Sgt. Floyd W. Weaver, and TSgt. Jesse E. Bunting—were dressed in Class "A" uniform with boots and overcoats.

Guards bound the prisoner's hands behind his back and then assisted him to climb the steps up the scaffold. After Williams stood on the center of the trapdoor, Martino bound the prisoner's feet. Kotzebue asked Williams if he had a last statement to make, to which the prisoner replied:

"I want to thank you for all you have done. I pass on to the hands of the Lord, holding no malice toward anyone." Williams then made a second statement to the chaplain: "I want to thank you, too, for all you have done, and if I could I would shake your hand." The two men began to recite the Lord's Prayer until Woods adjusted the black hood and the noose at 11:02 a.m. Kotzebue silently signaled the executioner, who cut the rope that released the weight and sprang the trap at 11:03:30. The name of the executioner was not provided in the official execution report, but it was almost certainly Woods. The trap mechanism operated perfectly, and the prisoner dropped through the opening and hung suspended with no sounds or muscular movement.[245]

At 11:18 a.m., the three medical officers marched to the understructure of the scaffold, made their examinations, and pronounced Williams dead at 11:21 a.m. The executioner cut the rope, and personnel led by 2Lt. Vincent W. Cantilla, from the 500th Quartermaster Battalion, a graves registration unit, removed the body.[246]

Ellsworth Williams would be the last American soldier that John Woods would ever hang.

Chapter 8
ON TO GERMANY

From June 1945 through September 1946, MSgt. Woods hanged thirty-two Nazi war criminals at Landsberg am Lech Prison and other locations in Germany. While the dates of eight German executions occurred during the period that John Woods was still hanging American soldiers, this study has chosen to break perfect chronological order and present them here.

Rheinbach Prison, Rheinbach, Germany

Peter Kohn, Matthias Gierens, and Peter Back, Friday, June 29, 1945

Rheinbach Prison was built in 1914, just outside the small city of the same name in North Rhine–Westphalia. The outside walls formed a square, with the inside prison building in the shape of an X. John Woods hanged his first postwar German war criminals on Friday, June 29, 1945. The event was dutifully reported by the *Stars & Stripes:*[1]

3 Germans Civilians Hanged for Murder of US Flyer

RHEINBACH, Germany, June 29 (UP)—Three German civilian war criminals climbed 13 steps to the gallows in the light of early dawn at the military prison in Rheinbach today, and were hanged.

They were executed for the merciless slaying last August of an unknown American flyer who had parachuted from a disabled bomber near their homes at Presit, in Germany.

"Jesus take me," screamed crippled Peter Back as the trap door in the floor of the wooden gallows sprung.

Back, who was the local Nazi party leader, was the last of the three to die. The executioner was M-Sgt. John Woods, former Texas penitentiary hangman, who slashed the cord opening the trap.

The executions were the first inside Germany of civilian war criminals. Besides Back, the executed were one-armed Peter Kohn, father of three children, whose wife is pregnant, and Matthias Gierens, who had admitted beating the flyer with a sledgehammer, but pleaded insanity....

Kohn was the first to die. Two stern-faced military policemen had to help him climb those 13 steps to the top of the gallows at 5 AM. His face was pale and his lips trembled as the sentence was read to him. He made one last request: "I wish that the American Army and government will protect my beloved wife and children, and that the German Government will give them all the aid it can."

Kohn kissed the crucifix held out to him by a black-robed Catholic priest who accompanied each of the condemned men to the gallows. He was pronounced dead by Maj. John Poutas of Newton, Mass.

Gierens was unemotional, and walked with a firm step. He climbed the stairway to the gallows without assistance, and stood firmly erect as Lt. Col. J. V. Roddy, deputy provost marshal, from San Francisco, Calif., read the order.

His only emotion was when he closed his eyes and his lips moved in silent prayer. He requested that two letters—one to his wife and the other to his father-in-law—be placed on his coffin and taken with his body to his home. In those letters he asked their forgiveness for the sadness which he had caused them.

Little Peter Back limped to the gallows clinging to the arms of MPs. His face was ashen white, and his lips quivered. He did not crack until the hangman reached to put the rope around his neck. Then he broke down and sobbed. He said:

"I have one wish that I discussed with my wife yesterday." He cried in a shrill voice: "I would like my body to lie in state in my home."

The black hood was placed over his head. Then, as the noose was being tightened, he screamed in German: "Farewell, Katherina, Angela and Ursula. Jesus, take me." Angela was his wife. Katherina and Ursula were his daughters.

• • •

Life Magazine followed up the story on July 16 with a story that began as follows: "The hand of American justice fell for the first time on German civilians on June 29 when three German murderers were dropped through a gallows trap in the Rheinbeck [sp. Rheinbach] prison. Their crime, which had gone unpunished in the perverted world of Nazi Germany, was particularly revealing of that world."[2]

The article described how defendant Peter Back shot a downed B-24 Liberator crewman twice; how defendant Peter Kohn clubbed the wounded man, causing him to fall on his face; and how defendant Matthias Gierens hit the American in the head with a stone hammer. The three men had two defense lawyers, a German civilian and an American Army major; they presented a mentally irresponsible defense for Gierens and a defense for Kohn that the loss of his left arm in the *Wehrmacht* on the Russian front had wrecked his nerves. Nine neighbors of the accused from the town of Preist testified for the prosecution. A forensics team exhumed the body of the victim but was unable to determine a name for the deceased. The trial, held at Ahrweiler, was open to the public, although few Germans attended. The eight-man commission, appointed by Lt. Gen. Leonard T. Gerow, commander of

the US 15th Army, returned a guilty verdict and a sentence of death.[3]

At the Rheinbach Prison, North Rhine–Westphalia, Germany, on Friday, June 29, 1945, the three condemned men met Woods, "the hand of American justice," for the first and last time. With Lt. Col. J. V. Roddy in charge, one-armed Peter Kohn, father of four with a fifth child on the way, mounted the gallows at 5:00 a.m. Standing behind Kohn, Woods tugged the black hood over the head and neck of the German, who was heard to utter: "God take pity on me!" At the rear of the scaffold, Woods cut the rope, which released a weight, and the trapdoor dropped at 5:05 a.m. Maj. John Poutas later pronounced Kohn deceased. Matthias Gierens was the next to mount the scaffold at 5:45 a.m. A thirty-seven-year-old father of three, he asked on the scaffold to have two letters delivered to his wife. Once again, Woods slipped the hood over the head and neck of the condemned man and followed this by placing the noose around his neck, tightening it.[4]

Then, Matthias Gierens specifically, and any German in general who heard what happened next or had seen *Life Magazine*, found out that John Woods had a little problem with botched hangings. At the rear of the scaffold, Woods cut the rope, which released a weight; the trap opened at 5:50 a.m. and away dropped the condemned man. It was not a "little" problem, though, for Gierens, who was obliged to hang for fifteen minutes until pronounced dead by Maj. John Poutas, although the canvas curtain hid the exact details of his final struggle from nearby queasy spectators. An American officer in attendance later said, "Some of these Krauts are hard to kill."[5]

Peter Back was next and had to be manhandled on the way to the gallows by two burly military policeman, each a half foot taller than the condemned. Back, wearing a mismatched suit and shoes with their laces removed, reportedly snarled at the Americans at the foot of the gallows but later said, "I respect the American Army and Army administration." Woods, wearing a helmet liner for the day's executions instead of his usual overseas cap, again slipped the hood and noose over the head and neck of the condemned, as Back began to sob, crying, "Farewell, Katherina, Angela, and Ursula. Jesus, take me." The witness list was small, but some of the authorized spectators had seen enough. Several of the eight American and British officers were observed to sway and turn pale when the trap was sprung at 6:35 a.m., after Woods "slashed" the rope, which released a weight causing this. Maj. Poutas now waited a full fifteen minutes before making his examination; once that was complete, graves registration personnel pulled a white mattress cover up over the body before it was cut down at 7:19 a.m. The *Life* caption for photo #26 of the article stated that "After this hanging [Back], as after the other ones, the hangman wept." It is the opinion of this study that assistant hangman Thomas F. Robinson wept, not Woods, and that the *Life* correspondent confused the two men. Robinson would do only one more execution, and it would be uncharacteristic of Woods to show this type of emotion.[6]

On June 30, 1945, the *New York Times* published an article titled "3 Germans Hanged for Slaying Airman," describing the triple hanging at dawn and adding a bit of color: "Birds chirped and chattered in the daybreak coolness as the trio dropped to their deaths, just as the American flier fell to his death at their hands at a point sixty miles southwest of Coblenz."

• • •

In an unusual description, the *Times* article mentioned the name and civilian address of the assistant hangman: SSgt. Thomas F. Robinson of 1933 Daly Avenue, Bronx, New York City.[7] A baker in civilian life, Robinson probably

accompanied Woods on thirty-two executions. Robinson, the son of John Robinson and Lillian Dunn, was born in New York in 1920; his mother passed away when he was seven. As a result, the family placed Thomas in the St. Joseph's Home for Children in Peekskill, New York, a facility for orphaned children or those youngsters in need of a stable environment; he remained there through sophomore year of high school, leaving about 1936 to become an apprentice baker.[8] Robinson married Mae Elizabeth Decker in Yonkers, New York, on June 14, 1942.[9] At the time of his enlistment on September 15, 1942, in Bayonne, New Jersey, he was living in Westchester, New York. He stood 5'11" tall and weighed 156 pounds. Thomas Robinson was assigned to the 554th Quartermaster Depot prior to working with Woods.[10]

Given that the soldier arrived in the States on September 6, 1945, and the schedule of hangings that summer, Robinson probably got out of the hanging business in July 1945 after the execution of Tom Gordon. Robinson was discharged from the Army on November 9, 1945, in New York City; he later lived in Mount Vernon, New York. Thomas and Mae Elizabeth had one son and one daughter, Peggy. His father, John Michael Robinson, died in Yonkers, New York, on December 19, 1959. Thomas Robinson later lived in Hernando, Florida.[11]

• • •

By November 1945, Woods had a new assigned headquarters and a new boss, Brig. Gen. Theodore F. Wessels. The general's office was located in the massive IG Farben Building in Frankfurt am Main, completed in 1930 as the corporate headquarters of the IG Farben conglomerate. At that time, the complex was the largest office building in Europe and remained so through the 1940s. Its signature features were the paternoster elevators, which consisted of a chain of small, open compartments that moved slowly in a loop up and down inside the building, without stopping. Passengers could step on or off at any floor they wished, although until a rider was familiar with it, the system was quite intimidating.

Even more intimidating was Gen. Wessels, who served previously as the assistant commander of the US 80th Infantry Division in 1943; commanded the Chinese Army Infantry School in Kunming, China, in 1944; and received a Silver Star for gallantry in action at the Siege of Myitkyina in Burma in 1944. He became the deputy theater provost marshal for the European theater in July 1945, and the provost marshal of the same command in December 1945.

Bruchsal Prison, Bruchsal, Germany

Johannes Seipel, Johann Opper, Phillip Gütlich, Joseph Hartgen, and Friedrich Wüst, Saturday, November 10, 1945

Woods's next stop in his German-war-criminal-execution tour took him on November 10, 1945, to Bruchsal Prison in the city of Bruchsal, 15 miles northeast of Karlsruhe. With construction finished in 1848, the prison copied the design of the Eastern State Penitentiary located in Philadelphia, Pennsylvania; it was built in the shape of an octagon, with four long walls connected by four shorter walls. Because of this, the prison became known as the "Star of Bruchsal" and "Café Eight Corners."

Once again, the American hangman had a date with German civilians who had murdered downed American fliers, as reported in the *New York Times* in an article titled "5 Germans Hanged for Killing Fliers." An American general military court, meeting on July 25, 1945, convicted all five of murder and sentenced them to death by hanging. The account stated that the first condemned man started mounting the gallows at 1:15 p.m.; the trap sprung for the last man at 4:10 p.m. The *Times* also reported that the weather was rainy and overcast.[12] A day later, the event was reported in the *Stars & Stripes*:[13]

American Airmen's Killers Hanged at Bruchsal Jail

BRUCHSAL, Germany, Nov. 11 (AP)—Five German civilians were hanged at Bruchsal prison Saturday for the murder of six American fliers who parachuted from a disabled plane near Russelsheim in August 1944.

They were plunged through the trap by an American Army sergeant, John C. Wood, who said he now had officiated at 299 hangings.

He expressed the hope that Josef Kramer, commandant of the notorious Belsen concentration camp, now on trial for alleged crimes there, would be his 300th assignment.

• • •

The following day, the newspaper published an interview with Woods that the United Press had conducted after the most-recent executions. Woods, whom the article stated was from San Antonio, Texas, and stood 5'3½", affirmed that he wanted to remain in Germany to hang senior German war criminals, including Hermann Göring. Woods continued, stating that he had hanged eighty-seven men in Europe already and that Göring's weight posed no problem, since Woods had already hanged a 280-pound man. The interview described that Woods's job consisted of preparing the gallows, securing the hood and noose around the prisoner's neck, cutting the rope that released the trapdoor, and watching the body before it was cut down—after medical officers had pronounced death. He also revealed that the trapdoor on the gallows weighed 200 pounds. Woods finished by stating that he always carried a sidearm, since his best friend and assistant had been killed in north France the previous summer "by a friend of a criminal we executed."[14] Three weeks later, the *Stars & Stripes* published three photos associated with the Bruchsal executions.[15]

The six victims were crew members of a B-24J bomber nicknamed "Wham! Bam! Thank You

Ma'am," based in England with the 8th Air Force. On August 24, 1944, their plane was hit by fire after a bombing mission over Hannover, and the men parachuted over Rüsselsheim, Germany, not far from Frankfurt. Angry Germans later captured them and killed six airmen.

Johannes Seipel was a farmer; he was born about 1879 and would be the first man to be hanged. The court had found that Seipel had kicked one of the airmen in the throat. Clad in a dark jacket and white skullcap, Seipel was nervous. After the execution order was read to him, Seipel shouted his final words: "I saw a fellow Engel throw rocks at them. I did nothing! Nothing!" The hangman first removed the man's white skullcap. As Woods put the black hood and noose over the condemned man's neck, Seipel continued to shout: "Nothing!" Woods pushed the lever about 2:45 p.m.; it appears that nothing went wrong in the hanging, even though the cold rain was lashing the gallows.

Johann Opper, born in 1884, was a railway switchman and also a Nazi Party member. At trial, he was found to have beaten the airmen with a broom.[16] Opper was the second to be hanged; his last words were "If the military won't give me another trial, could I be tried by the church?" Woods also removed the man's white skullcap before putting on the hood and noose. Woods pushed the lever about 3:10 p.m.[17]

Friedrich Wüst, born in 1905, worked as a blacksmith; he was also a Nazi Party member. He would be the third attacker to receive justice handed out in the rain by Woods. Wüst had been convicted of beating an airman in the head with a hammer, and it was becoming obvious that the hangman was getting tired of what he probably thought was whining by the condemned men, such as when Wüst gave his own last words: "With this I die with a clear conscience..."—the hangman grabbed the man's white skullcap and then pulled the black hood over the man's head before he had finished the sentence, and dropped the trapdoor about 3:30 p.m.[18]

The fourth man to die, Phillip Gütlich, was a farmer and tavern keeper. At trial he had admitted striking one of the airmen, but it was probably fortunate for him that Woods understood very little German, when Gütlich provided his last words of "I did only one thing, and only because an American stuck out his tongue at me." Woods dropped the trapdoor about 3:50 p.m., just after replacing Gütlich's white skullcap with the black hood and noose.[19]

Joseph Hartgen, born in 1903, was an air raid warden, Nazi Party member, and foreman of the nearby Opel automobile plant and was the last to die. He had shot several of the airmen in the head during the murders. As Hartgen, accompanied a priest reciting a prayer from an open bible, stopped at the foot of the scaffold steps, he kissed a silver crucifix. Hartgen then climbed the thirteen steps, thumping each with a solid footstep, perhaps to show everyone that he was not afraid. After an officer asked him for a last statement, Hartgen replied, "God forgive you because you don't know what you are doing." Just before John Woods—who did know what he was doing—pushed the lever, several flashbulbs lit the dark gray sky as Joseph Hartgen dropped at 4:10 p.m.[20]

After the last man was dead, Woods smiled and proclaimed "a perfect hanging." John Woods was content with his position. As so many soldiers with hardscrabble backgrounds had found, there was a home for them in the Army. And so, Woods now applied for and received appointment to the Regular Army. The service honorably discharged Woods on December 15, 1945, at the 2913th Disciplinary Training Center, paid him all back pay due, and accepted him into the Regular Army the following day.[21]

Bruchsal Prison, Bruchsal, Germany

Woods had a few days off, but then it was back to Germany and the Bruchsal Prison, where again the men to be executed had murdered American airmen during the war.

Clemens Wiegand, Friday, January 11, 1946

Clemens Wiegand was a Nazi Party district leader in Frankfurt-Ginnheim. On November 21, 1944, German antiaircraft fire brought down an American aircraft over Ginnheim. Several members of the crew parachuted to safety. One of the downed airmen, Anthony B. Martin, landed in a field and was captured; Wiegand approached and shot the airman in the head with a pistol. Wiegand believed that the American was dead and left the area, but later, learning that the airman was still alive, Wiegand returned and shot the airman an additional two times in the head; the wounds proved mortal and Martin died a few hours later.

An American general military court convened at the Grand Hotel at Heidelberg, Germany, on October 15, 1945. Wiegand's defense team offered no justification, and since he had admitted the murder, the court convicted him, but then sentenced him to death by decapitation, which had been the primary method of execution in Nazi Germany. A review panel changed decapitation to death by hanging. On Friday, January 11, 1946, Woods, assisted by Vincent J. Martino, hanged Clemens Wiegand at the Bruchsal Prison. It was quite cold; military policemen wore gloves, and the condemned man had a long-sleeved jacket and white skullcap.

Dominikus Thomas, Wilhelm Dietermann, and Karl Bloch, Saturday, January 12, 1946

The following day, Woods hanged another three men for killing downed American fliers. Wilhelm Dietermann, a police officer in Friedensdorf, helped arrest 1Lt. Joseph Roberts Jr., of the 361st US Fighter Squadron, near the village of Buchenau. Roberts's P-47D "Thunderbolt" had been shot down near Fritzlar by antiaircraft fire on October 7, 1944, but he had evaded capture for a week.

Dietermann and another man finally captured the pilot near Friedensdorf and decided to kill him. Roberts ascertained what was about to happen and began fighting, at which point Dietermann pulled the trigger.

An American general military court met at the Grand Hotel in Heidelberg on October 10–11, 1945. Wilhelm Dietermann pled self-defense, but the court convicted him of murder and sentenced him to death. Woods dispensed justice for 1Lt. Joseph Roberts when he hanged Wilhelm Dietermann at the Bruchsal Prison on January 12, 1946. Authorities buried Dietermann's remains there three days later but transferred them to his home town of Oberscheld in April 1946. 1Lt. Joseph Roberts Jr. is buried at Arlington National Cemetery at Arlington, Virginia.

Woods also hanged Karl Bloch that day. On December 1, 1944, Bloch and several other Germans killed four American airmen near Beltershain, Germany; after killing the Americans, Bloch helped loot their bodies before burying them in a ditch. The same court met at Heidelberg from October 12 to 15, 1945, and found Bloch guilty, giving him the death sentence. This court previously, on October 9, 1945, had sentenced Dominikus Thomas, a member of the Home Guard, to death for killing an American airman near Wollendorf on September 21, 1944. Given their dates of sentencing, Woods probably hanged Dominikus Thomas first, Wilhelm Dietermann second, and Karl Bloch third. The *Stars & Stripes* reported the January 12, 1946, executions three days later from a UP story:[22]

Three Germans Die for Fliers' Death

FRANKFURT, Jan. 14 (UP)—Three Germans, Dominikus Thomas, Wilhelm Dieterman, and Karl Bloch, were hanged this afternoon at Bruchsal Prison, near Heidelberg, for killing three American airmen.

Dieterman had been found guilty of shooting Lt. L. Roberts Jr. of Los Angeles. Bloch was one of the group that killed four fliers. Thomas shot an unidentified US aviator in September 1944.

The hangings were witnessed by five Russian correspondents now touring the American zone of occupation in Germany.

• • •

Additional details can be gleaned from Signal Corps motion pictures of the hangings. Each condemned man had the initial "T" on the back of his jacket, presumably indicating the German word *Tod*, or death. As each man marched to the gallows, he would have seen Woods and Technician Fifth Grade Martino, wearing raincoats and standing at parade rest on the scaffold platform. At least one condemned man, Dominikus Thomas, wore a dark skullcap, which Woods yanked off before putting the black hood on the man, while Martino held the noose. Woods did the same thing with the light-colored skullcap worn by Wilhelm Dietermann. A Signal Corps still photographer timed his shot at the instant the trapdoor opened. Three doctors went behind the scaffold canvas to pronounce each man dead. Woods, Martino, and a military policeman then went behind the canvas and carried the deceased man—now without the black hood—out, with the MP holding the body by a foot, Woods seizing the shoulders, and Martino grabbing an arm and a leg, to a nearby black, wooden coffin.

Enter Johann Reichhart

In some respects, Woods has been compared with three other prolific hangmen of World War II: Johann Reichhart of Germany, and the English duo of Tom Pierrepoint and his nephew Albert Pierrepoint. However, unlike Woods, Johann Reichhart knew all about his family history and was proud of the tradition—he came from a long line of state executioners!

Reichhart was born on April 29, 1893, in Wichenbach near Wörth an der Donau, into a family of executioners going back eight generations.

From the middle of the eighteenth century, the name Reichhart stood alongside the names of Keysser, Schellerer, and Kisslinger as famed royal Bavarian state executioners. Jakob Keysser, who is mentioned as far back as 1786, hailed from Würzburg and married into the Reichhart family. Jakob's successor in the service of the Bavarian state was Lorenz Schellerer, who also married into the Reichhart family. Lorenz began his tradecraft in 1836. He also made history when in 1854, at the Munich Heumarkt (known today as the Rindermarkt), he conducted the last execution in Bavaria with the massive two-handed sword. Not much had changed from the Middle Ages in good old Bavaria.[23]

In this final appearance as a swordsman, Lorenz stood dressed in all black, wearing a black hood with narrow eye slits. Standing on the scaffold, *Herr* Schellerer waited for the condemned to arrive. His assistant led the violently resisting criminal through a narrow alley past throngs of curious—and perhaps bloodthirsty—onlookers to the scaffold. Forced to kneel and wearing a blindfold, the condemned was to be dispatched with a mighty blow of the sword, but the condemned managed to jerk several times, causing the initial blows of the headsman to strike only thin air. Order soon returned, however, after some prodding by the assistant with a wooden stick so that the victim's head was properly positioned on the chopping block, when Lorenz finally hit his target and then held up the decapitated head to the roars of the assemblage.[24]

All this was too much for King Maximilian II, and a few weeks later, on August 5, 1854, the Bavarian ruler signed an order banning executions with the two-handed sword and substituting the guillotine in its place. Perhaps the fact that this last condemned person decapitated in Munich had been a woman had something to do with his majesty's decision.[25]

Bavarian craftsmen soon constructed their own version of the French guillotine. The height, only 1.5 meters, was much shorter than the French model, in which the blade fell 5 meters. The weight of the German blade was 29 pounds; however, the mass of the wooden frame surrounding the blade brought the overall weight to 90 pounds, which delivered sufficient momentum to cleanly sever the neck. Additionally, Bavarian authorities sought to remove executions from the view of the public. As time wore on, only eight officials would attend Bavarian executions.[26]

With the introduction of the guillotine, Lorenz Schellerer passed into history, another victim of advancing technology. In his place stepped Joseph Kisslinger, a wine estate owner, as the Crown's executioner. Three months after his selection, Kisslinger not only had learned the intricacies of the new machine but also managed to behead three criminals in Munich without a hitch. Normalcy had returned to Bavaria, at least where executions were concerned. During the period, Franz Xaver Reichhart—born in Mühltal in the Oberpfalz in 1851—became the primary assistant to Joseph Kisslinger in 1882. After learning at the foot of the master, Franz Xaver assumed Bavarian state executioner duties on May 1, 1894, when Kisslinger retired. Equally as important, the new executioner received an official rank within the Bavarian justice ministry.[27]

A day later, Franz Xaver Reichhart conducted his first execution at 5:00 a.m. at the Fronfeste Prison in Amberg, Bavaria. Speed was Franz Xaver's watchword. Over the years, he maintained a detailed diary of the fifty-eight beheadings, recording every facet of the procedures. He seemed quite proud, for example, that it generally took only three and a half minutes to complete his task. As Franz Xaver noted: "During his last walk [to the guillotine], as well as with the repeated reading of the judgment and sentence, the condemned trembled dreadfully and could hardly walk upright. From praying [in the cell], no more speech was possible and [the condemned] had to be strongly supported by assistants."[28]

At the end of the First World War, not only did the German monarchy fall, so did the monarchy of Bavaria. To make matters worse, a revolution broke out in the Bavarian capital of Munich. An unruly mob marched to the army barracks in the city, and by morning, most of the soldiers had switched allegiance to the side of the revolution. Hours later, Bavarian King Ludwig III went into exile. Kurt Eisner then declared Bavaria a "free state" and became the minister-president of Bavaria. Anarchy remained through April 6, 1919, when the insurgents formally proclaimed a Soviet republic. Finally, the Bavarian army rolled into Munich and defeated the Communists after bitter street fighting. The troops killed over 1,000 supporters of the Munich Soviet government, while the *Freikorps* arrested and summarily executed about seven hundred men and women by firing squads. During this period, the Bavarian justice ministry declared that all penalties of execution would be carried out by firing squad and not by guillotine. This policy would remain in effect for the next three years, until wiser heads prevailed.[29]

Meanwhile, the nephew of Franz Xaver Reichhart, Johann Reichhart, began life in the tiny hamlet of Wichenbach. Johann's father, Michl, was not in the execution profession but instead served as sort of a forest master in charge of disposing of the remains of animals that had died in the woods of that area; Johann's mother, Maria, tended house. Johann attended grade school and apparently began the lengthy apprenticeship to become a butcher. However, like many other young men in Germany, his professional pursuit took a back seat once war began in 1914.

The onset of the conflict that August found Johann Reichhart working in the northern German city of Hamburg in the butcher trade. Johann promptly visited a local military induction center and volunteered for service in the 76th Infantry Machine Gun Company, of the 76th Infantry Regiment assigned to the 17th Infantry Division.[30]

The unit joined the First German Army under *General* Alexander von Kluck, seeing action at the Belgian fortress of Liege, and then went into action against British forces on August 24, 1914, near Maubeuge. The following month, the unit took part in the Battle of the Marne, fighting at Châtillon sur Morin, Esternay, and Courgivaux. After the German withdrawal, the unit occupied defensive positions near Bailly, from the Oise River east of St. Mard. In early 1915, the German army reorganized and the regiment transferred to the 111th Infantry Division, manning the line along the Cotes de Meuse, near Verdun, before moving to Artois. In August 1916, the formation moved north of the Somme, where it suffered heavy losses at Guillemont and Guinchy, and returned to the Cotes de Meuse.[31]

The division returned to the Somme in October; in 1917, it fought in the Hindenberg Line north of St. Quentin and suffered serious losses defending at Ypres in July. In 1918, the unit fought in the Battle of Picardy, the Third Battle of the Somme, and at the bitter fighting at Lens.[32] Some 19,899 men rotated through the regiment during the war; of the 3,000 men who stood under the regiment's colors at the beginning of the war, only 647, including Reichhart, remained to the end of the conflict.[33]

With the carnage over, Johann Reichhart left the military and worked for the locomotive factory Krauss for a year and a half, before returning to his original profession as a butcher. In 1921, he married and worked as a landlord before driving a taxi in Neubiberg, a suburb of Munich. The Reichharts had a son, Heribert, in 1922, and a girl the following year. Meanwhile, Bavaria switched back to the guillotine as the approved method for execution and contacted Franz Xaver Reichhart. Now seventy-three years old, the elder Reichhart realized that his time had passed for such a demanding occupation. He suggested that his nephew Michael take over the job. Michael, however, was having none of it, and the offer fell to Michael's younger brother, Johann.[34]

On March 23, 1924, Johann Reichhart applied to the Bavarian state ministry of justice in Munich for the position of executioner. The administration accepted his offer, allocated 150 goldmarks for each execution he performed, and announced that "From April 1, 1924, Reichhart takes over the execution of all death sentences coming in the Free State of Bavaria to the execution by beheading with the guillotine." His career began on July 4, 1924—when he beheaded two men on the guillotine at Landshut.[35]

It was not a career to support his family, however. Reichhart executed only seven persons in 1924, nine in 1925, three in 1926, three in 1927, and one in 1928.[36] Moreover, Johann discovered that society viewed the state executioner as a necessary evil, and the Reichharts found that in many respects they had become social outcasts in the eyes of their fellow Bavarians, who often wanted nothing to do with them. The Reichhart children were mocked at school; neighbors made it clear that the neighborhood would be much better were the Reichharts to move elsewhere—which they finally did to the town of Deisenhofen, south of Munich. The family, which added a second son, Hans, in 1927, experienced difficult economic times, and Johann drifted from job to job, including for a time working as a dance instructor.

In 1929, his reputation was such that he fled Bavaria to Holland, opening a vegetable market in The Hague. During these years, he returned to Bavaria only when he received an encrypted telegram informing him of an assigned execution. With Hitler's rise to power in 1933, Reichhart permanently returned to the fatherland; he joined the Nazi Party four years later. The Nazis proved prolific employers, and Reichhart earned so much money as an executioner that in 1942 he purchased a home near Deisenhofen. During the Third Reich, Reichhart served as the chief executioner for Execution District VIII (*Vollstreckungsbezirk VIII*), which had three major centers for carrying out the death penalty: Bruchsal Prison, Stuttgart Remand Prison, and the Punishment Prison at Munich-Stadelheim. Reichhart executed 3,165 people, most of them during the period 1939–45, when, according to his own records, he put 2,876 men and women to death. In this Third Reich era, the executions derived largely from heavy sentences handed down by the *Volksgerichtshof* (People's Court) for political crimes such as treason, and included Sophie and Hans Scholl of the German resistance movement White Rose (Reichhart executed them at Munich's Stadelheim Prison on February 22, 1943).[37] Most of these sentences were carried out by the *Fallbeil* ("drop hatchet"), the shorter, largely metal, redesigned German version, which Reichhart had used for Bavaria, of the French guillotine.

Reichhart was very strict in his execution protocol, wearing the traditional German executioners' attire of black coat, white shirt and gloves, and black bow tie and top hat from his first days in the job in Bavaria. His work for the Third Reich also led him to many parts of occupied Europe, including Poland and Austria. He claimed during questioning that toward the end of the war, as the Allied armies closed in, he supposedly disposed of his mobile guillotine in a river, a claim that seems to be related to almost every guillotine in Germany at the end of the conflict. Following "Victory in Europe Day" in 1945, Reichhart, who was a member of the Nazi Party, was arrested for the purposes of denazification (to rid German society of any remnants of national socialism by removing from positions of power and influence those who had been Nazi Party members), but he was not immediately tried for carrying out his duty as one of the primary judicial executioners in the Third Reich.

Reichhart was subsequently employed by the occupation authorities beginning in November 1945, to help execute Nazi war criminals at Landsberg am Lech by hanging. On Monday, November 19, Reichhart hanged Albert Bury, Wilhelm Häfner, and Ernst Waldmann at Landsberg Prison. The trio had killed downed American airmen in separate incidents in December 1944. His next execution occurred on Monday, December 10, 1945, at Landsberg—the hanging of Franz Strasser, a former Nazi Party district leader in Bohemia, who killed two downed

American airmen outside the town of Kaplice in December 1944. The *Stars & Stripes* made scant mention of the event on page 2 of the December 12, 1945, edition: "Franz Strasser, Austrian-born Nazi, was hanged in Landsberg prison for the murder of two American airmen last December. Strasser was convicted of killing the fliers after they had been forced to land on German soil."

Johann Reichhart then executed Anton Schosser on Thursday, January 24, 1946, at Landsberg for murdering another downed American flier. Reichhart's next appearance at Landsberg was Monday, April 1, 1946, for the executions of Nicholaus Fachinger and Heinrich Flauaus. The condemned men had beaten two downed American fliers to death with an iron bar at the village of Gross-Gerau (near Darmstadt) on August 29, 1944.[38]

Bruchsal Prison, Bruchsal, Germany

Meanwhile, Woods returned to Bruchsal to hang four men; three had murdered German civilians and Russian and Polish prisoners at the Hadamar Euthanasia Center, while the fourth man had murdered another American airman.

Alfons Klein, Heinrich Ruoff, and Karl Willig, Thursday, March 14, 1946

The first three executions had to do with Hadamar, one of Nazi Germany's six primary euthanasia centers. Established at the end of 1940 as a killing center, between January and August 1941, medical personnel there used carbon monoxide to gas 10,000 institutionalized mentally and physically disabled persons, under the auspices of Operation T4. Designed to select patients deemed incurably sick, medical personnel were legally authorized to administer a mercy death, although the program was more about saving money than dispensing compassion, and the secrecy surrounding T4 certainly raised the specter of consciousness of guilt. Rising German public opinion helped temporarily halt the killings in August 1941, but a year later the center's medical personnel again began to murder disabled patients; it is estimated that from 1942 until the end of war in May 1945, the facility murdered an additional 4,400 victims by lethal overdoses of medication.

Karl Willig was born in 1894 in the town of Gräveneck in the Weinbach district in Hesse, Germany; he worked at the Hadamar Euthanasia Center beginning in July 1941 as an orderly and later deputy head nurse. Beginning in the summer of 1942, he helped select and kill German and partly Jewish patients either by lethal overdoses of medicine or slow starvation. In 1944 and 1945, he administered lethal injections to Polish and Soviet forced laborers suffering from tuberculosis. After their deaths, Karl Willig subsequently incinerated the remains of the victims to obfuscate the actual cause of death, a technique used throughout T4. According to postwar statements at his trial, Willig was regarded as particularly brutal, who also abused patients. Heinrich Ruoff was also a male nurse at Hadamar; he began working as chief male nurse at the asylum in 1936. Alfons Klein was the chief administrator for Hadamar. He was in charge of records, food, housing, and reports, and he knew of the deaths of the Poles and Russians. Klein received the original orders to kill forced laborers and transmitted these orders to other institution personnel.

An American general military court, meeting in Wiesbaden in October 1945, convicted the three men and sentenced them to death for the killings of about five hundred forced laborers between the summer of 1944 and March 1945. The court convicted several other individuals of lesser crimes at Hadamar and sentenced them to various terms of imprisonment. On March 7, 1946, the headquarters of the US 7th Army published *Military Commission Order Number 4*, stating that all three men would be executed at Bruchsal Prison on March 14, 1946, at times determined by the officer in charge, Maj. Willard W. Jensen.[39]

Present with Maj. Jensen were Lt. Col. Robert G. Thompson, Capt. Joseph B. Cherry, and Capt. Carlos Brewer, medical officers. Capt. Andrew J. White would serve as the chaplain. Four other US Army officers had duties as official witnesses, while 1Lt. Eldon C. Kunze served as the recorder. Sgt. William Aalmans of the Dutch army attached to the US 7th Army was the interpreter. Four German civilian prison officials were also in attendance.[40]

Maj. Jensen, Chaplain White, Kunze, Sgt. Aalmans, and two military policemen arrived at the cell of Karl Willig at 1:04 p.m. A minute later, the guards led Willig through the cellblock door; German Protestant minister of the prison August Schewerpflug walked with him. The procession reached the gallows at 1:06 p.m.; guards bound the prisoner's hands behind him and he climbed the thirteen steps. Maj. Jensen read the execution order in English, and Aalmans read an official German translation, during which "Willig showed signs of extreme nervousness and trembled considerably while the order was being read." Guards held the arms of the prisoner; Technician Fifth Grade Vincent J. Martino bound Willig's ankles. Maj. Jensen then asked if Willig had any last words, to which Willig replied, "I did my duty as a German official. God is my witness." The prisoner then said to Minister Schewerpflug: "Give my last regards to my wife and children."[41]

All personnel except for the condemned, Woods, the two MPs, and Martino departed the scaffold. Woods then placed the black hood over Willig's head, followed by the noose. At a silent signal from Maj. Jensen, Woods sprung the trap at 1:21 p.m. At 1:37 p.m., Jensen directed the medical officers to examine the prisoner. They did and declared him dead. Prison officials took possession of the remains four minutes later for disposal according to German law, while Lt. Col. Thompson signed the death certificate.[42]

Heinrich Ruoff was the next man up. The officials reached his cell at 1:50 p.m., departed his cell at 1:51 p.m., and began ascending the stairs at 1:52 p.m. Ruoff appeared calm at the reading of the execution order, although "he pressed his chin to his chest several times." The condemned man had no last words either for Maj. Jensen or the priest of the prison, Father August Dohn. Woods sprung the trap at 2:04 p.m. At 2:19 p.m. Jensen ordered the medical officers to make their examination; they did and pronounced Ruoff dead at 2:21 p.m. Prison officials took possession of the remains at 2:24 p.m.[43].

The official party headed straight from the gallows to the cellblock, since they had one more man to hang. Arriving at the cell of Alfons Klein at 2:33 p.m., one minute later the group reached the scaffold. After his hands were bound, Klein climbed the dreaded thirteen steps. The procedure on the platform was the same. While Maj. Jensen read the execution order, the recorder noted that "Klein showed signs of nervousness and trembled." At 2:50 p.m., Woods sprung the trap; medical officers declared Klein dead at 3:06 p.m. Prison officials took possession of the remains.[44]

August Kobus, Friday, March 15, 1946

August Kobus had been scheduled to be executed on March 14, 1946, but an interesting twist of fate delayed his hanging by one day. Kobus had been born on October 24, 1900, in Neuendorf in Pomerania. His early life was ordinary, serving in the First World War as an officer in the German army. He joined the Nazi Party in 1931 and by 1936 had become the mayor and Nazi Party local group leader of the city of Freilassing in Upper Bavaria.

On April 16, 1945, US Army Air Force captain Chester E. Coggeshall—flying a P-51 Mustang in the 343rd Fighter Squadron of the 55th Fighter Group—was shot down at Sillersdorf. A village policeman and a German soldier captured Coggeshall and took him 3 miles east to Freilassing. However, instead of receiving medical assistance, he was taken into a wooded area, where August Kobus killed him with two shots to the head from a 7.65 mm pistol. An American general military

court in Ludwigsburg on November 13–14, 1945, convicted Kobus of murder and sentenced him to death by shooting, which was later changed to death by hanging.

Kobus was disgusted, since he claimed that he had acted on telephone orders from his superior and the district Nazi Party leader for the area, Bernhard Stredele. Knowing that it would not affect his own sentence, Kobus agreed to testify against Stredele. That court met in early March, and on March 14, after Kobus's testimony, Stredele was condemned to death by shooting.

The next day at 3:06 p.m., a five-man procession led by Maj. Willard W. Jensen arrived at the cell of August Kobus at Bruchsal Prison and led the condemned man through the cellblock door and to the gallows. Military policemen then bound his arms and led him up the thirteen steps to the scaffold platform, at which point the assistant hangman, Vincent J. Martino, bound Kobus's ankles. The two MPs held the condemned man's elbows while the sentence was read to him both in English and German. Kobus had no statement to make and then asked the chaplain to write his wife. All personnel except for Kobus, the two MPs, Woods, and Martino departed the scaffold; Woods then placed the black hood over the head of August Kobus; he followed this with the noose. Upon receiving a silent signal from Maj. Jensen, Woods did his part in seeking justice for Capt. Chester E. Coggeshall by pushing a lever that sprung the trapdoor at 3:16 p.m. Fifteen minutes later, Maj. Jensen signaled the medical observers to come forward and examine the body of the condemned; they did and pronounced Kobus dead at 3:32 p.m.[45]

However, it would be Bernhard Stredele who would have the last laugh. On July 15, 1947, officials converted Stredele's death sentence to life imprisonment; their findings were approved by Gen. Lucius D. Clay. Stredele was subsequently released and he died in 1981.

• • •

These were the last executions in which Vincent Joseph Martino served as assistant to Woods. Born in Brooklyn, New York, on April 17, 1924, the son of Joseph Martino and Theresa Macri, Vincent served as a stock clerk after three years of high school. Martino was a stocky 5'6" tall and weighed 195 pounds. He enlisted on March 1, 1943, in New York City, Army Service Number 32819220, and arrived overseas on February 13, 1944, at the 2913th DTC as a military policeman. He had a military occupational specialty of 564—hangman. Vincent was married to Sylvia L. Martino, who was born on September 16, 1922. He departed Germany on April 21, 1946, and was discharged on May 3, 1946, at Ft. Dix, New Jersey, receiving the European–African–Middle Eastern Campaign Medal, Good Conduct Medal, and World War II Victory Medal. Martino and his wife lived in the Bronx in the 1970s, residing at 2549 Wilson Avenue; later the couple moved to 4765 Aston Gardens Way in Naples, Florida.[46]

Landsberg Prison, Landsberg am Lech, Bavaria, Germany

With a frontage in the art nouveau style designed by Hugo Höfl, the Landsberg Prison in the town of Landsberg am Lech, Bavaria, was completed in 1908, after four years of construction. Initially conceived as a facility for holding six hundred convicted criminals and those awaiting sentencing, Landsberg Prison soon became designated a *Festungshaft* (translated as fortress confinement) in which prominent prisoners received protective custody. Within its walls, the four brick cellblocks were constructed in a cross-shaped orientation, allowing guards to simultaneously watch all wings from a central rotunda location. The rotunda, over three stories high, was open in the center; each circular walkway was protected by iron railings that not only facilitated viewing down prisoner hallways on the same floor but did not obstruct observation to other floors. Each wing was three stories tall; the brick walls were covered with masonry and topped by a steep clay-tile roof. Acoustics inside the four wings was excellent; guards could hear even slight coughing from the hallways. The prisoners, after the American Army assumed control, could hear the loud clicking caused by the combat boots, with horseshoe-shaped heel plates, of the military police officers as they walked down the hallways.[47]

Almost every cell was designed for a single prisoner; male German prisoners were kept solitary, while the few women prisoners were in communal cells. Each cell had four plastered walls, a ceiling, and an outside window with eight vertical 1-inch bars set in concrete. The single entrance to each cell was a heavy oak door, framed with heavy steel. Five feet up from the bottom on this door was a small door, 15 inches square. This opening was hinged from the outside and had its own special lock. In the center of this small door was a glass peephole, 2 inches in diameter. Each morning, guards opened the small doors so that prisoners could receive books, mail, and food. During religious services conducted in the hallways, prisoners could stick their heads outward and participate in the proceedings.[48]

Inside each cubicle was a metal bunk bed secured by heavy steel bolts to the wall, so it could not be moved or tipped over. On each bed was a hard, straw-filled mattress. A short, three-legged wooden stool completed the furniture list. In one of the corners, farthest from the door, was a cylindrical radiator. Prison boilers pumped hot water to the cells—when the boilers were operating. The cells and hallways were cold in winter; American guards wore overcoats and field jackets in the hallways, while some prisoners suffered from frostbite. Each cell had a metal night pail for bathroom use. Work details of prisoners collected the pails every morning and dumped the contents at the prison farm outside the walls.[49]

Outside the cellblocks were twenty prison workshops, including those for tailoring, cobblery, sheet metalwork, carpentry, blacksmithing, photography, laundry, and locksmithing. Most prisoners had the opportunity to work in these areas during the day. German work foremen, after clearance by American authorities, supervised the efforts. Several exercise areas, enclosed by walls, were adjacent to but outside the four cellblocks. Around the entire prison compound stood a 20-foot-high concrete wall.[50]

After the Nazis assumed power, Landsberg Prison housed political prisoners as well as common criminals; by April 1933, some 385 of the former were incarcerated. During the Nazi period, the number of prisoners increased; by November 1944, there were 949. Most prisoners scheduled for execution were first transferred from Landsberg to a concentration camp, although records show that at least six condemned were executed at the prison itself in the last year of the war.

In May 1945, American forces occupied Landsberg Prison and designated it War Criminal Prison Nr. 1. The initial guard force consisted of American and French soldiers. A US Labor Service Company, a guard company of displaced Poles, soon joined the security force. Initial detainees arrived at Landsberg in the fall of 1945. Prisoner strength varied; in June 1946, there were seventy-four inmates, while this increased to 220 that fall. In January 1948, incarceration strength rose to 926 prisoners.[51]

The US Army found itself in a quandary. Initially after the war, military tribunals had issued a few individual death sentences, but by the end of the summer of 1945, dozens of Germans had been condemned to death, and it was presumed that their sentences would be upheld during the review process. Since the bulk of these tribunals occurred at Dachau, outside Munich, under American auspices, it would be the responsibility of the US Army to carry out the hangings.

Prior to the American occupation, executions at Landsberg had been by firing squad or guillotine. Construction of a gallows would have to occur

and occur quickly. The first gallows was a single structure in the prison church courtyard, used for seven executions between November 19, 1945, and April 1, 1946. However, it became apparent that during some periods, over twenty prisoners per day might be executed and a single scaffold would be insufficient. Prison officials added a second scaffold, about 10 yards to the left of the first. Both gallows stood at the corner between the hospital building and the C-wing of the prison. A door from the prison to the courtyard was located midway between the two. The courtyard had several linden and chestnut shade trees and a greenhouse. A wall, with two entrances, enclosed the yard; one was the aforementioned door, while the second entrance, which led to the cemetery, was at the rear wall. Under each scaffold, where the bodies would drop, heavy black curtains concealed the final seconds of life from onlookers.

With customary thoroughness, the Army developed procedures for these mass executions. Military police ringed the execution area. No civilian press was allowed; a *Stars & Stripes* reporter was present. A Signal Corps photographer would document the event with still photos; on May 28–29, a motion picture crew also recorded events. There was an officer responsible for the conduct of the execution; a captain from the Judge Advocate General's Corps served as the official witness. Two US Army doctors would certify the death of each prisoner, and the German mayor of Munich served as the chief German witness. Four military police sergeants would escort each prisoner from his cell to the scaffold. An American soldier fluent in German would translate the execution order to the condemned and translate into English the man's final statement. Two US chaplains, Peter Rush and Karl Almer, and one German priest provided religious support. Two prison inmates with carts stood at the gate to the cemetery to receive the remains.[52]

Friedrich Wilhelm Ruppert, Otto Förschner, Rudolf Heinrich Suttrop, Engelbert Valentin Niedermeyer, Klaus Karl Schilling, Walter Adolf Langleist, and Otto Moll, Tuesday, May 28, 1946

There was not a long wait until the first mass hanging at Landsberg Prison on May 28, 1945. A US military tribunal, in a proceeding termed the Dachau Camp Trial, had met in 1945 at the former concentration camp and tried forty German officials for their roles at the camp, not far from Munich. Under the direction of Brig. Gen. John Lenz, who served as the president of the court, the panel convicted thirty-six defendants under the auspices of a new legal theory, "common design," to violate the "Laws and Usages of War" under the 1929 Geneva Convention, and sentenced them to death on December 13, 1945; eight of the condemned had this sentence changed to life imprisonment.[53]

Twenty-eight men, however, faced the gallows at Landsberg, scheduled for late May 1946. Lt. Stanley Tilles was responsible for the logistics for the mass hangings. He found Woods building a second outdoor gallows at the prison. Tilles said that he had been warned that Woods was an unpredictable troublemaker with an unpredictable violent temper. In his later book, Tilles wrote that these descriptions were inaccurate: "He was respectful, friendly, and controlled when on duty. He did have a predilection for beer, and was given to verbal and physical outbursts when he was drunk. He freely expressed his hatred of Germans, a hatred rooted in the fact that he had lost several friends at the Malmedy Massacre.... He fraternized just as freely with German women, an apparent contradiction that was shared by most soldiers."[54]

Tilles added that in one "beer-fueled" conversation, Woods stated that his neighbor had been a hangman at a Texas prison and had invited Woods to watch a hanging, which he did and then became the man's assistant. Unknown to Tilles, these statements were false, but the lieutenant did provide a valuable description of hanging preparations. He stated that Woods stretched his hanging ropes with a duffel bag filled with sand, suspended from the end of the rope, to take the "stretch" out of them. On May 27, 1946, Johann Reichhart arrived at the prison; he and Woods tested both gallows for several hours.[55]

The morning of May 28 was a nice Bavarian spring day; that would swiftly change for fourteen men. The *Stars & Stripes* provided the following account:[56]

14 Germans Pay for Dachau Crimes

LANDSBERG, Germany, May 29 (AP)—The first 14 of 28 Dachau Nazis were executed yesterday, beginning the largest mass execution in the history of the US Army. Fourteen more were to walk up the 13 steps to the gallows today to pay for their part in causing the death of over 300,000 men, women and children in the Dachau concentration camp....

The black gallows, made darker by the shadows cast into the prison courtyard by the cell block in which Hitler wrote "Mein Kampf," ended the lives of the first group by a sprung trap and the punch of a 13-knot noose.

The Nazis were hanged at intervals of almost exactly 15 minutes, one being cut down as another, breathing, was led to the second gallows.

"This would be me," said an American soldier watching the scene, "but I just kept thinking about those thousands that these b—— got first."

Each man was led separately from the death cells of the old prison, and was escorted under the gallows beam by a guard of four soldiers and a clergyman.

Dr. Klaus Schilling, 74-year-old physician and scientist, shuffled broken and trembling to the foot of the gallows. Asked if he had a last word he replied, "No, hurry please, hurry."

A few seconds later the trap dropped.

Small Simon Kiern, who used to use prisoners for pistol practice, carried a bouquet of white and pink flowers in his pale hand as he walked to the gallows.

A photograph of Woods putting the black hood over Klaus Schilling appeared in the *New York Times* on May 30 with the heading "A German War Criminal Pays the Penalty for his Acts."[57]

On May 29, another fourteen Nazi war criminals met their end on the two gallows at Landsberg. The *Chicago Tribune* provided this report of the second day's events:[58]

DACHAU'S LAST TORTURERS DIE ON THE GALLOWS
Most of 14 Drop Silently into Oblivion

LANDSBERG, Germany, May 29 (AP)—Fourteen more Nazis were hanged by the United States army today in a grim four-hour drama, completing the execution of 28 men found responsible for the sadistic torture killing of 300,000 inmates at the infamous Dachau concentration camp. The first 14 were hanged yesterday.

In the shadow of the old Landsberg prison where Hitler wrote "Mein Kampf," his followers walked one by one up the 13 steps to one of the twin scaffolds and oblivion. Most died in silence. Some made final melodramatic gestures.

Lie in Unmarked Graves

All 28 will lie in unmarked graves in the prison cemetery. They came from all walks of life. Among them were scientists; artists played Bach and Brahms; ham-fisted brutes who delighted in sadism; men like Anton Endres, who aided in such experiments as the effect of freezing on the human body.

There were men like Christoph Knoll, 50, habitual criminal and pre-war Dachau prisoner who, because of his specialty of brutality, was made a trusty and given authority to beat inmates into unconsciousness.

The seventh to die today was Martin Gottfried Weiss, 40, commandant of Dachau in 1942/43. Until the last minute he had hoped for a reprieve, after a former Dachau inmate volunteered a statement that Weiss had done all he could for the prisoners.

Dies for Germany, He Shouts

But the army saw no reason to reverse the war crimes court verdict pronounced upon the man accused of allowing hangings and experiments to be conducted during his administration of the camp and of having personally conducted some executions. As the hangman placed the black hood on Weiss's head, the doomed man shouted: "I am giving my life for Germany!"

One of the prisoners, the hood over his eyes, shouted loudly that he had been framed. Another expressed a dying wish that his son, a war prisoner in the British zone, be freed. A third died with a picture of his wife pinned to the lapel of his gray and black striped prison coat.

The last to mount the 13 steps was one-legged Leonard Eichberger, who was carried in the arms of two military policemen. He was held upright while prepared for the noose.

• • •

Actual events were somewhat more detailed than the Army plans delineated or the newspapers reported. The death sentences had originally been published on December 13, 1945, by a US general military government court. For the next several months, defendants submitted appeals and clemency requests. These procedures were completed by mid-April. On April 15, 1946, the commanding general for US forces in the European theater, Gen. Joseph T. McNarney, the confirming authority for each of the cases, issued an order to Lt. Gen. Geoffrey T. Keyes, commander of the US 3rd Army, to "carry the sentences into execution," stating that each man had been convicted of the crime of Violation of the Laws and Usages of War. On May 17, 1946, Gen. Keyes signed an order directing the assistant provost marshal, Lt. Col. James J. Fogarty, to carry out the executions of the twenty-eight condemned men over a period of two consecutive days as soon as possible.[59]

US officials determined that fourteen condemned men would be executed on May 28, 1946, in the order that they were sentenced as a major factor. According to Irving Dilliard of the *Stars & Stripes*, another consideration concerning the order of death was the religious affiliation of each of the condemned. To allow appropriate chaplains adequate time for their duties, Catholic and Protestant condemned would be executed in an alternating sequence.[60]

Although he was quite junior, 2Lt. Stanley Tilles was designated as the witnessing officer who would sign the certificate of execution after each man was declared dead. The proceedings would commence about 9:30 a.m. each morning, with a break about 11:30 a.m. for lunch. The executions would resume about 1:30 p.m. and end in midafternoon. Woods would use a new rope for each hanging; on his scaffold was an 8-foot step ladder, which the hangman employed between each execution to remove the old rope and affix a new one to the crossbeam. Woods would adjust the rope for each hanging so that the knot was directly behind the condemned man's head; Reichhart did not, preferring that the knot be immediately behind the left ear.

Friedrich Wilhelm Ruppert

Ruppert was the first man that morning to be led separately from the death cells of the old prison by four soldiers and a clergyman outside to the courtyard to the gallows, on which stood MSgt. Woods. The time was approximately 9:30 a.m. After an American Army officer read the execution order, Ruppert made his final remarks: "I was wrongfully convicted. I hope that my family does not have to suffer. I ask that my wife be informed that I was thinking of her at my death and that I died bravely." Woods placed a black hood over the head of Friedrich Wilhelm Ruppert and followed this by placing the noose of the execution rope around the man's neck and tightening it. While assistant hangman Joseph Malta held the heavy rope vertical, Woods spun around and pushed the lever dropping the trapdoor. Ruppert was pronounced dead at 9:54 a.m. Burial personnel interred Ruppert's remains in grave #139 at the Spöttinger Friedhof (cemetery) next to Landsberg Prison.[61]

Born in Frankenthal near Ludwigshafen on February 2, 1905, Friedrich Wilhelm Ruppert served from 1933 to 1945 at various concentration camps, including Dachau, Majdanek, and Warsaw, as an *SS-Hauptsturmführer* (captain). At trial, witnesses accused Ruppert of being the officer in charge of executing condemned prisoners at Dachau, also testifying that Ruppert often personally kicked and beat prisoners with a whip so hard that the victims lost consciousness. Most damning, he was linked to the September 13, 1944, executions at Dachau of British Special Operations Executive agents Yolande Beekman, Eliane Plewman, Madeleine Damerment, and Noor Inayat Khan.[62]

• • •

Serving as Woods's assistant this day, and remaining in this position through the Nürnberg executions in October 1946, was Joseph Vincent Malta, nicknamed by some of his fellow soldiers as "Dirty Dom."[63] Malta was born on November 27, 1918, in Revere, Massachusetts, to Stellario (a carpenter) and Antoinette Malta.[64] One postwar source stated that he was the youngest of twenty-one children of an immigrant Sicilian family, but census records show that he had a younger sister. He later told an interviewer that he never attended church in St. Anthony's Parish.[65] Malta enlisted as a private at Ft. Bragg, North Carolina, on December 12, 1945, for the military police, Army

Service Number 31504814. He stated that he had attended grammar school through eighth grade and was married.[66] In 1996, Malta told an interviewer that he had volunteered for the job of assistant hangman, and concerning the executions of Nazis, "It was a pleasure doing it. I'd do it all over again."[67]

Malta also later said that he had been in the 403rd Military Police and that John Woods approached him about being his assistant. Malta was bored patrolling through the cinemas and bars in occupied Heidelberg, so he volunteered, as did two other men. The three men met Woods, who took one man at a time to a scaffold for a dry run with a stuffed mannequin to see how they would perform. Malta later said he was the last candidate and had watched through a window to see how the first two men performed, so he would not make their mistakes. Woods apparently was impressed, asking Malta, "Did you do this in your hometown or what?" Malta said that he had not, but that he had watched Woods carefully with the other two men.[68] Malta was hired and would serve as the assistant hangman in twenty-five executions.

In another interview, Joseph Malta said of Woods, "He was a great teacher; I had the best."[69] "Dirty Dom" appears to have been fired from his position in February 1947, when he insisted that he ride in an Army sedan to an execution instead of a winterized jeep. His lieutenant informed him that a jeep was good enough for a major and that if unpleased, Malta could seek employment elsewhere.[70] Malta left the Army soon after—his final rank was private first class—and returned to Massachusetts and his former job of floor sander. In later life, he stated that his wife was Jewish.[71] In his later years, "Dirty Dom" kept a small model of the Landsberg Prison scaffold, which he had had at Landberg in 1946, in his apartment.[72] This study was unable to confirm the legend that "Dirty Dom" occasionally took his scale model scaffold to show condemned men the evening before their execution.

• • •

While Friedrich Ruppert was dangling at the end of the rope on Woods's gallows, Simon Kiern was the next man to be led from the death cells to meet his fate, although Woods would not hang him. A former *SS-Hauptscharführer* (master sergeant), Kiern began his service at Dachau in 1941; he was born about 1913, serving in the German army from 1932 to 1936, and he was married and had two children. He soon joined the SS and was first assigned to Dachau on February 1, 1937. His career took a turn for the worse in 1942, when he was arrested for stealing the contents of mail; he wound up at the Waffen-SS punishment camp at Danzig until February 12, 1945, when he was sent to the front. Given that this punishment camp served as a source of recruits for the notorious 36th *SS Waffen Grenadier Division Dirlewanger* (which had brutally helped suppress the Warsaw Uprising in 1944), it is possible that Simon Kiern was assigned to that notorious unit prior to the end of the war.[73]

At Dachau, however, Kiern served as a block leader at the camp; he also participated in killing many Russian prisoners of war at the rifle range. Now it was his turn to die. Once outside the prison building about 9:45 a.m., his escort led him to the gallows that would be worked on this day by hangman Johann Reichhart. Kiern reportedly carried a bouquet of white and pink flowers in his hand as he walked. The procedure at the gallows was the same; the escorts led the condemned man up the steps and placed him on the center of the trapdoor. After an American Army officer read the execution order, Johann Reichhart placed the hood over Kiern's head and neck and then put the noose over the man's head as Woods had done. Reichhart quickly turned about and pushed the lever, causing the trapdoor on this gallows to drop open; unlike Woods, Reichhart was operating without a formal assistant hangman. Physicians pronounced Simon Kiern dead at 10:13 a.m.[74]

Otto Förschner

Guards escorted Otto Förschner out of the prison about 10:00 a.m. Förschner, a former *SS-Sturmbannführer* (major), was born on November 4, 1902, in Dürrenzimmern near Nördlingen in Bavaria; he served during the war as a commander of the SS guard battalion at the Buchenwald concentration camp, and later as the commandant of the Mittelbau-Dora concentration camp and still later as the commandant of all nine Kaufering subcamps of Dachau. Prior to these assignments, Förschner served in the 5th *SS Panzer-Grenadier Division Wiking* until he was seriously wounded in action in Russia. Witnesses at the trial claimed that he was responsible for the brutal conditions at the Kaufering subcamps, most specifically the execution of prisoners; he also beat a prisoner to death with an iron pipe. Otto Förschner was led to John C. Woods's gallows and followed the same procedures as the previous men. Physicians declared him dead at 10:22 a.m. Burial personnel buried Förschner's remains at the Spöttinger Friedhof in grave #133.[75]

•••

It was Franz Trenkle's turn next; in other times he might have evoked sympathy since he was a widower with four children—but not today. The former *SS-Hauptscharführer* had been born on December 23, 1898, in Pfronten in Upper Bavaria and started his career at Dachau in 1933. Five years later he transferred to a subcamp of Dachau St. Gilgen on the Wolfgangsee in Austria. He also served at the Sachsenhausen concentration camp at Berlin and the Neuengamme concentration camp at Hamburg. In late 1944, Trenkle served at the Belsen concentration camp. At the end of the war, he transferred to another Dachau subcamp at Lauingen, Bavaria. Evidence at the postwar trial indicated that he had mishandled prisoners and participated in executions. Trenkle stood 5'9" and weighed 165 pounds. Johann Reichhart

hanged Trenkle without fanfare; he had entered the courtyard about 10:25 a.m., dropped through the trap at about 10:29 a.m., and was pronounced dead at 10:44 a.m. Relatives requested his remains be interred at Pfronten.[76]

Rudolf Heinrich Suttrop

The next of the condemned marched to John Woods's scaffold. Rudolf Heinrich Suttrop looked like a successful businessman more suited to Wall Street than Dachau. He was born in Horstmar (Lünen) in North Rhine–Westphalia on July 17, 1911; he was married and had three children. Suttrop joined the SS on September 5, 1933, and the Nazi Party in September 1937. As an enlisted man early in his career, he served as a guard at the Sachsenburg and Buchenwald concentration camps. Later, he fought in Waffen-SS combat units in Poland, the Netherlands, and France before transferring to the Gross-Rosen concentration camp in September 1941 and later to Dachau; at both he served as camp adjutant. In 1945, now an *SS-Obersturmbannführer* (lieutenant colonel), Suttrop spent two months in the replacement battalion of the 17th *SS Panzer-Grenadier Division Götz von Berlichingen* before returning to Dachau in the final week of the war. Woods hanged Suttrop after the condemned man uttered his final words: "My last greetings to my wife." Medical officers pronounced Suttrop dead at 10:54 a.m. Burial personnel interred his remains at the Spöttinger Friedhof in grave #134.[77]

•••

Standing 5'11" tall, Joseph Jarolin was a bad character. He was born on March 6, 1904, at Rehpoint and joined the SS on March 6, 1935. Early in the war, he worked at the overall concentration camp headquarters at Oranienburg. At Dachau, *SS-Obersturmführer* (first lieutenant) Jarolin worked for Dr. Sigmund Rascher and killed at least three personnel in 1942 in lethal pressure chamber experiments. During the war, he received the War Service Cross Second Class. After his arrest, he submitted numerous statements revealing where his fellow SS personnel were hiding. Johann Reichhart hanged Jarolin just before lunch; the former SS officer entered the courtyard about 10:48 a.m., dropped through the trapdoor about 10:54 a.m., and was pronounced dead at 11:11 a.m. He was originally buried at the Spöttinger Friedhof, but his remains were transferred to Munich two years later.[78]

Engelbert Valentin Niedermeyer

Johann Reichhart may have gone to lunch, but John Woods and Joseph Malta had one additional morning appointment, Engelbert Valentin Niedermeyer. He was born December 26, 1911, and his father died in the First World War; Niedermeyer joined the SS in 1934 and was assigned to Dachau on April 1, 1938. He transferred to the Waffen-SS and later served at the front as an enlisted man. Niedermeyer walked into the execution courtyard about 11:00 a.m. His last words were "I am dying not guilty." John Woods pushed the lever that dropped the trapdoor at approximately 11:10 a.m. Physicians pronounced Engelbert Niedermeyer dead at 11:21 a.m. Burial personnel interred his remains at the Spöttinger Friedhof in grave #138.[79]

• • •

After lunch, Vinzenz Schöttel was the next man slated to be executed, and he walked out into the sunshine of the execution courtyard between 1:00 p.m. and 1:10 p.m. Born at Appersdorf on June 30, 1905, *SS-Obersturmführer* Schöttel served at Neuengamme (1941), Majdanek (1941), and Auschwitz-Monowitz (1942–45) concentration camps during the war. He was an old Nazi, joining the party in 1928, and was also an early member of the SS, receiving SS number 5630 when he joined. He first worked at Dachau from 1933 to 1937 as a guard, later working in the Lublin Ghetto in 1940. In 1945, Schöttel was commandant at the Kaufering #3 subcamp of Dachau. Johann Reichhart pushed the lever at approximately 1:15 p.m., and two physicians pronounced Vinzenz Schöttel dead at 1:27 p.m.[80]

Klaus Karl Schilling

It was back to work for John Clarence Woods and time to die for Klaus Karl Schilling. One of the oldest of the condemned men, Schilling was born on July 5, 1871, at Munich. He stood just over 6' tall and weighed 176 pounds, but prison had made him appear older and thinner; his wife lived in Bad Aibling. Dr. Schilling, who graduated from the University of Munich in 1894 as a physician, was an expert in tropical diseases; at Dachau, where he arrived in February 1942, he strapped special containers on the arms of prisoners so malaria-exposed mosquitoes could infect his subjects, and almost four hundred prisoners died as a result it would seem that Schilling especially preferred priests for his experiments. He remained at Dachau into 1945. Schilling's last words were "No, hurry please, hurry." Woods and Malta hanged Schilling about 1:20 p.m.; while Woods remained on the platform, Joseph Malta descended the thirteen steps and went behind the canvas. Doctors pronounced Schilling dead at 1:37 p.m. German prison workers placed the body in a black, rough, wooden casket; on the lid were a white wooden cross and a shipping tag with Schilling's name. The remains were transferred to Hamburg for burial.[81]

SS-Hauptscharführer Josef Seuss was born on March 3, 1906, in Nürnberg. During the war he served as a reports leader at Dachau, where he was first assigned on April 20, 1933. In 1939–40, Seuss was assigned to the Flossenbürg concentration camp. Seuss marched out to the execution courtyard about 1:30 p.m. After Johann Reichhart prepared Seuss for execution, the condemned man made his final remarks: "I hope Germany will be strong, no, I mean will be again." Reichhart pushed the lever at about 1:42 p.m. Physicians pronounced that Josef Seuss was deceased at 1:54 p.m. Burial personnel interred his remains at the Spöttinger Friedhof in grave #146.[82]

Walter Adolf Langleist

Both hangmen were hitting their stride now. The next SS man to face Woods was former *SS-Hauptsturmführer* Walter Adolf Langleist, who, wearing a cap and dark shirt and trousers, entered the courtyard with his guards about 1:45 p.m. Born in Dresden on August 5, 1893, Langleist had served at Buchenwald, Auschwitz, Majdanek, and Dachau. His highest position was as commandant of the Kaufering #4 subcamp; he also served as the guard battalion commander of the main Dachau camp. Langleist joined the Nazi Party in 1930; he was also an early member of the SS, joining in 1931, with SS number 8980. Woods pushed the trapdoor lever about 1:55 p.m.; doctors pronounced Langleist dead at 2:07 p.m. His remains were transferred to Remsdorf, south of Leipzig.[83]

• • •

Anton Endres was born in Schwaben on June 3, 1909; he was married and the father of three children. He joined the SS on September 7, 1939, but early on was involved in a serious automobile accident and spent several months in a hospital. He then served in the SS guard detachment at Oranienburg in 1940 and subsequently as a medical *SS-Unterscharführer* (corporal) at Dachau before transferring to Majdanek in May 1942. He finished the war as an *SS-Oberscharführer*; he also served in the 3rd *SS Panzer-Grenadier Division Totenkopf*. Endres walked into the courtyard at Landsberg Prison about 2:00 p.m. Johann Reichhart pushed the execution lever at about 2:10 p.m., and physicians pronounced Endres deceased at 2:23 p.m. His remains were interred at Spöttinger Friedhof in grave #147.[84]

Otto Moll

SS-Hauptscharführer Otto Moll, born in Höhen Schönberg in Mecklenburg on December 4, 1914 (another source gives March 4, 1915), joined the SS on May 1, 1935, and spent most of the war assigned to the Auschwitz-Birkenau concentration camp; for a while, he supervised the operation of the crematoria there. Prior to that assignment, Moll was at Sachsenhausen; he may have been in an execution commando for a short time at the Ravensbrück women's concentration camp. Moll, who stood 5'8" tall and weighed 165 pounds, briefly served in the 17th *SS Panzer-Grenadier Division Götz von Berlichingen* in the antitank detachment. In January 1945, Moll transferred to Dachau and ended up at the Kaufering subcamp.[85] Although Moll was convicted at the Dachau Lager Process for criminality at that location, his worst offenses had occurred at Auschwitz.

His shirtsleeves rolled up above his elbows, Moll entered the courtyard at approximately 2:00 p.m., just after Woods had tied a new rope to the gallows crossbeam. Guards at the bottom of the scaffold stairs strapped Moll's wrists together. A military police captain at the door of the courtyard read the execution order. Moll's final words were "I am not guilty. I was not in Dachau, where the crimes for which I am accused were committed." His claim fell on deaf ears as Woods placed the black hood and noose over Otto Moll and subsequently pushed the lever about 2:20 p.m., as Joseph Malta held the knot of the hanging rope upward so it would drop smoothly. Two American Army physicians pronounced Otto Moll dead at 2:36 p.m. A pair of German workers took Moll, now in his casket, from under the scaffold, and burial personnel subsequently interred the remains at the Spöttinger Friedhof in grave #111.[86]

• • •

Viktor Johann Kirsch was the last man to be hanged that afternoon, as he entered the courtyard about 2:30 p.m. and was escorted to Johann Reichhart's gallows. Born on February 15, 1891, in Marpingen in the Saar region of Germany, he fought in the First World War (and was wounded) and served in the German army again in World War II until the summer of 1944, when he transferred to the Waffen-SS; the assignment would prove fatal. Kirsch trained for three weeks at Auschwitz and then was assigned to Dachau; he would spend time in subcamps Kaufering, Mittergars, and Mühldorf, serving as an *SS-Hauptscharführer* and commandant of Kaufering #1. Reichhart went through the execution protocol and dropped Kirsch about 2:35 p.m. American doctors pronounced Viktor Kirsch dead at 2:47 p.m. Burial personnel subsequently interred the remains at the Spöttinger Friedhof in grave #149.[87]

Arno Lippmann, Wilhelm Welter, Wilhelm Wagner, Johann Kick, Fritz Hintermeyer, Johann Baptist Eichelsdörfer, and Leonhard Anselm Eichberger, Wednesday, May 29, 1946

That was only half the mission, and the final fourteen condemned men would be executed the following day by using the same alternating-gallows procedure; Johann Reichhart would hang the first man. Fritz Becher was escorted out of the prison about 10:00 a.m., bound for Johann Reichhart's scaffold. Born on October 24, 1904, he had originally been a political prisoner at Dachau from May 1938 to June 1943; he was married and had one child. He appears to have been made a *kapo*, a prisoner-trustee who cooperated with the SS administration of the camp, and his excessive actions caused suffering and even death for several prisoners. At one time, his block contained most of the inmates who were priests; witnesses said he had personally killed Father Kowilinski, a Polish priest. Two

American doctors pronounced Becher dead at 10:26 a.m. Burial personnel subsequently interred Becher's remains at the Spöttinger Friedhof in grave #151.[88]

Arno Lippmann

Professional pride may have entered the execution of Arno Lippmann, since he entered the courtyard at almost the same time as Fritz Becher so that an observer could simultaneously watch Woods and Reichhart at their craft. Lippmann, who was born on July 25, 1890, in Lippelsdorf, had been with the SS almost from its beginning and had SS number 439. He also had the Nazi Golden Party Badge, being the 8,891st person to join the Nazi Party in its infancy. Lippmann was a veteran of the First World War, winning the Iron Cross Second Class in that conflict. Reaching the grade of *SS-Obersturmführer*, he served as a commandant of Kaufering #7 subcamp. Lippmann's last words were "My last greetings go to my wife." John Woods pushed the lever releasing the trapdoor about 10:15 a.m.; physicians declared Arno Lippmann to be dead at 10:31a.m. Burial personnel subsequently interred Lippmann's remains at the Spöttinger Friedhof in grave #152.[89]

• • •

Wilhelm Tempel served at the Kaufering #4 subcamp and was accused of shooting and beating prisoners to death. He was born November 1, 1908, near Posen, was married, and had five children. Tempel joined the SS in 1932. He served at Majdanek starting in October 1942, and subsequently at Auschwitz until July 27, 1944. He arrived at Dachau in August 1944. Johann Reichhart hanged Wilhelm Tempel about 10:40 a.m. Physicians declared him dead at 10:52 a.m. Burial personnel subsequently interred the remains in grave #132 at the Spöttinger Friedhof.[90]

Wilhelm Welter

Wilhelm Welter helped select prisoners for experiments and slave labor projects at Dachau, serving there from April 1940 to July 1943. Standing 5'8" tall and weighing 132 pounds, he then served in the 3rd *SS Panzer-Grenadier Division Totenkopf* on the Eastern Front from August 1943 to January 17, 1944, when he was wounded in the head by shrapnel. Welter was married and had three children. Woods put the black hood and noose around Welter's neck about 10:50 a.m. and then pushed the lever. Two US Army physicians pronounced Welter dead at 11:06 a.m. He was later buried at Dachau.[91]

• • •

Former *SS-Hauptsturmführer* Michael Redwitz was the next Dachau official to face Johann Reichhart. Born in Bayreuth, Bavaria, on August 14, 1900, Redwitz had served in the Waffen-SS as a staff officer of the First SS Panzer Corps. Unfortunately for him, he also served at the Mauthausen, Ravensbrück, Buchenwald, and Dachau concentration camps, and that service got him executed. Redwitz, who received the War Service Cross Second Class, was also the recipient of the Nazi Golden Party Badge; he was married with four children. At Dachau, where he served from November 1942 to March 1944, and also at the Gusen subcamp of Mauthausen, Redwitz served as lager commandant. Johann Reichhart pushed the lever on the gallows about 11:00 a.m., and doctors declared Redwitz deceased at 11:16 a.m. His remains were later interred in Munich.[92]

Wilhelm Wagner

SS-Scharführer Wilhelm Wagner was born on November 28, 1904, in Augsburg, Bavaria. From September 18, 1933, to the end of the war he served at Dachau, except from August 1938 to November 1939, when he was at Mauthausen in Austria. Wagner probably walked outside into the courtyard about 11:10 a.m., and after Woods placed the hood and noose over the condemned man about 11:20 a.m., Woods pushed the lever. Physicians declared Wagner deceased at 11:35 a.m. His remains were later interred at Augsburg.[93]

• • •

It was now time for Johannes Reichhart to administer justice to arguably the most significant war criminal executed at Landsberg over the past two days. Former *SS-Obersturmbannführer* Martin Gottfried Weiss had been born on June 3, 1905, in Weiden in the Oberpfalz. He joined the SS on April 1, 1932. Weiss served two tours at Dachau (1933–39, 1942–43), as well as stints at Neuengamme (1940–42) and Majdanek (1943–44), and at the concentration camp administrative headquarters at Oranienburg (1944–45). At the very end of the war, Weiss was at the Mühldorf subcamp. Weiss received the War Service Cross First Class for this service; he also was the recipient of the Nazi Golden Party Badge. During his trial, Weiss stated, "I had nothing to do with the camp." Weiss entered the courtyard about 11:25 a.m.; his last words were "I am giving my life for Germany!" Reichhart released the trapdoor about 11:30 a.m., and doctors proclaimed Weiss dead at 11:46 a.m. Burial personnel interred his remains at the Spöttinger Friedhof in grave #150.[94]

Johann Kick

Johann Kick was born in Waldau in the Oberpfalz on November 24, 1901. The *SS-Untersturmführer* (his police rank was that of *Kriminal-Sekretär*) was the leader of the Gestapo political section at Dachau from 1937 to August 1944, carrying out numerous orders of execution that had been sent from the security service in Munich. Kick stood 5'9" tall and weighed 152 pounds. He entered the courtyard about 1:00 p.m. Woods received the silent signal to push the trapdoor release lever about 1:05 p.m., which he promptly did; physicians pronounced Johann Kick dead at 1:19 p.m. Burial personnel then interred his remains at the Spöttinger Friedhof in grave #136.[95]

•••

Alfred Kramer served as the commandant of Kaufering #1. Born on November 7, 1898, in Waldenburg, Silesia, he joined the SS on April 20, 1933. Kramer had fought in the First World War. He served at Buchenwald from September 1939 to September 1941, when he was transferred to Majdanek. In late July 1944, he took a convoy of prisoners from Lublin to Dachau, where he was subsequently assigned. He stated that after his arrest, he had been beaten by a US counterintelligence officer with sticks and rubber hoses. Johann Reichhart hanged Alfred Kramer about 1:15 p.m., and doctors declared the man deceased at 1:27 p.m. Burial personnel then interred his remains in grave #125 at the Spöttinger Friedhof.[96]

Dr. Fritz Hintermeyer

SS-Obersturmführer Dr. Fritz Hintermeyer was the chief physician at Dachau from October 1, 1944, to April 25, 1945. Born at Grafing near Munich on October 28, 1911, he graduated from the University of Munich in 1937. Dr. Hintermeyer was assigned to the overall concentration camp headquarters at Oranienburg in 1938. He served in the Waffen-SS with the 6th *SS Panzer-Grenadier Regiment Theodor Eicke* of the 3rd *SS Panzer-Grenadier Division Totenkopf* from 1941 to January 1944. While assigned to this unit in Russia, he received the Iron Cross First Class and also received a concussion. He arrived at Dachau in February 1944.[97] Guards escorted Hintermeyer, who claimed that he had earlier been beaten by American authorities, to the courtyard at Landsburg prison about 1:30 p.m. Woods received the silent signal to push the trapdoor lever about

1:35 p.m., and physicians pronounced Hintermeyer dead at 1:48 p.m. His remains were later buried at Grafing.[98]

•••

Christof Ludwig Knoll had been a political prisoner at Dachau from September 1933 to the end of the war. Born on April 20, 1895, he became a *kapo* about 1941. Johann Reichhart hanged Knoll at about 1:45 p.m., and physicians declared him dead at 2:01 p.m. Burial personnel then interred his remains at the Spöttinger Friedhof in grave #123.

Johann Baptist Eichelsdörfer

SS-Untersturmführer Johann Baptist Eichelsdörfer rose to become the commandant of three Kaufering subcamps. Born in Hallstadt, near Bamberg in Bavaria, on January 20, 1890, he served in the First World War with the 5th Royal Bavarian Infantry Regiment, seeing extensive combat in Flanders. He also served as a lieutenant and truck company commander in the German army in World War II in France and Russia until 1943. At Dachau, Eichelsdörfer served as the commandant of Kaufering #8, then Kaufering #7, and finally Kaufering #4. He stood 5'4" tall and weighed 135 pounds. At approximately 2:00 p.m., Eichelsdörfer entered the courtyard. Joseph Malta bound Eichelsdörfer's ankles together; shortly afterward, John Woods pushed the trapdoor release lever about 2:04 p.m. Military physicians pronounced Johann Baptist Eichelsdörfer dead at 2:14 p.m. His remains were later interred at Nürnberg.[99]

•••

Franz Böttger was a junior enlisted man who first arrived at Dachau in June 1940. He was born July 11, 1888, was married, but had no children. He had joined the SS in 1940. He later admitted that he had performed minor duties at prisoner executions but denied pulling a trigger. Reichhart placed the hood and rope over Böttger's head and neck, and the attending priest made the sign of the cross. Seconds later, Johann Reichhart hanged Böttger at 2:13 p.m., and doctors declared him dead at 2:25 p.m. Into the black coffin he went, and burial personnel later interred his remains at the Spöttinger Friedhof in grave #124.[100]

Leonhard Anselm Eichberger

One-legged former *SS-Hauptscharführer* Leonhard Anselm Eichberger was the last man to die. Born on January 22, 1915, at Pensberg/Weilheim, he stood 5'7" tall and weighed 132 pounds. He had served in France in 1940 with the German army's 19th Infantry Regiment and was seriously wounded; doctors later amputated his lower left leg. Married with one child, Eichberger later transferred to the SS and served in the Dachau concentration camp. He admitted killing fifteen Polish and Russian prisoners of war there. Eichberger emerged into the sunlight of the courtyard at about 2:10 p.m. Eichberger hopped up the thirteen steps, Woods pushed the lever at about 2:20 p.m., and doctors pronounced Eichberger dead at 2:36 p.m. Burial personnel buried his remains at the Spöttinger Friedhof in grave #137.[101]

• • •

These executions marked the end of Johann Reichhart's career as a *Scharfrichter* (executioner). He apparently spoke to the prison commandant sometime after the May 29 hangings, stating that he was worried that he was executing some innocent men. Although he was afraid of repercussions, Reichhart believed that he would rather face his own potential judicial proceedings than continue as a hangman. One source indicated that one of his sons assisted him at Landsberg in the executions; photographic records do not confirm that anyone else aided him on the scaffold platform. Reichhart has been credited with hanging

forty-two war criminals after the war; he was not involved in any way with the Nürnberg executions later in 1946. However, this study believes that he actually hanged twenty German war criminals. Perhaps those upcoming Nürnberg executions caused Johann Reichhart to rethink his position, not wanting to be forever linked with the deaths of these senior leaders of the Third Reich.

His work at Landsberg terminated, Reichhart was finally arrested at his home in May 1947 and taken to an internment camp at Moosburg, Bavaria. Court proceedings began on December 13, 1948, at Munich. On November 29, 1949, in a German tribunal, Reichhart received "strict" punishment, including two years confinement in a labor camp and confiscation of 50 percent of his financial and property assets. He was forbidden from ever holding public office, voting, or the right to engage in politics, as well as being denied ownership of a motor vehicle or a driver's license. He also was ordered to pay court costs of 26,000 marks.

Financially ruined, his marriage failed, and one of his sons, twenty-three-year-old Hans, committing suicide in 1950, Johann Reichhart retreated to private life. In 1963, during a series of taxi driver murders, there were public demands for the reintroduction of the death penalty—which had been abolished in West Germany on May 23, 1949—and Reichhart was vocal in his support for this legislation. He maintained that the preferred method of killing should be the guillotine, since it was the fastest and cleanest method of execution.

Johann Reichhart died in a nursing home at Dorfen near Erding, Bavaria, on April 26, 1972, from dementia. On May 2, 1972, his body was cremated at the Ostfriedhof (East Cemetery) in Munich. His remains are buried in the Ostfriedhof in a family grave (section 47, row 2, #21) that also contains both his sons, a daughter, and his uncle, Franz Xavier.

• • •

Justus Gerstenberg, Thursday, September 12, 1946

John Woods would hang one more man at Landsberg, Justus Gerstenberg, on September 12, 1946.[102] Gerstenberg was born at Witzenhausen near Kassel on September 6, 1897; he was married and had four children. During the First World War, Gerstenberg served in the 5th Dragoon Regiment. He was a painter and later a police officer.[103]

On July 16, 1944, the accused murdered an American airman, who had just surrendered and was a prisoner of war; a tribunal in Ludwigsburg met and convicted him in January 1946. Pvt. Joseph Malta served as Woods's assistant, and Lt. Stanley Tilles served as the officer in charge. The evening before the hanging, Woods stretched his ropes at the same gallows that he had used the previous May. A photograph of the event shows it was sunny and good weather; there were approximately thirty American soldiers present. The trapdoor dropped at 8:00 a.m. Prior to the execution, Woods had modified the trapdoor with a latch that prevented it from springing backward and striking the falling condemned man, and that modification appeared to work on this morning, although Malta later said a German had designed the latch.[104] Woods had previously explained the need for such a modification to Lt. Tilles: "In May, one of the trap doors swung back up and hit the guy in the face as he dropped. I've never seen it happen before, but it broke the guy's jaw and teeth and bloodied him up pretty good. I'm not going to let that happen again, and this latch will hold the trap door open until I release it. No one else will get hit like that."[105]

Justus Gerstenberg's body convulsed for a few seconds but then went still.[106] Burial personnel interred his remains at the Spöttinger Friedhof in grave #127.[107]

Chapter 9
NÜRNBERG

Preparation for the Nürnberg executions actually began in August 1946, when Lt. Stanley Tilles met with five enlisted members of the military police, including Pvt. Malta. These men would build three gallows, each 15 feet tall, at Landsberg Prison that could then be tested, disassembled, transported to Nürnberg, reassembled, and then used on the date of execution. Estimates ranged upward of five weeks, at least, to accomplish these tasks through reassembling. Woods thought that the construction would take up to thirty days, including painting all the wood olive drab, which required 25 gallons of the hard-to-find paint.[1] One observer described the scaffolds as being black in color instead of olive drab.[2]

When assembled, each gallows had three components: the framework, the platform, and the thirteen steps. The area below the platform, which was 8 feet wide, was boarded up with wood on three sides and shielded by a dark canvas curtain on the fourth. The trapdoor was at the center of the platform; the lever Woods would use to release the trapdoor was located at the rear of the platform, just as it had been in May at Landsberg. A square timbered arch extended about 8 feet above the platform; it had a large eyebolt in the center of the arch to secure the rope. Woods prepared thirteen ropes on October 9, stretching each one with the sand-filled duffel bag.[3]

However, Woods had a small problem: he needed a reliable method to tie each condemned man's hands behind his back. He did not like handcuffs but wanted to ensure that the men could not break free. Woods found his solution in a small German shop, when he spotted a roll of black, 1-inch-wide girl's hair ribbon. Made of imitation silk, it was strong and after the execution could be cut off easily with a knife. As Woods

later stated, "I guess the clerk thought I was up to some heavy fraternizing." The team would use regulation GI web belts, with the buckles sewn down to bind each prisoner's ankles.[4] Woods and his team were billeted in the prison; they ate incognito in the International Military Tribunal mess. Woods later said that after the executions, the mess sergeant said to him: "You guys pulled a fast one, all right. I never thought hangmen ate so hearty."[5]

The trial proceedings of the International Military Tribunal occurred at Nürnberg's Palace of Justice (*Justizgebaude*). At the rear of the palace stood a prison, consisting of four wings that radiated like the spokes of a wheel. One of the wings held the war criminals on trial. Inside the outer wall of the prison were a courtyard and a gymnasium. The executions would occur in that building. The judges, lawyers, and other officials lived nearby at the Grand Hotel. The tribunal announced the verdicts on October 1, 1946. Tribunal officials decided shortly thereafter to hang those men sentenced to death on October 16, but they kept this news secret.[6]

On October 15, the three gallows had been assembled and tested when an unplanned event occurred. The senior member of the Soviet delegation of observers to the execution, Maj. Gen. Iona T. Nikitchenko, requested to examine the gallows and observe a mock hanging with a sand-filled duffel bag. The demonstration occurred at 2:00 p.m. that day. Lt. Tilles met the Russians outside the gymnasium, escorted them inside, and introduced them to one MSgt. Woods.[7]

Woods took charge; he was in his element and he knew it. He took a good half hour to show Gen. Nikitchenko and his "strap-hangers" every facet of the gallows, including Woods's modification of the latch to keep the trapdoor open. Woods, with the exquisite timing of a Shakespearean actor, then gave a slight visual signal to "Dirty Dom," and when Malta pushed the handle, the duffel bag dropped with such force that the Soviet officers jumped backward, recovered, smiled broadly, and vigorously shook hands with the American hangman. Shortly after the Russian delegation departed, Woods strolled over to Stanley Tilles and said, "Told you it would be all right, lieutenant!"[8]

• • •

Some of the fragmentary information we know about John Woods during this period comes from Sgt. James J. Gibilante, a US Army mess sergeant (technician fourth grade) from Abington, Pennsylvania, professed best friend of John Woods and as unafraid to grant an interview to the press as Woods was.[9] As they had for Woods, however, it appears that the newspapers printed some incorrect information about Gibilante. James J. Gibilante appears to have actually been Anthony Joseph Gibilante (Army Service Number 33582004), who had been born in Willow Grove, Pennsylvania (just north of Philadelphia), on December 9, 1924. Anthony was the son of Italian immigrants Frank E. Guibilante, born in 1891, and his wife, Marianna, born in 1901. Frank arrived in the US in 1911; he was a cemetery laborer. Marianna arrived in the country in 1912. Anthony had two younger sisters, Rita and Carolina, an older brother, Frank, and a younger brother, Victor. The family soon moved to Abington, about a mile from Willow Grove.[10]

Anthony Gibilante attended two years of high school; he entered the Army at Cumberland, Pennsylvania, on February 10, 1943. He stood 5'9" tall, weighed 152 pounds, and had brown hair and brown eyes. This enlistment ended three years later; on January 23, 1946, Sgt. Gibilante reenlisted for a period that would terminate on December 1, 1948. During his tour in Germany, it appears that Anthony married Katharina

(Katherine) Wimmer, who had been born August 14, 1926, in Bad Tolz, Bavaria. She came to the US on the *General M. M. Patrick* from Bremerhaven, with their young son, James, on August 18, 1948.[11]

However, Anthony Gibilante had run into trouble before her departure. On September 4, 1947, Gibilante forged four American Express travelers checks in the name of Milton W. Schreyer at Bad Tolz, Bavaria. Authorities apprehended Gibilante, and the US 1st Infantry Division, to which the soldier now belonged, assembled a general court-martial. Anthony Gibilante pled not guilty, but the court ruled otherwise and sentenced him on February 13, 1948, to be discharged from the service, to forfeit all pay and allowances, and to be confined at hard labor for one year. He began his imprisonment at the European Command Military Prison at Mannheim; he was scheduled to be confined for the remainder of his sentence at the US Disciplinary Barracks at Ft. Hancock, New Jersey, after returning to the US on May 15, 1948.[12]

It is not clear when Gibilante was released from Ft. Hancock, but by 1950, Anthony was living at 202 Huntington Road in Abington. His wife died on August 15, 1996.

• • •

Nürnberg Prison, Nürnberg, Germany

Joachim von Ribbentrop, Wilhelm Keitel, Wilhelm Frick, Ernst Kaltenbrunner, Hans Frank, Alfred Jodl, Alfred Rosenberg, Julius Streicher, Fritz Sauckel, and Arthur Seyss-Inquart, Wednesday, October 16, 1946

MSgt. John C. Woods was now on his greatest stage, since early the morning of October 16, 1946, he hanged ten senior Nazi war criminals at Nürnberg. Dana Adams Schmidt of the *New York Times* was one of the first to describe the story the same day: "Guilt Is Punished: No. 2 Nazi a

Suicide Two Hours before the Execution Time." The article described the mood at the executions, concentrating on Herman Göring's suicide, but did provide an often-overlooked detail that Woods had two assistants, one American and one German.[13] One of the best-written accounts surfaced twelve days later in *Time* magazine:[14]

INTERNATIONAL: WAR CRIMES:
Night without Dawn

9 p.m. The eleven men for whom this night held no dawn ate a last supper of potato salad, sausage, cold cuts, black bread and tea. At 9 p.m., the prison lights were dimmed. At 10:45, US Army Security officer Colonel Burton C. Andrus walked across the courtyard to set the night's lethal machinery in motion. The whole prison was permeated by the thought of impending death. (The Courthouse movie announced the next day's attraction: Deadline for Murder).

Just then Hermann Göring was crunching a phial of cyanide (no one knew where it came from). When guards and a chaplain rushed into his cell, he was dying. Meanwhile, near Nürnberg's old imperial Castle, a band of German children hung Göring in effigy. Then they burned the makeshift scaffold and silently marched around the fire, watching it scatter weird shadows among the rubble.

In the small gymnasium of the jail (its floor dusty, its walls dirty grey), three black gallows had been erected with more attention to numerology than to efficiency. The platforms were eight feet apart, stood eight feet above the ground, measured eight feet square. From each platform rose two heavy beams, supporting a heavy crosspiece with a hook for the rope in the middle. An inconspicuous lever served to open the traps. The space beneath the traps was hidden by curtains.

1:11 a.m. Two white-helmeted guards led Joachim von Ribbentrop from his cell down the corridor and across the courtyard. He walked as in a trance, his eyes half closed. The wind ruffled his sparse grey hair. Overhead, the same wind whipped clouds into bizarre patterns.

At 1:11 a.m. he entered the gymnasium, and all officers, official witnesses and correspondents rose to attention. Ribbentrop's manacles were removed and he mounted the steps (there were 13) to the gallows. With the noose around his neck, he said: "My last wish . . . is an understanding between East and West . . ." All present removed their hats. The executioner tightened the noose. A chaplain standing beside him prayed. The assistant executioner pulled the lever, the trap dropped open with a rumbling noise, and Ribbentrop's hooded figure disappeared. The rope was suddenly taut, and swung back & forth creaking audibly.

The executioner was US Master Sergeant John C. Woods, 43, of San Antonio, a short, chunky man who in his 15 years as US Army executioner has hanged 347 people. Said he afterwards: "I hanged those ten Nazis . . . and I am proud of it . . . I wasn't nervous . . . A fellow can't afford to have nerves in this business. . . . I want to put in a good word for those G.I.s who helped me . . . they all did swell . . . I am trying to get [them] a promotion . . . The way I look at this hanging job, somebody has to do it. I got into it kind of by accident, years ago in the States . . ."

2:14 a.m. While the late Joachim von Ribbentrop was still swinging from the first gallows, Field Marshal General Wilhelm Keitel, in well-pressed uniform and gleaming boots, mounted the second scaffold briskly, as though it were a reviewing stand, and said: ". . . More than two million German soldiers went to their deaths for the Fatherland. I follow now my sons."

Then Ernst Kaltenbrunner: ". . . I have loved my German people and my Fatherland with a warm heart. . . . Germany, good luck . . ." Then Philosopher Alfred Rosenberg, who had nothing to say. Then Hans Frank: "I am thankful for the kind treatment during my imprisonment and I ask God to accept me with mercy." Then Wilhelm Frick: "Long live eternal Germany!" Then Julius Streicher, who looked wild-eyed and yelled "Heil Hitler" . . . at 2:14 the trap swallowed him. Reported Sergeant Woods: ". . . he kicked a little while, but not long."

2:57 a.m. Woods and his assistants seemed to be getting impatient as they moved from one scaffold to the other, using a new rope for each man. At 2:26 it was Fritz Sauckel's turn. When summoned for his last walk, he had refused to dress, so he went to the gallows coatless. He cried: "I am dying innocent . . . I pay my respects to US soldiers and officers, but not to US justice." (Conflicting versions claimed that he did not mention "US justice" but "US Jews.") Then Colonel General Alfred Jodl. Then, finally, Arthur Seyss-Inquart, who limped as he mounted the steps. He said: "I hope this execution is the last act in the tragedy of World War II . . ." It was 2:57 when he was pronounced dead. Said Woods: "Ten men in 103 minutes. That's fast work." He added that he was ready for a "stiff drink afterwards" . . .

• • •

The article may have been eloquent, but the problem was it was horribly incomplete, which would cause not only immediate problems for the four-power commission appointed to organize and supervise the executions, but also—perhaps more importantly—for historical accounts over the next seven decades, although the *Chicago Tribune*, the same day as the executions, published a more accurate timeline concerning the precise moment each man fell through the trap.[15]

The condemned men ate their final meal at 5:30 p.m. on October 15.[16] That evening, intermittent heavy rain fell. At 10:00 p.m., Col. Burton C. Andrus, commandant of the Nürnberg Prison, accompanied by about ten witnesses including Bavarian premier Dr. Wilhelm Hoegner and a German interpreter, went to the cell of each prisoner scheduled to die and told them that this was the

night.[17] Rumors had been rampant, although until this moment Andrus and his staff made every attempt to maintain secrecy. Meanwhile, Lt. Tilles, Woods, and the assistants assembled in a wood-paneled room. Sitting on folding chairs, some sipped coffee waiting for Maj. F. C. Teich, the prison operations officer. At 11:30 p.m., Col. Andrus strode in and informed the group that Hermann Göring, former chief of the Luftwaffe—among his many titles—had taken poison and died. Göring was the only defendant that night to cheat the hangman.[18] Joseph Malta later confirmed that Göring would have been the first to be hanged had he lived.[19] For the rest of his life, John Woods regretted not being able to hang "the fat man." Col. Andrus noticed that Woods's face looked puffy.[20] The faces of the men he subsequently hanged would look far worse.

Maj. Teich took over the meeting and explained the procedures that would be used that night. A prison staff lieutenant colonel would go to the cell of the condemned man scheduled to die first. He would escort the prisoner, who had his ankles shackled, from his cell, down a corridor, and outside the building down a flight of stairs, then turn left and proceed to the closed door of the gymnasium. He would then knock on the door. Two military policemen would open the door, and the lieutenant colonel and the prisoner would take three steps inside the gymnasium. The lieutenant colonel would remove the shackles, leave the chamber, and go to the cell of the next man scheduled to be executed and repeat the process. Teich's meeting lasted until 12:25 a.m. (October 16).[21]

Meanwhile, inside the gymnasium, the interior dimensions measuring 33 feet wide by 80 feet long, two MPs would hold the prisoner by the arms while two other MPs stepped behind the prisoner. Behind the last MPs was either a Protestant or Catholic chaplain; an interpreter was next, and Lt. Tilles would bring up the rear. In front of the prisoner, two lieutenant colonels from the Provost Marshal Section of the US 3rd

Army would lead the procession (which would march to the appropriate gallows) and halt, and the prisoner would state his name. Two gallows were used alternatingly to keep the flow moving. They stood next to each other, 8 feet apart and slightly left of the door through which the prisoner had entered the room. To the prisoner's right stood a third gallows that could be used as a backup if a malfunction occurred on one of the two primary gallows. The prisoner, if he took in his surroundings, would have noted that the room's plaster walls were cracked in many places—it was a shabby place to die.[22]

The MPs holding the condemned man's arms would assist him up the thirteen steps to the platform; standing on the closed trapdoor at the gallows, each prisoner had his hands tied behind his back with black shoelaces/ribbon, while their lower legs were strapped together using Army web belts. Meanwhile, the two MPs in the rear would peel off behind the gallows to retrieve a canvas stretcher that was located behind a separate long, black curtain. Behind the curtain were also eleven pine coffins leaning against a side wall. The prisoner would make a final statement, at which point Woods would hang him. Once the prisoner was declared dead, the rope would be cut and the two MPs with the stretcher would transport the body behind the long, black curtain and place it on top of one of the empty coffins. When all the executions had taken place, official Army photographers would take two pictures of each body lying on top of his coffin.[23]

Joachim von Ribbentrop, First Gallows

Nicknamed "Ribbensnob," Joachim von Ribbentrop, minister of foreign affairs, entered the gymnasium at 1:11 a.m. and proceeded to the first gallows. Born April 30, 1893, in Wesel in North Rhine–Westphalia, he was wounded in the First World War and also won the Iron Cross First Class. At the International Military Tribunal he occupied cell #7 of the first floor of the main

section of the prison. Psychiatrists at the trial measured his IQ at 129. The tribunal convicted him of crimes against peace, war crimes, and crimes against humanity, sentencing him to death.[24] Ribbentrop initially did not answer the question of who he was, but at a second query he shouted, "Joachim von Ribbentrop!" Ribbentrop's final words were "God protect Germany. My last wish is that Germany's unity be preserved and that an understanding be reached between East and West." Pvt. Joseph Malta put the hood on the condemned man; Woods followed by putting the noose around the condemned man's neck, and then, as he would for each, Malta held the slack in the rope until the instant the trapdoor opened.[25] The two-man team would follow the same procedure for every man that night. At 1:14 a.m., Woods activated the lever. A Russian physician, carrying a stethoscope, and an American doctor, carrying a flashlight, stepped under the black curtains and examined Ribbentrop; they emerged and stated, "This man is dead."[26] The time was 1:30 a.m.[27]

Wilhelm Keitel, Second Gallows

Field Marshal Wilhelm Keitel, chief of the armed forces high command (*Oberkommando der Wehrmacht*—OKW), entered the gymnasium about 1:18 a.m., climbed the thirteen steps of the second scaffold, moved to the center, and did a crisp "about-face." Born in Helmscherode in Lower Saxony on September 22, 1882, he did not serve at the front in World War II but did survive the bomb explosion at Rastenburg during the July 20, 1944, attempt to assassinate Adolf Hitler.

At the International Military Tribunal, Keitel occupied cell #8 on the first floor of the main section of the prison. Psychiatrists measured his IQ to be 129. The tribunal convicted him of crimes against peace, war crimes, and crimes against humanity, sentencing him to death. According to Col. Andrus, Keitel's final words as he hurtled through the trap opening at 1:20 a.m. were a scream: *"Deutschland über Alles!"* That jerky movement may have caused the condemned man to wobble, since his face later looked as though it had violently struck the front edge of the trap. However, a witness later said that the trapdoor had swung back after opening, and it was this object that smashed into Keitel's face. In any case, while Keitel was swinging from the end of the rope, two soldiers carrying stretchers arrived about 1:33 a.m. As these men went to the first scaffold, either Woods—who had returned from the second gallows—whipped out his "commando knife" and cut through the rope, or Joseph Malta did (accounts vary), causing the body to drop to the floor.[28] Woods would later say in an interview that an infantryman, who was later killed in action, had given him a hunting knife, and it was this knife that Woods used at Nürnberg; the hangman said of his infantryman friend: "He asked me always to carry that knife with me."[29]

The two MPs then carried Ribbentrop's body on the stretcher to behind the long curtain. The black hood was still over Ribbentrop's head; the time was 1:35 a.m. Under the second gallows, physicians pronounced Keitel dead at 1:44 a.m. The field marshal, whose nickname among some German military officers had been "the Nodding Ass," wrote his autobiography, *In the Service of the Reich*, in prison; it was published after his death.[30]

Ernst Kaltenbrunner, First Gallows

After Woods cut the rope at the first gallows, former *SS-Obergruppenführer* (four-star general) Ernst Kaltenbrunner could arrive at the chamber, which he did at 1:36 a.m., wearing a blue suit over a tattered sweater to combat the chill in the air. He then mounted the first scaffold. Born on October 4, 1903, at Ried am Inn in Austria, Kaltenbrunner assumed command of the dreaded Reich main security office (*Reichssicherheits-hauptamt*—RSHA) after the assassination of Reinhard Heydrich. During his career in the SS, Kaltenbrunner received the Nazi Golden Party Badge, the Blood Order (officially known as the "Decoration in Memory of 9 November 1923," one of the most prestigious decorations in the Nazi Party), and the Knight's Cross of the War Service Cross. At the International Military Tribunal he occupied cell #26 of the first floor of the main section of the prison. Psychiatrists at the trial measured his IQ at 113. The tribunal convicted Kaltenbrunner of war crimes and crimes against humanity, sentencing him to death.

He had a lengthy final statement: "I have loved my German people [Kaltenbrunner was Austrian] with a warm heart. And my Fatherland. I have done my duty by the laws of my people, and I regret that my people were led, this time, by men who were not soldiers, and that crimes were committed of which I have no knowledge."[31] He may also have added "Good luck Germany." The black hood and noose went over Kaltenbrunner's head and neck. Woods activated the lever at 1:39 a.m. and then strutted to the second gallows and cut that rope; the two troopers carried Keitel's body, also with the head covered by a black hood, to behind the long curtain. At 1:52 a.m., the Russian and American physicians declared that Ernst Kaltenbrunner, whose nickname had been "the Gorilla," was dead. Malta later stated that under the gallows, he had to lift Kaltenbrunner's body upward a bit "to take the slack off" and then cut the rope.[32]

Alfred Rosenberg, Second Gallows

Alfred Rosenberg, former Reich minister for the Eastern Occupied Territories and a national socialist ideologist, just wanted to get the whole ordeal over. With sunken cheeks and a pasty complexion, he walked into the gymnasium at 1:47 a.m., climbed the steps of the second scaffold, and had no last words.[33] He had about said it all during the trial, when he uttered: "We didn't contemplate killing anybody in the beginning."[34] Rosenberg, an ethnic German, had been born in Reval (now Tallinn), Estonia, on January 12, 1893.

Winner of the Nazi Golden Party Badge and author of *The Myth of the Twentieth Century*, he was convicted at Nürnberg of crimes against peace, war crimes, and crimes against humanity and sentenced to death. At the International Military Tribunal he occupied cell #16 of the first floor of the main section of the prison. Psychiatrists at the trial measured his IQ at 127. Woods dropped the trapdoor at 1:49 a.m., and the doctors pronounced Rosenberg dead at 1:59 a.m. Joseph Malta later cut the rope, and MPs took the body away as before.

Hans Frank, First Gallows

Then there occurred the first preventable mishap of the night. Col. Andrus was in the process of escorting Dr. Hans Frank, former *Gauleiter* of Poland, into the gymnasium at 1:56 a.m. Frank stopped for a moment, turned toward Andrus, and said, "Colonel, I want to thank you for your great kindness to me." That was not in the plan, and an American major grabbed Frank and pushed him toward the first scaffold.[35] Frank announced his name, climbed the steps, and made a final statement: "I am thankful for the kind treatment during my captivity, and I ask God to accept me with mercy."[36] Hans Frank had been a *Reichsleiter* of the Nazi Party; the term was used to describe members of the executive committee and departmental heads of the organization. Born on May 23, 1900, in Karlsruhe, he served in the post–First World War *von Epp Freikorps*, was president of the Academy of German Law, served as governor-general of the General Government of Occupied Poland, and received the Blood Order. At the International Military Tribunal he occupied cell #15 of the first floor. Psychiatrists at the trial measured his IQ at 130; during his imprisonment Frank converted to Roman Catholicism. The tribunal convicted Frank of war crimes and sentenced him to death.

Frank swallowed hard as Woods put the black hood over his head.[37] The trapdoor dropped at 1:58 a.m., and at 2:09 a.m. the physicians pronounced Frank dead. A second misfortune, albeit minor, now occurred. An unnamed, but obviously nervous, American Army officer walked over to Woods and asked, "How are you doing?" In characteristic Woods fashion the hangman replied, "Okay; when's early chow?," at which point the officer retched.[38] "Dirty Dom" probably chuckled inside at the officer's discomfort but was able to cut the rope, and MPs moved Frank's body behind the curtain. During his trial, Hans Frank wrote *In the Face of the Gallows* (*Im Angesicht des Galgens*), completing it just twenty-one days before his execution.

Wilhelm Frick, Second Gallows

Wilhelm Frick was next; the procedure returned to normal, although the sixty-nine-year-old former Reich minister of the interior stumbled on the top step of the scaffold; the MPs holding his arms held him up so he would not fall. Born on March 12, 1877, in Alsenz in the Rhineland-Palatinate region of Germany, he was a participant in the 1923 Nazi "Beer Hall Putsch" and thus a recipient of the Blood Order. Frick had previously been the minister of the interior for Thuringia before assuming the Reich-level position. At the International Military Tribunal he occupied cell #28 of the first floor of the main section of the prison. Psychiatrists had measured his IQ at 124. The tribunal convicted him of crimes against peace, war crimes, and crimes against humanity, sentencing him to death.

Frick's final words were "Long live eternal Germany."[39] The trapdoor dropped at 2:08 a.m.; at 2:20 a.m. doctors pronounced Frick dead. Joseph Malta later cut the rope. Frick's posthumous photograph shows the condemned, dressed in a checked coat, with blood around his eye sockets, but the procedure had transpired exactly by the book and followed Frick's own comments on April 24, 1946, when he stated, "I wanted things done legally."[40] Behind the long, black curtain, it was getting crowded with bodies.

Julius Streicher, First Gallows

The most significant mishap of the proceedings occurred next. Julius Streicher, *Gauleiter* for Franconia and editor of *Der Stürmer* magazine, entered the gymnasium about 2:10 a.m., wearing an old blue shirt buttoned to the neck and a threadbare suit. When asked to state his name, Streicher replied, "Heil Hitler!," and while the shocked assemblage digested that outburst, Streicher added, "You know my name very well!" For those in the gymnasium who did not know Streicher, he had been born on February 12, 1885, in the village of Fleinhausen, a few miles west of Augsburg, Bavaria. During the First World War, Streicher received the Iron Cross First and Second Class; he was nicknamed "the King of Franconia." At the International Military Tribunal he occupied cell #25 of the first floor. Psychiatrists at the trial measured Streicher's IQ at 106. The tribunal convicted him of crimes against humanity, sentencing him to death. To say that Streicher hated Jews was a gross understatement. For example, he told Dr. G. M. Gilbert, the Nürnberg Prison psychiatrist, in an interview on July 26, 1946, "Oh, I don't think we have exterminated as many as they say. I don't think it was six million. I figure maybe it was four million."[41]

Julius Streicher mounted the first scaffold, although the MPs had to push him the final 2 feet to the center of the trapdoor, as Streicher screamed, "The Bolsheviks will hang you one day."[42] Woods placed the black hood over Streicher's head, followed by the noose. Hissing through the hood, Streicher uttered, "Purim Fest 1946."[43] Woods understood almost no German. Had the Kansan recognized the phrase, he would have known that it referred to an Old Testament account of the Purim Jewish holiday celebrated each spring that commemorated the execution of Haman, an ancient persecutor of the Jews. Streicher then added, "Adele, my dear wife."[44] Woods pushed the lever at 2:14 a.m., and down went Streicher.

Julius Streicher was dying hard, kicking as he went down. His bald head may have hit the trapdoor on the way down; later Woods thought so. The rope snapped taut and Streicher's body swung wildly, although the witnesses could see only the movement in the rope. Woods knew more, and as the official witnesses heard Streicher groaning, the American hangman came down from the scaffold and disappeared behind the black curtain. Woods still had his commando knife, but its use in this situation was not in the manual concerning executions, although the Soviet observers would not have complained. Within seconds after Woods had stepped behind the curtain, the rope stopped moving and Streicher ceased gurgling. A very small number of witnesses, although they would never be certain due to the opaque curtain, were convinced that Woods had grabbed Streicher's body and lifted his own feet off the floor, the combined weight causing the Nazi to strangle or perhaps even severing his spine. Whatever the case, doctors pronounced Streicher dead at 2:28 a.m. Pvt. Malta quickly cut the rope, since the first gallows had one more visitor to accommodate.

Almost every correspondent in the chamber heard Streicher's tortured gasps, although many of them, with the exception of Kingsbury Smith, later denied that, since they denied watching Woods step behind the curtains (Col. Burton Andrus never mentioned a word of it in his book *I Was the Nuremberg Jailer*, nor did Malta, on later televised interviews, admit that this happened). What each man, other than John Woods, had undoubtedly wondered was if something gone wrong, or was this more than a horrible accident?

Lt. Stanley Tilles later claimed that he had seen Woods deliberately place the coils of the hangman's noose off-center from the rear of Streicher's neck, an anomaly that would make it more likely that Streicher's neck would not be broken during the fall; as a result, Streicher would slowly strangle. Equally as chilling, Tilles insisted that he observed a small smile cross Woods's lips as he pushed the lever to release the trap.[45] Tilles made an assumption that Woods may have been seeking revenge for those comrades he had known who had been murdered by the Waffen-SS at Malmedy, Belgium, during the "Battle of the Bulge," but Woods's old unit, Company B of the 37th Engineer Combat Battalion, never fought in that battle.

This study does not believe that Woods intentionally caused the slow death of Julius Streicher because the Nazi earlier said "Heil Hitler!" He did not punish Streicher further because of what the Nazi said on the scaffold, or to take revenge for the victims of the "Malmedy Massacre," or even—as Woods would say later—that Streicher had spit in his face, "and for a moment I felt like striking him."[46]

To be sure, Woods moved the knot, knowing that Streicher would strangle by inches. However, Woods committed the act not for the above reasons, but because during a hanging, Woods considered himself to be the major actor in the drama; it was his show, and woe be it to the intruder—condemned man or overbearing American officer—who attempted to "steal the scene." Julius Streicher was trying to wrest "top billing" in this spectacle, and Woods decisively put Streicher in his place in the only way John knew how—he strangled him, to show everyone at Nürnberg and around the world, who was running this show.

Fritz Sauckel, Second Gallows

With that ruckus going on at the first gallows, Fritz Sauckel, former *Gauleiter* of Thuringia and plenipotentiary for labor allocation, entered the gymnasium at 2:24 a.m., wearing a sweater but no overcoat. We do not know if Sauckel saw the final twitches of Julius Streicher. Looking confused, he stated: "I am dying an innocent man. The sentence is wrong." He may have believed that assertion, but the tribunal had convicted him of war crimes and crimes against humanity,

sentencing him to death, but then again, he always denied responsibility, stating at the trial on December 15, 1945: "I was like a seaman's agency. If I supply hands for a ship, I am not responsible for cruelty that may be exercised aboard ship without my knowledge. I just supplied workers to places like the Krupp Works at Hitler's orders. I am not to blame if they were later mistreated."[47]

At the International Military Tribunal he occupied cell #11 on the first floor. Psychiatrists had measured his IQ at 118. Fritz Sauckel had been born in Hassfurt am Main in Lower Franconia, Bavaria, on October 27, 1894. An honorary *SS-Obergruppenführer*, he was a recipient of the Nazi Golden Party Badge.

Sauckel was escorted up the steps. His final words were "I pay my respects to US soldiers and officers, but not to US justice." Lt. Tilles later wrote that some observers thought Sauckel's final phrase was "US Jews" (*Jüden*) instead of "US justice" (*Justiz*), although Tilles believed it was the latter. Sauckel continued: "God protect Germany and make Germany great again. Long live Germany. God protect my family."[48] What he did not restate was a comment he had made in November 1945 concerning the deaths of foreign workers, when he said, "I'd choke myself with these hands if I thought that I had the slightest thing to do with those murders!"[49] Woods, administering "the choke" for every one of the millions of foreign slave-laborers who were worked to death in Nazi work projects and munitions factories, dropped Sauckel at 2:26 a.m.; as had Streicher, Sauckel uttered a loud groan when the rope snapped tightly.[50] At 2:40 a.m. physicians pronounced him dead. Malta then cut the rope.

Alfred Jodl, First Gallows

Generaloberst Alfred Jodl, chief of the operations staff of the German armed forces high command, entered the death chamber at 2:30 a.m., just a minute after two soldiers had removed the body of Julius Streicher. Jodl, a career soldier, had been born on May 10, 1890, in Würzburg in the Franconia area of Bavaria. During the First World War, he served in the artillery, winning the Iron Cross First and Second Class; he was wounded in action as well. A winner of the Knight's Cross of the Iron Cross with Oak Leaves, he survived the bomb explosion at Rastenburg during the July 20, 1944, attempt to assassinate Adolf Hitler. The tribunal convicted Jodl of crimes against peace, war crimes, and crimes against humanity and sentenced him to death. Most damning to the general at the trial were his signatures on documents directing that captured Soviet political commissars and captured allied commandos were to be executed immediately without trial.

At the International Military Tribunal he occupied cell #6; psychiatrists at the trial measured his IQ at 127. His final words were "My greetings to you, my Germany."[51] The trapdoor dropped at 2:34 a.m., and doctors pronounced him dead at 2:50 a.m. Minutes later, Joseph Malta cut the rope, and the MPs took his body on the stretcher to join the others.

Arthur Seyss-Inquart, Second Gallows

Dr. Arthur Seyss-Inquart was the final Nazi to be hanged that night—and as it would turn out, he was the last man that Woods would ever hang. Born in Moravia in the Austro-Hungarian Empire on July 22, 1892, the former governor of Austria (after the Nazi *Anschluss* (Germany's annexation of Austria), deputy governor general of Poland, and Reichs commissioner of the Netherlands entered the gymnasium at 2:39 a.m.; he would have to wait two minutes as doctors were still examining Fritz Sauckel. At the International Military Tribunal, Seyss-Inquart occupied cell #14 of the first floor of the main section of the prison. Psychiatrists at the trial measured his IQ at 141, the highest of any man that Woods would hang that night. The tribunal had convicted him of crimes against peace, war crimes, and crimes against humanity, sentencing him to death.

Arthur Seyss-Inquart uttered his final words about 2:43 a.m., saying, "I hope that this execution is the last act in the tragedy of the Second World War, that lessons will be drawn from this world war, and that peace and understanding between peoples will be the result. I have faith in Germany."[52] Pvt. Malta bound Seyss-Inquart's ankles and pulled the black hood over the condemned man's head, and Woods adjusted the noose around his neck, as he had done previously for all ten executions. Woods dropped the trapdoor at 2:45 a.m.; the condemned man was pronounced dead at 2:57 a.m., and Malta later cut the rope. Woods, now concentrating so hard and not realizing that Seyss-Inquart was the last man to be executed, yelled down to a member of his team, probably Sgt. Billy Ford: "Hey kid! When are you going to bring the next one up?"[53]

Now the press could really begin the feeding frenzy. Sgt. Gibilante elaborated on his relationship with Woods that was captured in another article, published in the *Indiana Gazette* of Indiana, Pennsylvania, on October 17, 1946:

Sgt. Hoped to Hang Nazis—and He Did

By DONALD DOANE, FRANKFURT, Germany, Oct., 17—(UP) Master Sgt. John C. Woods hoped he would get the job of hanging the Nazi war criminals convicted at Nuernberg—and he did. Now the veteran of 233 executions and four years of overseas army duty is ready to go back to his home near San Antonio, Tex., his friends said yesterday. "He was going to stay overseas until he could hang those Nuernberg Nazis and then he was ready to go back to the states," said the T-4 James J. Gibilante of Abington, Pa., a mess sergeant at one of the leading army hotels in Germany. "But, gee, I'll bet he hated to see Goering get away from him," Gibilante added. Gibilante was waiting tonight for Woods to come back from Nuernberg so they could have a celebration they planned. But nobody—not even his buddy Gibilante—seemed to know where Woods was today or when he would return.

"I think the Army may be hiding him out so he won't talk about the Nuernberg executions," one GI suggested. Apparently, Woods doesn't talk much about his work, even without an army gag, however. "He wouldn't even tell us whether he was going to do the job on those Nazis," Gibilante said. "But he said several months ago he hoped he would get it and we all thought he would. He's supposed to be good at this hanging business."

•••

Back in Wichita, there was shock. Newsmen raced to interview Hazel Woods, who was now employed at the Archer Taylor Laboratory and lived at 621 North Emporia. Hazel said she was stunned to know that John was the executioner, but stated, "It was his job—he received his orders from the higher command." The reporters also located Mrs. Martha A. Green, John's mother, who was residing at 628 West Osie. She had her own opinion on her son's duty: "As long as it had to be done it might just as well have been my son, and I am sure it was done in the line of duty."[54]

The day following the executions, the public became aware that photographs had been taken at the event. The following short article from the *Chicago Tribune* gave basic details:[55]

TAKE 2 PICTURES OF EACH NAZI AFTER HANGING

NUERNBERG, Germany, Oct. 16 (AP)—The official army photographer selected to make a pictorial record of the executions of the 11 Nazi leaders took only pictures of the corpses after they had been removed from the gallows, it was learned today.

Two photographs were made of each of the ten men executed and of the body of Hermann Goering, who committed suicide—one picture in each case of the body as it was dressed at the time of execution, and the other was of the nude body. The photographer's name was withheld.

The photographs, labeled top secret, were taken to Berlin—probably to be filed for record and historical purposes only. The allied coordinating committee will meet tomorrow to decide whether any will be released.

•••

The photos finally were released, and back in Wichita they appeared in the *Wichita Beacon* on October 24, 1946, but not all were shown to the public. Photography experts at the US National Archives have repeatedly stated that the photos of the naked corpses were never provided to their facility. Meanwhile, on October 19, 1946, Woods in a copyrighted story to the Associated Press told his account of the Nürnberg hangings. An accompanying photograph had the following caption: "(NY12-Oct.18) NUERNBERG HANGMAN—M/Sgt. John C. Woods (above), soldier hangman at the Nuernberg, Germany, executions last Wednesday morning, told in a copyrighted story for the Associated Press today his story of the hanging of the ten former German war leaders. This picture was made at Bruchsal Prison, Germany, Nov. 10, 1945, where Woods was Army hangman at execution of five German civilians who killed six US fliers."

On October 20, 1946, the *Stars & Stripes* published the letter that John Woods had written exclusively for the Associated Press. It would be the most comprehensive revelation of information that Woods would ever publicly provide.[56]

GI Hangman Tells Story of Top Nazis' Executions

(EDITOR'S NOTE: The soldier-hangman who executed the 10 Nazi leaders at Nurnberg wrote the following account exclusively for the Associated Press. Master Sergeant John C. Woods, short, chunky, 43, and growing bald, has been in the US Army off and on for the past 19 years. He landed in Normandy on D-Day and saw combat

in Africa. He won't divulge his home town, because "there's no use bringing my family into this.")
By M/Sgt John C. Woods
(Copyright by the Associated Press)

HEIDELBERG. Oct. 19 (AP)—I hanged those 10 Nazis at Nurnberg and I'm proud of it.

That was a job that needed doing for a long time, and I did a good job of it too. Everything clicked perfectly. I've hanged 347 people in the last 15 years, and I never saw a hanging go off any better. I'm only sorry Goering escaped. I wanted him especially.

No, I wasn't nervous. I haven't got any nerves. A fellow can't afford to have nerves in this business.

But this Nurnberg Job was one I really wanted to do. I wanted that assignment so badly I stayed over here after I could have gone back home just to do it. Those guys really deserved hanging.

Frick Weakened at End

I'll say this for those Nazis, though. They died like brave men. Only one of them showed any signs of weakening. When Frick was climbing those 13 steps of the gallows one leg seemed to go bad on him, and the guards had to steady him.

They were all arrogant. You could see they hated us. Old Jew-baiter Streicher looked right at me when he said: "The Bolsheviks will hang you, too, some day." And I looked him right back in the eye. They can't bother me.

There's not much to tell about the actual hangings. They went off just off like any routine hangings. Ten men in 103 minutes. That's fast work.

Only one of them even moved after the drop. That was Streicher, the one who shouted, "Heil Hitler!" He kicked a little while, but not too long. Another one, Sauckel, I think, started to shout "Heil Hitler!" too, after I put the hood over his head. But I cut him off short with the rope.

New Rope for Each

I used a different rope and different hood on each man. I fixed the nooses and stretched the ropes myself to make sure nothing would go wrong.

The ropes and hoods were burned up with the bodies, leaving nothing for the souvenir hunters. Why, one souvenir hunter from Havana, Cuba, wired an offer of $2,500 for one of those ropes.

I want to put in a good word for those GIs who helped me on that Nurnberg job. Only three of them had ever helped in a hanging before, but I trained them all for three weeks and they all did swell.

I noticed they were ready for a stiff drink afterwards though. So was I. I am trying to get those soldiers, who helped me, a promotion, and I think they will get it too. They don't want their names mentioned.

As for my name, well, I guess it's too late to keep my name out of it. I'm too well known over here already. After I started hanging these German war criminals last year somebody tried to poison me here in Germany, and somebody shot at me in Paris, but the poison only made me sick and the bullet missed me.

Somebody Has to Do It

The way I look at this hanging job, somebody has to do it. I got into it kind of by accident years ago in the States. I attended a hanging as a witness, and the hangman asked me if I'd mind helping. I did, and later I took over myself.

I just don't let it bother me. There was one soldier went crazy, though, after helping me on a five-man execution. Something went wrong on one of those hangings and the guy cracked.

Now that this Nurnberg job is over, I'm ready to go back to the States, and I'm planning to leave in a few days. But I may come back to Germany. There are more than 120 war criminals waiting to be hanged, including those 43 sentenced for the Malmedy massacre. I had some buddies killed in that massacre, and I'll come back here just to get even for them.

I am glad that this Nurnberg thing is over, though. That was a strain. They told me in August I'd be the one to do it. I've had to keep it a secret all that time.

I never saw any of the condemned men until they walked through the door of that execution chamber. I tried several times to get in to see some of the trial, but never succeeded.

I followed it pretty closely in the papers, and studied their pictures, and they gave me their names as they came to the scaffold.

But still, it was hard to keep them straight, and it's hard to remember just what each one did or said. Hanging 10 men one after the other is fast, you know. And that was a rope I had in my hand, not a notebook.

• • •

Pvt. Joseph Malta and Sgt. Billy Ford assisted Woods at Nürnberg.[57] Ford, Army Service Number 37701723, appears to have been from Collins, Mississippi, where he was born on October 28, 1924, the son of Homer W. Davis and Annie L. Rigdon. His draft card from 1942 listed his residence as Pueblo, Colorado; he was 5'9" tall, weighed 150 pounds, and had blond hair and gray eyes. He enlisted for the first time on June 19, 1943, and was released from the service on January 15, 1946. But the Army was in his blood, and he enlisted for a second time on April 15, 1946, at Ft. Logan, Colorado, for the Corps of Military Police. At that time, he was single and had one year of high school. In 1952, he listed his name as Billy Floyd Davis; he reenlisted again on November 4, 1952, remaining in the Army until March 31, 1964. He changed his name again to Billy F. Davis.[58]

Concerning the assistant who "went crazy, though, after helping me on a five-man execution," prior to Nürnberg, Woods had executed five or more men on only three occasions: November

10, 1945, at Bruchsal with assistant Vincent J. Martino, and both May 28 and May 29, 1946, at Landsberg with assistant Joseph Malta. Neither man cracked; it is more likely that Woods was talking about Thomas F. Robinson, who assisted him in hanging three men at the Rheinbach Prison on Friday, June 29, 1945; *Life* had reported that "the executioner" wept then, but probably was referring to Robinson.

Woods arrived in Heidelberg, Germany, and the US 3rd Army headquarters from Nürnberg just after noon on October 18, 1946, where he was met by numerous noncommissioned officer friends and acquaintances. He had just missed lunch, but a mess sergeant—probably Sgt. Gibilante—prepared a big steak sandwich for him as he described to his buddies what had occurred.[59] John also celebrated the Nürnberg executions with a few shots of Old Crow. An Associated Press photograph of Woods released October 24 had the following caption:

"(NY12-OCT.24)—JOB OVER, HANGMAN CELEBRATES—M/Sgt. John C. Woods (*right*), of San Antonio, Texas, the soldier-hangman who executed the ten Nazi leaders at Nuernberg Oct. 16, celebrates the end of his difficult job with a buddy, Sgt. James Gibilante of Abington, Penns. at Heidelberg, Germany, on Oct. 18."

The photograph ran in newspapers across the United States; for example, the *Chicago Tribune* ran the picture on November 10, 1946, with the caption "THE MAN WHO HANGED 10 NAZI LEADERS at Nuernberg, Germany, Master Sgt. John C. Woods (*right*), pours a drink for a friend, Sgt. James Gibilante."

Woods also started changing the story of his background. Previously, he had told the press that he was from San Antonio, Texas; now he said that was untrue. After telling the Army in September 1944 that he had participated in four hangings in Oklahoma and Texas as an assistant, he now stated that he had been a civilian hangman in "scores" of hangings but would not say where. He now gave his age as forty-three, but that would have made his birth date 1903, not 1911 as all his other background documentation indicated. The Army knew he had not served "off and on" in the Army for the last nineteen years, as he had now stated. Woods said that he had fought in Africa, but that campaign had ended in May 1943, some three months before Woods was inducted.[60] Army brass must have been fuming; Woods was shooting his mouth off to anyone with a pencil and a pad of paper, and he couldn't even keep his story consistent, let alone truthful.

However, more hell soon broke loose. It started in Germany on October 24, 1946, in the *Stars & Stripes*; once again John Woods was talking with the press.[61]

Nazis' Executioner "Never Missed One"

HEIDELBERG, Oct. 23 (UP)—Press reports that the hanging of the 10 Nazis war criminals at Nurnberg Oct. 16 was a "botched job" were decisively quashed today by M/Sgt. John C. Woods, the man who hanged them.

A report quoting unidentified sources who had seen the bodies or watched the hangings said some of the condemned men had taken an abnormally long time to die after the drop, that they had been strangled to death instead of being killed instantly, that several of the men hit the trap going through, and that most of the bodies were bloody after death.

"The only people who spread reports like that are people who don't know anything about hangings," Woods declared. "All the medical officers present and several people who had witnessed many hangings said it was one of the fastest, cleanest jobs they had ever seen. Even the Russian general came up afterwards and told me it was a first-class job."

"Got Them All"

In answer to reports that death had taken too long in some instances, Woods said, "If you don't want to take my word for it why don't you ask the medical examiners. The medical officer told me right after it was over, 'you got them all. You never missed a single one.'"

"He was referring to their necks which were all broken when they dropped. I've seen enough hangings to know by the way they hang whether the neck is broken or not, and besides I went and felt their necks with my own hands."

"If a man is healthy and has a good heart it will continue to beat from five to 12 minutes after his neck is broken, no matter how he is hung. But he doesn't feel anything because he is unconscious from the instant he drops and that knot hits the back of his head."

"Sometimes if a man has a weak heart it stops beating sooner, maybe almost right away, but that is not normal. And so far as strangling is concerned, if those men made any sounds or motions after they dropped it was purely what doctors call reflex action."

Woods was referred to the practice at inquests following British hangings to declare death instantaneous.

"That is impossible," said the sergeant.

As for hitting the trap door going through, "that happens occasionally when a man is off balance at the last second when the trap is sprung. One of these men, Streicher, I believe it was, hit his head on the trap. But he never knew what hit him."

And about the blood on their faces? "There's nothing unusual about that," said Woods, who has hanged more than three hundred men. "Sometimes they open their mouths at the drop, and the blow of the knot makes them bite their tongues. But they never know that either. That might happen in any hanging."

Defends Gallows

Woods said his portable gallows were not inadequate for a proper death-bringing drop. "The standard drop is the condemned man's height plus six inches," he said. "But I always judge a man's weight and give a light man a longer drop than a heavy man."

But the tough Texas hangman, who executed the top Nazi war criminals as the climax of almost 20 years of hanging criminals, announced that Wednesday night for him was not only the climax but the end of his career.

"I've hung my last man. I'm through," he revealed.

Why? The answer he gave belied the reports that Woods is a man without nerves.

"Terrible Nervous Strain"

"Have you seen this man Pierrepoint, the British expert who has hung more than a thousand men?" he asked. "Well, it made an old man out of him. He goes around all bent over like his hands and his head were going to drag. A man is under a terrible nervous strain. I don't think it was dishonorable, because someone had to do it, but I've had enough. I'm through."

Woods is going home, probably in the next few days. He admits it is risky to stay in Germany after hanging this nation's erstwhile leaders, and that "There's no use taking unnecessary chances."

"But someone is with me all the time," he said, "and besides, I always carry two .45s with me. If some German thinks he wants to get me, he better make sure he does it with the first shot, because I was raised with a pistol in my hand and I'm an expert shot with either hand."

• • •

Woods was undoubtedly referring to Thomas W. Pierrepoint. The Pierrepoints, a Yorkshire family, provided three of Britain's chief executioners,

often called official executioners–number one, and sometimes termed "scaffolders," for over fifty years. Henry Pierrepoint (March 1878–December 14, 1922) took up the craft first; he hanged a total of 105 men from 1901 to 1910. According to reputable sources, Henry could execute a man in the time it took the prison clock to strike eight—leading him from his cell to the adjacent death chamber on the first stroke, and having him suspended, dead on the rope, by the eighth and final stroke. However, the work proved to be a pressure cooker, and on July 13, 1910, when he arrived at Chelmsford Prison to prepare for an execution the following day, Henry was intoxicated and physically assaulted his assistant, John Ellis. Nine days later, authorities removed him from the list of executioners, and he never worked again as a scaffolder.[62]

However, a few years before, Henry had persuaded his older brother Thomas to take up the calling. By 1913, Thomas was the number two to John Ellis, who had succeeded Henry as chief executioner. Ellis resigned his position in 1923, which left Thomas as the Number One. Five months later, John Ellis attempted suicide by shooting himself in the jaw but survived the wound.[63]

Born in 1870, in Sutton Bonington, Nottinghamshire, Thomas W. Pierrepoint served as a hangman from 1909 to 1946; he is credited with having carried out 294 hangings, not the over 1,000 that Woods had asserted. Thomas served as the chief executioner of seventeen American soldiers—sixteen in Great Britain and one in France. He died on February 10, 1954, in Bradford, England. Later, Albert Pierrepoint recalled that Uncle Thomas on one occasion counseled him on how to conduct an execution, stating, "If you can't do it without whisky, don't do it at all."

Albert Pierrepoint would be highly critical of John Woods, in part because Pierrepoint was the British hangman of Nazis war criminals in the British sector of occupied Germany and used a far different method of hanging than did Woods. There also may have been a slight professional jealousy that he had not been selected to hang the top Nazis at Nürnberg. Albert, born March 30, 1905, in Clayton, West Yorkshire, Henry's son and Thomas's nephew, outdid his father and uncle combined and executed 434 people (including sixteen women) between 1932 and 1956. During World War II, Albert served as assistant executioner for Thomas in seven hangings of American soldiers in Britain.

In 1956, Albert resigned over a disagreement about fees, when not paid the full amount of 15£ for an execution. In his later memoirs, on the final page, Albert Pierrepoint concluded, "The trouble with the death sentence has always been that nobody wanted it for everybody, but everybody differed about who should get off." In later years, he opposed capital punishment. Pierrepoint also served as the proprietor for two pubs, "Help the Poor Struggler" and the "Rose and Crown." Albert died at the Melvin Nursing Home in Southport, Lancashire, on the coast of the Irish Sea, on July 10, 1992, after spending the last four years of his life there. The physician's certificate listed the causes of death as bronchopneumonia and Alzheimer's disease. Soon afterward, the *News of the World* announced Albert Pierrepoint's death under the title "King of the rope dies."[64]

In his autobiography, *Executioner: Pierrepoint*, published in 1974, the British hangman would not discuss Woods by name, simply terming him "a sergeant of the American Army." In the book, Albert synthesized the executions at Nürnberg: "There were indications of clumsiness, the newspapers alleged, arising from the unalterable five-foot drop and the, to me, old-fashioned four coiled cowboy knot, which resulted in each bloodstained rope having to be cut above the halter to remove the body, since the noose was unusable for a second time."[65]

• • •

The firestorm of criticism could not be contained, and on October 30, 1946, several newspapers in the US ran the following story:[66]

NAZI HANGINGS BUNGLED, SAYS BRITISH REPORT

BY JOHN THOMPSON
[*Chicago Tribune* Press Service]
BERLIN, Oct. 29—Because of objections by the American representative, the allied control authority has rejected a British request for investigation of reports that 10 top flight Nuernberg Nazi war criminals were hanged in inhumane fashion on Oct. 16, it was learned tonight.

The paper submitted by the British called attention to reports that the condemned Nazis died by strangulation in the hangman's noose instead of having a quick death by broken necks, and that because of bungling, one Nazi was smashed in the face by the trap door as he dropped to his death.

The British paper was prepared after consultation with Brig. E. J. Paton-Walsh, British member of the four power commission appointed to superintend the execution, which was carried out by the American military authorities at the Nuernberg prison. Paton-Walsh is regarded as an authority on British prisons.

Believe Part of Reports True

The British paper, which was stricken from the control council agenda after the Americans refused to accept it, said that Paton-Walsh, who was an execution eyewitness, believed at least part of the published press reports were true. Study of official photographs of the bodies taken after the execution, the paper stated, lent further support to the belief that the execution was badly bungled in that the condemned men were killed in a distinctly inhumane manner.

The paper suggested that the council could adopt any of three courses: Make no public announcement, since the stories could not be denied; call for and publish a complete report from those responsible for the hangings, or deny what could be denied and publish a short statement.

In their proposed draft of the statement, the British suggested that the council not state that reports that the condemned men took from 10 to 16 minutes to die were erroneous. Instead it should say that the method of execution was the approved method used throughout the American zone and one common in several states of the United States; that death intervened rapidly, and that the times quoted merely referred to the moment when the doctors examined the corpses and pronounced death.

Seems a Tacit Admission

The council's lack of action on the matter appeared to be a tacit admission that the published stories were true. The gallows used were 15 feet high with automatic trap 7½ feet above the ground. The hangman, American Master Sgt. John C. Woods who had at other executions here and in the United States, used a noose with 13 knots.

The hangman asserted that the long rope almost always broke the neck, while the 13 loop knot acted as a clout when the rope pulled taut, knocking the victim unconscious so that subsequent death, even by strangulation, was painless.

Eyewitness reports were to the contrary. One expert who had witnessed many hangings described this as the worst job of incompetence he had ever seen. This witness asserted the victims strangled for upward of three minutes. In some cases, the weight of heavier criminals was misjudged, so that the rope stretched and their toes touched the ground, prolonging the inevitable. He added that there was no evidence of any dislocation of necks of the victims.

Trap Incorrectly Set

In the case of one man [apparently Field Marshal Keitel] this witness said, the trap was incorrectly set so that as the man plunged to his death, the trap snapped back, striking him full in the face. The faces of both Keitel and Wilhelm Frick were covered with blood in the official photographs.

Another objection raised by this witness was that the rope—a new one was used in each case—was too pliable. In British executions, the hangman tests the rope for months ahead of time, suspending a heavy iron weight at one end. Before the executions, the rope is again tested innumerable times with a dummy, which simulates the weight of the victim.

In place of the large hangman's noose, the British place a steel pad under the rope at the base of the victim's neck. This is said to immediately fracture the neck when the victim drops thru, so that there can be no possible strangulation.

In later years an interviewer appeared to want to know about Master Sergeant John Woods's proficiency at Nürnberg and asked Joseph Malta on camera if they had conducted any dry runs of the hangings prior to the actual executions. "Dirty Dom" Malta snorted disdainfully, shook his head "no" at what he apparently thought was a stupid question, and tersely replied, "John knew what to do."[67]

Chapter 10

OLD SOLDIERS NEVER DIE, THEY JUST FADE AWAY...MAYBE

John Woods remained in Germany slightly longer than he had anticipated in his interviews, but Army brass were not waiting too long for the garrulous hangman to spout off again. Woods, fabricated claims of service longevity and all, received his orders for home, and on November 9, 1946, on the troopship *St. Albans Victory*, he departed Bremerhaven, Germany, with 1,427 other soldiers, bound for New York City.[1] On November 19, 1946, the troopship arrived at the "Big Apple" at Pier 3 of Army Base Brooklyn. An Associated Press photograph of Woods in his bunk on the ship has the following caption:

"NEW YORK, NOV. 19—NUERNBERG HANGMAN RETURNS—M/Sgt. John C. Woods, 35, of San Antonio, Tex., hangman of ten Nazi chieftains at Nuernberg last month, holds a noose he fashioned, as he waits in his bunk for the troopship St. Albans Victory to land here today after a voyage from Bremerhaven, Germany. Woods will rejoin his wife who lives at Wichita, Kas. denied that he had bungled his Nuernberg hanging assignment and said he will not quit his job as hangman. The rope he is holding is NOT one used at Nuernberg."

The following day, the *New York Times* reported on an interview made with Woods upon his arrival in New York. It was full of melodrama—and numerous inaccurate statements made by Woods, who revealed that two attempts had been made to kill him. The first had occurred about a year prior, according to Woods, when an unknown gunman fired a shot at him in front of a Paris, France, perfume store. Woods stated that a second attempt had occurred the previous summer about five months prior, when two German cooks at a US Army mess facility had tried to poison him.[2]

Joseph Malta would later state, "When Woods left, there was no replacement; it [executions after October 16, 1946] was slow."[3]

The *Times* then reported, presumably from information provided by Woods, that the sergeant had served in the Army for fourteen years, three of which were overseas duty. Then Woods asserted that he had spent 116 days in combat. Mentioning that he had once been an assistant hangman in Texas, Woods estimated that he had hanged two hundred men, of which 134 had occurred in Europe. Woods stated: "Hanging is awfully hard work. It's hard on your nerves and it wears you out. It's time for me to quit but I won't."[4]

The article ended that Woods, a native of San Antonio, Texas, would go soon to Wichita, Kansas, to rejoin his wife.[5]

Woods must have hustled off the pier and onto transportation, since he gave an interview to *True: The Man's Magazine* at Ft. Dix, New Jersey, this time supervised by the Fort Dix public relations officer, Maj. Cornelius T. Morris.[6] Woods revealed a few more "trade secrets" not previously recorded. He stated that to construct a gallows he preferred hard wood, since it stayed tight, but since such wood was scarce in Germany he could get by with green lumber such as native pine. He added that when a 200-pound condemned man was hanged with a trap mechanism weighing 265 pounds, the entire gallows wobbled. In fact, he added that the heavy trap fell so fast that for a split second one could see daylight between the condemned man's feet and the falling door. To dampen those vibrations, Woods used 8-by-8-inch beams and headers instead of 6 by 6, although at Nürnberg the smaller size was all that was available. Woods carried another technique forward from Landsberg; instead of wrapping the rope around the top beam, Woods bored a shaft in the beam, bolted a 4-inch-diameter iron ring through the hole, and attached the rope to the ring, although another account said the fixture was an iron hook and not a ring.[7]

Concerning the rope, Woods preferred a real manila ⅝-inch that was well oiled. He then began the stretching process, tying a 200-pound weight to the rope and dropping that weight thirty to forty times, which would stretch an 18-foot rope an additional 3 to 5 feet in length. Once the ropes were stretched, Woods began to work on the nooses. He preferred what he called "the Thirteen Knot" noose, which he said was his own invention. Woods stated that it took 6.5 feet of rope just to construct the noose, but what made it special was that the thirteen turns of the rope created a heavy, substantial mass.[8]

That was important, Woods added, since when the condemned man fell and the rope went taught, the knot propelled forward to hit "him on the back of the head like a sledgehammer, and his head has a tendency to go forward. In other words, when that knot hits him on the back of the head, he is knocked out cold." Woods finally added that for Nürnberg, he prepared fourteen ropes, and before their use he hung them in a warm room.[9]

Finally, the hangman from Nürnberg added two anecdotes, for the benefit of his readers, which were pure John Woods. The first was about the officer vomiting after Woods had hanged Hans Frank. Woods then added that he and his crew were never nervous but were "so tuckered out" they could hardly get back to their billets. Woods ended the interview by stating: "We went straight over to our billet, and I never saw three quarts of whiskey disappear so fast in my life. We weren't drowning our sorrow or anything like that, understand. We were just plain thirsty."[10]

On November 20, 1946, Woods's hometown paper, the *Wichita Beacon*, published an article under the title "Nuernberg Hangman Proud of Executions." The article began "'GI' John C. Woods, the roly-poly hangman from Nuernberg,

arrived from Europe yesterday and immediately announced he was not going out of business."[11]

The article quoted Woods as saying that he began his hanging career in Texas as an assistant hangman when he was eighteen years old and served for the first time as the primary hangman when he was twenty-one. The report also referred to him as "The Army's No. 1 Rope Artist." Woods added, "It's nerve-racking all right, and you need some good stiff drinks when it's over, but you sleep alright."[12]

The article ended saying that Woods would first go to Ft. Sheridan, Illinois, for reassignment orders before joining his wife. He probably went to Illinois fairly quickly, since by November 27, 1946, John was in Wichita. The following day was Thanksgiving, and the Woodses attended a local church service, an event that was documented by the Associated Press in a photograph of the two leaving church, with the following caption:

"WICHITA, KANS., NOV. 29—NUERNBERG HANGMAN AND WIFE ATTEND CHURCH. Master Sgt. John C. Woods, 35-year-old army hangman at Nuernberg, and his wife Hazel Marie, attend church here Thanksgiving Day. Woods is on 90-day furlough."

The *Wichita Beacon* published an article on the event, stating that the service was at the First Methodist Church and the sermon, titled "Think and Be Thankful," was given by Dr. F. B. Thorn, pastor of the First Baptist Church. Reporters closed in on the Woodses. Hazel told newsmen: "We only want some privacy. Give us a little consideration and ask other people to do the same," while John discussed getting crank letters: "After all, this is my home. People seem to think I'm a racketeer or something worse. My job was no worse than any other soldier's." After the service, the Woodses departed for a Thanksgiving dinner with relatives. The couple finished the day with a movie.[13]

The same day as the article, the *Wichita Beacon* rolled out the red carper for their former delivery boy. Johnny Woods was on top of the world and so was the *Beacon*, with photo after photo of the hometown hero, many of which circulated around the globe. The paper made him the "editor for the day," and a photograph showed the happy hangman behind his new tool of the trade—a typewriter. The newspaper published two articles, the first of which dealt with the man who got away from Woods, Hermann Göring. Woods said, "I had looked forward to hanging Goering. As a matter of fact, I had stretched a rope for him six months before. . . . Rope was stretched on the basis of the weight of the man to be hanged. For example, Göring weighed 196 pounds. We attached 250 pounds of sand to a rope and dropped it thru the trap time and time again until it had been fully stretched. That was to make certain that when Göring himself was hanged there would be no give in the rope."[14]

Woods continued, discussing his return recently by troopship, stating, "One of the passengers on the boat coming over told me I would make a good Santa Claus."[15] In a sidebar, John went into a lengthy discussion concerning the men he hanged at Nürnberg.[16]

"I had no feeling that I was executing human beings when I executed war criminals. I could see before me the white crosses of the graves of my buddies who were killed at Omaha Beach. I went thru one concentration camp and saw something I will remember as long as I live. I saw the mutilated body of a woman who was about to become a mother. She had been cut open and maggots were eating her and the unborn baby. At Landsberg I executed 28 of the Nazis found guilty of that and other crimes. Do you think I had any feeling about executing them?

"These men were like animals—like black panthers. An animal is always ready to kill you regardless of what you do for him. If you happen to be in his way, he will kill you. The Nazis not only were animals—they were training other Germans to become animals and kill. Germany was becoming a whole nation of animals waiting for their prey."

John then switched gears and talked about his home life, laughing and saying, "while I'm in the Army, I'm the boss. While I'm at home, she's the boss," nodding to Hazel next to him. Woods then wrote a special editorial for the *Beacon* readers, which reflected a whole new side of the man who had dropped out of high school after just one year.[17]

Hanging Nazis Didn't End All Their Ideals
By M/S John C. Woods
Don't kid yourself—this war isn't over yet.

There are millions of people yet to be fed with winter coming on.

Holding things up like they are here in the states—such as the coal and other strikes—isn't helping things out a bit.

When a man, or a woman for that matter, won't fight for anything else, he'll fight for something to eat.

Our occupation forces in Europe have done a swell job so far, but if we don't stand back of them here, everything they've done will be ruined. As long as the Germans and the other countries and displaced persons are fed they will not cause any trouble.

But if we don't feed them, you can count on it, they'll be plenty of trouble. A man isn't going to let his family starve.

I have spent four years in the Army and three and a half years of that has been overseas. Before that I worked at Boeing and before that I did construction work with my father, Roy Woods. As a boy I sold Beacons at Market and Douglas.

Home Means a Lot
My trip home now is the first one in more than years. Home means just as much to those people in Europe. I would fight for my home and so would they. That's what we all fought for.

Soldiers come home and find this country torn up like it is and they wonder what the hell has been going on while they were overseas.

I don't know what the government plans to do about the strike situation now, but I know what we would have done in the Army if we had some of the strike leaders over there.

During the Battle of the Bulge my company went five days without any ammunition or food at all on account of such stuff as is going on in the United States right now.

When I hanged those Nazis, that didn't put an end to the ideas they had put in the people's mind.

Even up to the last minute of their lives, those men were arrogant. One of them—Streicher—even spit in my face.

Wanted to Make Showing

They wanted to make a good show so the German people would think they actually believed all the stuff they've been preaching.

When they were hanged there were representatives there from four countries including their own and they didn't want to show any weakness.

Now, if this nation shows weakness by letting a few people try to run it, the German people will be the first to begin thinking stronger than ever that their leaders—the ones I executed—were right and we are wrong.

If we let these strike leaders get away with some of the things they are trying, why wouldn't the German people think we are weak and for that reason think that their own leaders were that much stronger?

The majority of the soldiers look to our leaders over here as the greatest in the world, but now that I am over here, it begins to look to me as tho they are letting us down.

This is the time when America has a chance to prove that it is the greatest in the world and should set an example for the rest of the world if it is going to be the teacher.

Strike "Disgusting"

It was disgusting to me when I got back in the United States that every time I picked up a paper or talked to anyone, all I could find was strikes.

No one loves America better than I do: but I know that the other countries where I have been are looking to America for leadership and they are getting a poor example.

We wouldn't tolerate things like this in the Army—so why tolerate them in civilian life?

Thousands of our boys came back to go to work and couldn't even get a job.

I hope when my furlough ends and if I am sent back overseas or wherever I go that I can take back a message that things are better than they were when I got here last week. America is my home and it is a home of which I always want to be proud.

The tens of thousands who gave up their lives for this country would probably turn over in their graves if they could see how it is being run today.

• • •

The next few months were the happiest of John's life. Nieces and nephews would take the train from Toronto to Wichita and stay in John and Hazel's small basement apartment, amazed at a trundle bed that folded down from the wall. John, a voracious smoker, told jokes and mysteriously could blow smoke out of his ears, amazing the children.[18] He always wore his uniform, now pressed and neat; one nephew recalled that John even shined his shoes during the visits. A niece said that John "was very funny, always joking around and teasing."[19] A nephew recalled that "Uncle John" snored loudly when he slept. When awake, John found the time to speak to several civic groups.

John Woods took advantage of his three-month furlough and remained in Wichita until February 15, 1947. That Saturday night, he said goodbye to Hazel at Wichita's picturesque Union

Station and took a train to Ft. Dix, New Jersey.[20] When he departed, according to reporter Ernest A. Warden of the *Wichita Beacon*, Woods was unhappy; he disliked leaving his wife for a protracted period of time—which had first happened in 1943. However, he also had a premonition of impending disaster. Warden noticed that during their last meeting, one of the rare occasions when Woods did not have a grin on his face, the hangman lowered his voice and said, "I don't think I'll ever come back to Wichita alive again."[21]

This study concludes that Woods went east to Ft. Dix and possibly Ft. Belvoir for training as a senior noncommissioned officer in the Corps of Engineers. In 1944, he had been elevated from private to master sergeant, and he needed to be taught just what a senior noncommissioned officer needed to know and do. He departed the US on April 15, 1947, and probably arrived in Germany by ship about April 22, 1947.[22]

The question remains: What did Woods do in Europe from 1947 to 1948? A logical assumption could be that he resumed hanging American soldiers, German war criminals, or both. Reality is not that exotic. Woods was initially assigned to the 3rd Replacement Depot in Marburg, Germany; his roughly ten days there were probably spent in routine in-processing. The company morning report of May 2, 1947, for the 507th Engineer Service Company in Russelsheim, Germany, commanded by Capt. Daniel J. Murphy, stated that Woods joined this organization effective May 1, 1947.[23]

It was not to be a lengthy assignment for Woods. The company morning report for the same organization on May 8, 1947, showed that Woods was placed in detached service to the headquarters of the Greater Hesse area engineer for a period of eight days, although what this service would include was not mentioned. Whatever the duty was, Woods quickly returned to Russelsheim on May 16, 1947, according to the company morning report.[24] The following

week, on May 22, 1947, another company morning report placed Woods on temporary duty with the 559th Engineer Service Battalion, based in Gelnhausen, Germany, for an indefinite period, although the duration would prove short since the battalion inactivated on September 1, 1947.[25]

It is not clear when Woods rejoined the 507th Engineer Service Company. However, on June 20, 1947, the unit was redesignated the 507th Engineer Utility Company. This unit was in existence only a short time and was inactivated on September 1, 1947. Shortly thereafter, a special order from the 555th Engineer Composite Group, which until March 5, 1947, had been designated the 1103rd Engineer Combat Group, assigned Woods to Company B of the 1st Engineer Combat Battalion, in the US 1st Infantry Division, effective September 10, 1947.[26]

A later company morning report, dated October 1, 1947, for Company B, located in Kastel (Mainz-Kastel), Germany, shows Woods transferred again, this time to the 7801st Station Complement Unit of the 2nd Military District in Wetzlar, Germany.[27] Woods's specific duty would be with the Wetzlar post engineers, jacks of all trades who could fix plumbing, replace electrical wiring, repair heating units, conduct general contract construction—in short, fix anything on post when it broke or did not function correctly. Woods subsequently returned to Company B of the 1st Engineer Combat Battalion, which during the year served primarily at Grafenwöhr in Bavaria. In early 1948, Woods transferred again, this time to the 7809th Station Complement Unit (Heidelberg); he returned to the 1st Engineer Combat Battalion, under the command of Lt. Col. Eugene E. Moyers, on February 18, 1948. He would bounce back and forth between these two organizations for the next two months.[28]

Unfortunately, the frequency of the moves caused clerks of the company morning reports to have frequent headaches when they incorrectly reported Woods AWOL on several occasions.

These mistakes were finally rectified; it was a far cry from Woods's halcyon days as hangman. However, there was a silver lining to the problem, and he subsequently received a coveted twenty-one-day leave from his unit to be spent at Garmisch, Germany, on the mountainous border with Austria. He departed on leave on April 27 and returned on May 17, 1948. Two days later, Woods, with the assistance of his company commander Capt. Jasper N. Cohen, extended his three-year enlistment—which had been initiated on December 16, 1945, when he entered the Regular Army—to six years. This extension would extend John's Army service to December 1951.[29]

Woods remained in Company B until September 24, 1948, when the battalion assigned him to Headquarters and Service Company in Darmstadt, Germany. He still had until April 14, 1950, to serve in Germany, but perhaps he felt he was on borrowed time and that too many former Nazis still in the Fatherland were gunning for him. Whatever the reason, the Army soon transferred Woods back to the US, and he departed Germany for the last time on October 22, 1948, bound for the personnel center at Camp Kilmer, New Jersey.[30] Although John Woods hinted that he flew back to the US, he probably took a ship instead, which would have placed him at Camp Kilmer (an installation of the New York Port of Embarkation) about November 1. It is possible that Woods remained there for the next two weeks, or he could have traveled to Ft. Belvoir, the Corps of Engineers center.

His premonition about never making it alive back to Wichita had been incorrect. When Woods returned to Wichita on about November 20, 1948, he was interviewed by Ernest A. Warden about the imminent execution of Hideki Tojo, the former prime minister of Japan, during the war.[31] The International Military Tribunal for the Far East had sentenced Tojo to death on November 12, 1948, and "scuttlebutt" was rife concerning when the hanging would occur. At the end of the interview, Warden noted that in this latest stint

in Germany, Woods had been assigned to the "First Division," and that can only be the US 1st Infantry Division, "Big Red 1." Woods began the interview by discussing the impending execution: "I think I ought to get a crack at one of the big shots. . . . Whoever hangs Tojo will have a tough job on his hands. Those little fellows have to drop farther in order to break their neck. They just don't have the weight."[32]

"There has to be a representative of each nation present. Where the secrecy comes in is the time that the hanging will take place."

John Woods ended his discussion about Tojo's execution by opining that perhaps it would occur on December 7, 1948, the seventh anniversary of the attack on Pearl Harbor: "He pulled a sneak attack on us—why shouldn't we pull one on him?"[33]

Woods ended the interview by stating that he was under orders not to talk about his own recent activities in Germany—which appear to have been routine engineer duties—and expected to receive orders soon showing his next destination. He also indicated that he would be speaking to numerous civic groups in Wichita.[34] Woods would soon be proven incorrect in his speculation of the death of Hideki Tojo; the former Japanese leader was not hanged on December 7 but instead had a date with the hangman—not John—on December 23, 1948.

By then, Woods and his wife, Hazel, were not in Wichita. The two departed their home on Sunday, December 19, 1948, headed for Ft. Belvoir, Virginia. Hazel probably stayed at Ft. Belvoir until the following fall or the holiday season of 1949, when she traveled to Boise, Idaho, to visit two brothers and their families. Hazel told her family that Virginia was intolerably hot and humid. She had lost a significant amount of weight in the climate, stating, "It is too humid to even eat."[35]

Already, the lengthy separations of the couple during the war led Helen, Hazel's sister, to opine that perhaps the couple should get a divorce. In March 1950, the ever-hopeful Hazel Woods moved to 1708½ North 8th Street, in Boise, Idaho. Three brothers, John William, Max, and Kenneth, lived in Boise; Hazel later said that she and John had planned to settle there when he retired from the Army in November 1951. Anna Dale, the daughter of Hazel's brother Dale, recalled that John was a good letter writer to Hazel; his correspondence mentioned that he was enjoying his work, and he also told funny stories of Army life.[36]

• • •

Whether John Woods realized it or not, his time had passed as the preeminent US Army hangman. In the Pacific, the Army had found a different hangman, who would obey orders, keep his mouth shut, and search for more-innovative ways to successfully complete the difficult job of hanging a man. An MP officer, 2Lt. Charles C. Rexroad, seemed to be everything that John Woods was not; his award recommendation in September 1946— weeks before Woods hanged the ten top Nazis at Nürnberg—clearly shows those qualifications.[37]

"As executioner for all condemned War Criminals in AFWESPAC [US Army Forces, Western Pacific] Lt. Rexroad has been given an unusual, unique, extremely trying and exacting assignment which requires an officer of certain definite and decided qualifications. In addition, Lt. Rexroad has been assigned a T/O position as Motor Officer of the 795th MP Bn. In both assignments this officer has displayed unusual attentiveness to and diligence in the execution of his designated duties. He is an officer of Merit distinguished by his ingenuity, aggressiveness in attacking the problem; he is level headed, stable under pressure and exacting in all details concerning his own duties and those of his subordinates.

"As executioner, Lt. Rexroad has executed thirty-four (34) War Criminals, thirty-two (32) by hanging and two (2) by Musketry. The techniques of hanging have been altered and reorganized in many ways due to the detailed analysis of methods employed. Thru a change in rigging of the gallows he has halved the time required in execution by

hanging in that he has made it possible to complete four (4) hangings in the period of one (1) hour rather than four (4) hangings in the period of two (2) hours as required by former methods.

"He has eliminated the 'hangman knot' and substituted a plain loop with a wooden sliding keeper resulting in a sharper impact and distinct and definite severance of the spinal cord, reducing the average dying time by four (4) minutes.

"With his personal training of his subordinates he has eliminated the confusion and delay incident to a matter of this kind. The condemned are brought to the gallows and dropped thru the trap in a maximum time of seven (7) to eight (8) seconds reducing thereby mental cruelty and suspense to the condemned. This officer approached every assignment without thought of self and in a deliberate, calm and resourceful manner characteristic of him."[38]

• • •

Meanwhile, the last Army unit to which Woods would be assigned was the newly formed 7th Engineer Brigade at Ft. Belvoir, which was activated on October 22, 1948, under the command of Col. Charles H. McNutt.[39] A month later, the brigade was assigned to the US 3rd Army; under this command, the brigade was located at Camp Gordon, Georgia, from January 4, 1949, to November 15, 1949, when the unit was relieved from the US 3rd Army and reassigned back to the chief of engineers at Ft. Belvoir. Brig. Gen. Frederick B. Butler assumed command of the unit on December 5, 1949. However, the unit would not be assigned to the chief of engineers for long; effective January 1, 1950, the brigade was subordinated to an obscure organization titled Joint Task Force Three.[40]

According to the official company morning report of Headquarters and Headquarters Company (commanded by Captain Willard C. Taft) of the 7th Engineer Brigade, Master Sergeant John C. Woods was assigned to that organization on January

12, 1950.[41] He had been previously assigned to the 7071st ASU (Area Support Unit), a personnel administration battalion at Fort Belvoir. While in this battalion, Woods received a set of movement orders for selected officers and noncommissioned officers, dated January 4, 1950, which indicated that John would depart individually (privately owned automobile authorized) from Ft. Belvoir on January 19, 1950, and travel to Camp Stoneman, California, as part of the 7th Engineer Brigade. He was authorized to take six days leave along the way; his address while on this leave was listed as 1312 6th Street, Boise, Idaho. Should John choose not to take leave, he understood that he was to arrive at Camp Stoneman during daylight hours on February 6, 1950.[42]

Meanwhile, the bulk of the brigade traveled by train to California, and from February to April–May 1950, the engineers prepared for overseas deployment at Camp Stoneman, located between Oakland and Sacramento. The brigade advance party departed San Francisco on January 25, 1950, for Joint Task Force Three.[43] Another brigade element departed Camp Stoneman by ferry at 6:15 a.m. on March 4, 1950. Woods was almost certainly in this contingent. Once at the San Francisco port of embarkation, the soldiers boarded the USAT Gen. A. W. Brewster and began their journey across the Pacific.[44] A photograph indicates that Woods arrived at Eniwetok on March 16, 1950.[45] The rest of the brigade sailed later on the USS Zelima, an Alstedes stores ship, bound for the same destination.[46]

Headquarters and Headquarters Company was a relatively small organization; on any given day, the unit had roughly thirty-three officers and 188 enlisted men. These men, many of them senior noncommissioned officers, would provide much of the technical expertise; the actual muscle would come from attached battalions. The 7th Engineer Brigade had the 79th Engineer Construction Battalion as its major construction force. The battalion, which had fought in World War II in the New Guinea and Philippine campaigns

and then participated in the occupation of Japan until 1947, when it returned to Hawaii for deactivation, was reactivated on February 28, 1949, at Ft. Sill, Oklahoma. The battalion departed from Ft. Sill on February 5, 1950, for Camp Stoneman. On March 16, 1950, also on the USAT Gen. A. W. Brewster, it arrived at Joint Task Force Three—to prepare existing air base facilities for greater capabilities.

That's what members of the general public were led to believe, but it wasn't correct—not by a long shot.

Joint Task Force Three (JTF-3) was not interested in improving simple air base facilities; JTF-3 was interested in testing atomic bombs and business was booming. On December 2, 1947, US authorities announced that tiny Eniwetok Atoll in the Pacific would be used for a series of nuclear tests, and that its inhabitants would be moved immediately to Ujelang Atoll, which had only one-fourth the land area of Eniwetok. In April 1948, Operation Sandstone began on Eniwetok, consisting of atomic bomb tests on April 14, April 30, and May 14 of that year.

In charge of the testing facility on Eniwetok in 1950 was JTF-3, under command of Lt. Gen. Elwood R. "Pete" Quesada, who had commanded the 9th Air Force in the skies over Normandy in 1944 and was one of the true fathers of close air support. It had its administrative headquarters located in the Main Navy Building in Washington, DC, but had an operational headquarters on Parry Islet (now Medren) in the Eniwetok Atoll. After the war, Quesada had become the first commander of the Tactical Air Command. But the mercurial Quesada quickly found that most of the new US Air Force's emphasis was on the heavy Strategic Air Command. After numerous run-ins with superiors, Pete Quesada was put in charge of the Joint Technical Planning Committee for the Joint Chiefs of Staff in September 1949. In November 1949, Quesada was elevated to command JTF-3, which had been activated on November 1, just before it assumed control of the 7th Engineer Brigade.[47] General Quesada had to hustle the troops on Eniwetok since Operation Greenhouse—the first true tests of thermonuclear fusion—was just around the corner.

The Army component of JTF-3 was Task Group 3.2, commanded by Brig. Gen. Don G. Shingler; he also had assumed command of the 7th Engineer Brigade. This task group had its operational headquarters located at Eniwetok Islet, the largest island of the atoll. Given that force projections assumed that the total number of military and civilian personnel on Eniwetok Atoll would be 3,000 men, existing facilities were abysmal, but over the next two years, engineers constructed 197 buildings and poured 450,000 square yards of asphalt. Permanent power-generating facilities would ultimately produce 3,000 kilowatts, although that was not enough, and six smaller portable generators, each of 75 kilowatts, were placed into operation.

• • •

It was power generation expertise that would involve MSgt. John C. Woods.

During the hours of darkness, at approximately 10:30 p.m. on July 21, 1950, on Eniwetok Islet, Woods was called to fix a faulty electrical line running from a power source in a small shed (known as the tool shack) to a light set at a nearby quarry. As a result of the damaged electrical line, the lights in the light set had been extinguished. Because the mission of the engineers at the quarry was round the clock, power and light needed for quarry operations had to be restored and restored quickly.[48]

The quarry was much different than those in the continental US. Eniwetok has an average elevation of only 10 feet above sea level, so the quarry was not a deep pit. It did not have to be, since Army engineers there mined coral—not rock—as a substitute for cement, so the latter heavy material would not have to be shipped in from other locations. At high tide, seawater flowed into parts of the floor of the quarry, which was

located in the northeast corner of Eniwetok Islet and extended to a coral reef in the ocean. The quarry was close to the bachelor officers' quarters.

The problem appears to have occurred more than once, since on two occasions, Woods went to the shack and carefully turned the switch controlling the flow of electricity to the lights to an "off" position prior to returning to work on the damaged line. With the electricity now off, Woods moved to the break in the line and began repairing it.[49] Unknown to the soldiers at the line break, however, Cpl. Ernest L. Blanchard of Company A of the 79th Engineer Construction Battalion—who normally worked in another section of the rock quarry—came on duty with the next work shift. Due to the darkness, Blanchard was unable to see Woods and his team down in the quarry. Although nothing in the report reflects the distance between the shack and the line break, it was apparently substantial enough that Blanchard also could not hear the men at the line break talking.[50]

According to 1Lt. Avery L. Granger—who had been appointed the incident investigating officer early on July 22 by Task Group 3.2 chief of staff Col. Samuel N. Lowry—Cpl. Blanchard entered the shack, located the appropriate switch, and threw it to the "on" position. The lengthy Army report of the incident stated that this act caused the current to flow through the line and electrocute Woods. The file stated that the switch was subsequently checked and "found to be in good working order." The bulk of the witnesses interviewed supported the assumption that Blanchard acted in good faith and that he should be absolved of any responsibility on the tragic incident.[51] The following is Blanchard's official statement: "My name is Ernest L. Blanchard, RA11144666, Corporal, Company A, 79th Engineer Construction Battalion. My duty in the rock quarry is Chief Driller. My crew was supposed to be to work on 21 July 1950, the night of the accident. I left the tool shack with Corporal [Calvin H] Mahone at approximately 2220 hours [10:20 p.m.] to go to chow. We hadn't started working yet. When we left the quarry the lights were on. On our way back to the quarry, at approximately 2245 hours [10:45 p.m.] we met Sergeant Adkins and another soldier. Sergeant Adkins is one of the crane operators. When we got to the quarry all the lights were out except those on the crane. We wanted to get set up to drill. I took my fatigue jacket and hung it up behind the tool shack, then entered the tool shack to switch on the lights. I hadn't seen anyone on the reef. I no sooner threw the switch when Private [Richard G.] Griffin came running up shouting, 'Somebody, come with me. Turn off the switch. Woods is dead. Get an ambulance.' I immediately turned off the switch; [I] then ran to the Company B Orderly Room to call the ambulance. I then ran out to Lagoon Road to direct the ambulance to the quarry."[52]

The aforementioned Pvt. Richard G. Griffin also made a statement, which added valuable details of the incident: "My name is Richard G. Griffen, RA17260969, Private, Company A, 79th Engineer Construction Battalion. I work in the quarry at Eniwetok. Just before we quit hauling rock on the night of 21 July 1950, two lights went out. I told Sergeant Woods about it and he said that we would have to fix them because the drillers were going to work. He sent me after two light bulbs because he thought the other two were burned out. We put the two new bulbs in but they still didn't work. We started to check the line running to the switch box and I saw where it was broken and told Sergeant Woods. He told me to turn the switch off. I did, and then went into the building next to the one the switch is located in to get some friction tape and a pair of pliers. When I came out of the building Sergeant Woods hollered to turn the switch off. I told him I had already done it but he said some current was coming through so he came up and turned it off again. We went back down to splice the wire. He was telling me about some man that got killed by working with electricity in water. About that time I felt a shock and threw my wire down. Sergeant

Woods screamed and fell backwards into the water. I yelled to Corporal Blanchard to call the ambulance. He took off and I called to Corporal Mahone to hold the switch down. Mahone and someone else then pulled Woods out of the water. I don't know who the other man was. In just a few minutes the ambulance came, the Medics gave Sergeant Woods artificial respiration."[53]

The story about the man standing in water was pure Woods. He was always telling anecdotes, and that made him popular with other enlisted men, if not always with the officers. PFC Thomas W. Sanders made a statement that added no additional details other than after the incident, he and two other men carried Woods's body to the beach a few minutes before the doctor arrived.[54] PFC Jacob H. Rasely also made a statement, which added a key point that at the incident site, Capt. Robert S. Tolmach, the surgeon for Task Group 3.2, instructed Rasely to take the jeep to the dispensary and get a resuscitator.[55]

Capt. Robert S. Tolmach submitted an official statement the next day that certified that the cause of death of MSgt. Woods was electrical shock and that the time of death was 10:55 p.m. on July 21.[56] Pvt. Justin C. Smith of Company A provided a short statement that confirmed details in the other statements and added that after Woods yelled, he fell backward into the water.[57] Finally, Cpl. Calvin H. Mahone of Company A submitted his statement. He did not actually see Woods get shocked, but when he quickly went to the scene, Woods was "floating in the water, face up."[58]

The company morning report for Headquarters and Headquarters Company of the 7th Engineer Brigade was the initial official document that dealt with the death of John C. Woods. Prepared late the night of the incident, the report read: "Woods, John C., RA37540591, M/Sgt, Duty to died by electric shock sustained at Rock Quarry, Eniwetok, Marshall Islands, LD [line of duty] Yes."[59]

First Lt. Avery L. Granger finished his report in several hours, and the same day Brig. Gen. Don G. Shingler approved and signed the report of investigation. In his half page of findings, Lt. Granger stated the following: an enlisted man had thrown the unguarded switch to the "on" position, the accident was not the result of gross negligence, and there was no indication of foul play. The Army shipped Woods's body by air to Hawaii, where an extensive autopsy confirmed that electricity had indeed killed John Woods.[60]

• • •

However, buried deep in the voluminous report was a crucial statement made by 1Lt. Forest K. Weaver, a platoon leader in Company B of the 79th Engineer Construction Battalion, and the supervisor of the electrical shop on Eniwetok. Forest stated that at 11:10 p.m. (twelve minutes after Woods had been electrocuted), he was in the mess hall and was told to go to Company B immediately, but was not told why. He departed the mess hall about 11:14 p.m., returned to the electrical shop, and called Company B; the answering soldier from that unit reported that a soldier had just been electrocuted.[61]

First Lt. Weaver then went to Company B and spoke with two soldiers who said that they had been with Woods at the rock quarry when Woods had noticed a short circuit in the wire near the waterline in the quarry, and that the men then went to the shack, "pulled the switch," and returned to the location of the short circuit. Noticing that the wires were "still hot," Woods returned to the shack and carefully turned the switch off himself and then went back out and started "skinning the wires" to repair the break, when he yelled and fell back into the water. One of the men quickly returned to the shack, where he found the switch to be in the "on" position, pulled the switch, and went back to the accident location, and then the two men pulled Woods out of the water.[62]

Later that night, Lt. Col. Walsh, commander of the 79th Engineer Construction Battalion, asked 1Lt. Weaver to check the switch on the generator. Weaver took a voltmeter and checked the switch both in the "off" and "on" position. Weaver wrote in his statement that "I took a voltmeter and checked the switch in an "on" position and an "off" position. When I found the switch to be "off" there was no voltage across the terminals at any time. *After checking the switch with the voltmeter, I found the voltage to be 110 Volts while the switch was on and 113 Volts when it was off*" [emphasis added].[63]

What exactly had happened? Weaver's statement is confusing; did he make two checks of the system or only one? This study showed Weaver's statement to Rich and John Closs, co-owners of Closs Electric; both men have over fifty years' experience as qualified electricians. Both men read the entire statement and first discussed Lt. Forest Weaver's procedure in measuring the power switch.[64]

"The statement seems to indicate that First Lieutenant Weaver measured the voltage in the switch twice, the second time with a voltmeter, although if he checked it without a voltmeter, we are not sure how he accomplished this. He needed to measure the current from the terminal to a ground; that would have been a proper measurement. And to get these numbers, 110 and 113, he had to measure correctly. If he measured across the terminals, instead of a ground, there would have been no current across them, and that may be what he was inferring in the first part of his statement."

Both men then agreed concerning the serviceability of the switch.[65]

"Our conclusion is that if the voltmeter was operating properly and if Lieutenant Weaver operated the voltmeter properly, then the switch was faulty. What cannot be determined from this statement is how long the switch had been faulty; in other words, when did it go bad?"

The experienced electricians then offered an opinion on the investigation.[66]

"At the very least, Weaver's statement is ambiguous and the investigating officer, First

Lieutenant Granger, should have gone back to First Lieutenant Weaver and asked him to better explain what he did and what he found. Then, Granger should have expanded the investigation and focused on equipment failure at the switch, rather than concentrate on the soldier who flipped the switch to the "on" position, while Master Sergeant Woods was fixing the line. With a faulty switch, in which current flowed in either the "on" or the "off" position, it did not matter how Cpl. Blanchard set the switch—there was going to be current going through the line to the lights in the rock quarry."

John and Rich Closs then offered opinions on the current itself, on the basis of their experience, including a few times of being shocked.[67]

"You know, 110 volts is not a lot; we would have thought it would have been much higher. Current is what kills you. Current is directly proportional to the voltage and inversely proportional to the resistance. Add in the resistance of the line, say a couple of hundred feet from the generator. They would have had to have a 30-amp circuit. We have been shocked by 110 volts before and it is not a pleasant experience. The length of the wire from the power source is going to help Woods survive, the longer it is. However, Woods was standing in water and that certainly is not going to help him, but in our experience, that amount of current is not necessarily lethal."

Armed with only this knowledge, both men came to a tentative conclusion that Woods's death was accidental, but that the root cause was faulty equipment, not human error by Cpl. Blanchard.

• • •

A day after the incident at Eniwetok, the *Wichita Beacon* reported Woods's death but provided scant details.[68] On July 28, 1950, the death of John C. Woods was reported in the *Stars & Stripes*, European Edition, on page 3:

Nurnberg Hangman Killed in Accident

BOISE, Ida,, July 27 (AP)—Hazel Woods, wife of the Army sergeant who hanged the Nazi war criminals after the Nurnberg trials, said yesterday her husband had been accidentally electrocuted.

Mrs. Woods said the Army had informed her that her husband, M/Sgt John C. Woods, was killed last week on Eniwetok Atoll in the Marshall Islands. No details were given.

Mrs. Woods came here, where three of her brothers reside, in March. She said her husband's home was Wichita, Kan., but they had planned to make their home here when he was discharged.

• • •

Anna Dale, who was age nine at the time, was present with "Aunt Hazel" in Boise when the official telegram arrived stating that John was dead. A Western Union deliveryman brought the telegram to the residence. Hazel opened the message, quickly scanned it, and fainted—falling to the floor. Anna Dale ran to get an adult, who revived Hazel, but the distraught new widow fainted several more times over the next few minutes.[69]

Meanwhile, the military flew Woods's remains to Hawaii for an autopsy, which was performed at 4:00 p.m. on July 25, 1950—almost four days after the incident—by Capt. John K. Frost at Tripler Army Hospital. His summary, approved by Maj. Gilbert B. Stansell, chief of laboratory service, reads as follows: "The anatomical findings in this case are minimal. They are listed to a very mild atheromatosis of the aorta, a few well-healed plural adhesions, and various superficial injuries to the skin and subcutaneous tissue. No cause of death is thus demonstrable. However, the two areas of dessicated necrosis present within the tissues over the left clavicle and the multiple, ruptured papules over the lower legs, are not only compatible with but highly suggestive of electrical injury. The lack of tissue reaction at the margins of the areas indicates that the injury did not long precede death. The probable cause of death is electrocution."[70]

After the autopsy, technicians Reynold F. Reep and Jean S. Bilbe embalmed the body at the US mortuary at Tripler Army Hospital.[71] After the procedure, authorities placed the remains in a casket, which was delivered to Hickam Field. An aircraft numbered 6535, flight number C-51A-30, with the remains of John C. Woods (and PFC Merle C. Dockery of the US Air Force, whose death was unrelated), departed Hickam Field at 1:30 p.m. on August 1, 1950. The aircraft arrived at Fairfield-Suisun Airfield (now Travis Air Force Base, California) at 1:30 a.m. on August 2, 1950.

The story of the bizarre death of the former Army hangman hit the mainstream press stateside a week later, in "Armed Forces: Hangman's End" (*Time*, August 7, 1950). The account reads as follows: "In postwar Germany, husky, bull-necked Master Sergeant John C. Woods of San Antonio had gone about his business with a craftsman's pride and enthusiasm. As official US hangman, he credited himself with more than three hundred successful executions, topped off his career four years ago by hanging ten of the Nazi leaders condemned in the Nürnberg trials. "Never saw a hanging go off any better," he said cheerfully afterwards. He was not disturbed when bald, squat Julius Streicher, the Jew baiter, had snarled at him: "The Bolsheviks will hang you, too, some day.

"But, as time went by, Hangman Woods was more and more disturbed by the way the German people began to look at him. He took to packing two .45s, remarked loudly, "If some German thinks he wants to get me, he better make sure he does it with his first shot, because I was raised with a pistol in my hand." Once, just after chow in an Army mess, he turned violently ill, was certain the German cooks had poisoned him. He was delighted when the Army returned him to the US, felt better still last March when it shipped him half a world away from Germany, to duty on Eniwetok Atoll in the mid-Pacific.

Then, the Army reported tersely last week, Hangman Woods died. Cause of death: accidental electrocution."[72]

●●●

A hearse transported Woods's body to the port mortuary in San Francisco, where it was transferred to the Oakland Army Base. Hazel took a train to California and escorted the remains by train back to Wichita.[73] The train arrived at Wichita at 3:24 p.m. on August 12, 1950, and the casket was promptly transported to the Broadway Mortuary. At 10:00 a.m. on August 14, 1950, one hundred visitors attended Woods's funeral at the mortuary chapel. Chaplain William H. Teed, of the Wichita Veterans Hospital, delivered the sermon, during which the flag-draped coffin was open. Musical selections in the half-hour ceremony included "In the Sweet By and By" and "Lord, I Am Coming to Thee," which Hazel Woods said were her husband's favorites. The six pallbearers included Fred Woods, Wilbur Woods, Floyd Gunsaullus, Jack Garrett, George Lanning, and George Magruder. After the ceremony, a hearse drove the remains to Toronto, Kansas, where members of the American Legion post conducted the burial with the family in attendance.[74] John Woods was buried in his uniform at the Toronto Cemetery, Toronto, Kansas.[75]

●●●

Then rumors began to surface that John Woods's death may not have been accidental. A Kansas newspaper article with the heading "Did Nazi Kill Hangman of Hitler Gang?" reported that *Ici Paris*, a French magazine founded in 1941, reported that Woods had been killed on July 25, when an electric chair exploded as he was preparing for another execution. The magazine added that the incident had been carefully arranged by German scientists who had been recruited after the surrender of Nazi Germany, may still have been faithful to the Third Reich, and were working on atomic research at Eniwetok. Within weeks, the story appeared in newspapers from Lubbock, Texas, to Columbus, Indiana. German magazine

Der Spiegel piled on in an article stating that after John Woods left Germany and returned to the US, he joined the "intelligence service," but he was unsatisfied with that duty and so returned to execution duties using an electric chair. *Der Spiegel* continued that before the first execution with the device, Woods switched on the current and received a lethal shock of 25,000 volts.[76]

Army officials dismissed the reports, but their obtuse reply of "your version is incorrect, but further information on the subject is barred for security reasons" did nothing to quell imaginations. After he retired from the service, Pete Quesada added to the firestorm in a 1956 interview with journalist Bob Considine about Eniwetok, when he stated, "'The only man we lost on that job,' Quesada remembered today. 'And one of the strangest stories I've ever encountered.' I asked him why. 'The sergeant was the executioner at Nuremburg,' Pete said."[77]

What did Gen. Quesada mean? Did strangest mean macabre or that the circumstances surrounding the incident did not add up?

Virg Hill of the *Topeka Capital* quoted that the *London News of the World* had an even more interesting story concerning Woods's death, indicating that a Nazi underground agent on Eniwetok had caused the fatality. Hill quoted the British newspaper as writing that "Almost everywhere in the world there were men who swore death to Woods. Wherever he went, this man who brought justice to the Fuehrer's lieutenants was specially guarded by American authorities. He always carried with him a pair of loaded revolvers."

• • •

The last sentence was pure Hollywood, but was this accusation of murder pure fantasy? Herman Obermayer thought not. Fifty years after the hangman's death and armed with a copy of the death investigation and autopsy findings, Obermayer enlisted the assistance of several retired forensic

pathologists, who independently found that intentional causing of death could not be ruled out. They noted that the sheer magnitude of the investigative report was quite unusual for an enlisted soldier. They did opine that the electric-chair episode was pure fantasy and that Woods had been killed by the electricity passing through the wire from the generator to the light set.[78]

"Obe" believed that if the death was intentional, it was not at the hands of a fellow American soldier, for the simple reason that in his experience, every fellow soldier liked Woods and there were only Americans on the atoll. Then "Obe" began to pry into Operation Paperclip, a secret Joint Intelligence Objectives Agency (JIOA) program to bring over 1,600 German scientists, technicians, and engineers to the US for government employment, beginning at the end of World War II. Although many of these men had been members and, in a few cases, significant leaders of the Nazi Party, that hindrance was overshadowed by the prerequisite to gain US military advantage in the budding Cold War and the future race into space. The US started with a position of disadvantage, since the Soviet Union's recruiting of German scientific talent, in its own Operation Osoaviakhim, used coercive tactics that the West would not entertain.

The program, originally termed called Operation Overcast, began on July 20, 1945. By November 1945, authorities changed the name to Operation Paperclip; according to project lore, this new name was based on US Army Ordnance Corps recruiting officers, who would attach a paper clip to the folders of those German experts whom they wished to employ in the US or its territories. By March 1947, over four hundred Germans had been hired. Each participant was to be thoroughly vetted, but those who had lived or worked in what had become East Germany (which in 1949 assumed the name German Democratic Republic [*Deutsche Demokratische Republik*]) were difficult to investigate.

It was Herman Obermayer's theory that some of these Operation Paperclip men were on

Eniwetok Atoll in 1950, helping prepare for additional atomic bomb testing. He knew that in Operation Sandstone, three weapons had been detonated in 1948: a 37-kiloton burst on April 14 at Engebi Islet, a 49-kiloton burst on April 30 at Aomon Islet, and an 18-ton burst on May 14 at Runit Islet. He also knew that the next series of atomic tests at Eniwetok did not occur until April 1951, although on November 29, 1949, the Department of Defense and the Atomic Agency Commission notified President Harry Truman that a new series of weapons tests were being planned at Eniwetok Atoll, which probably is why the 7th Engineer Brigade began deploying there just three months later. "Obe" also knew that most of the buildings and other structures on Eniwetok Atoll were concentrated on two small islets, Eniwetok and Parry; at the apex of the program, six hundred persons were on Parry and three thousand on Eniwetok, although there were many fewer present in July 1950.[79] Island residents had been relocated away from the atoll.

Personnel generally lived in large tents or aluminum Quonset huts; to improve morale, Eniwetok would have had a library, a hobby shop, several movie theaters, a gymnasium, three athletic fields, and several clubs. The smaller Parry Islet had a community club, 400-person mess hall, small base-exchange store, and an open-air theater.[80] Today, the total landmass of all islets in the atoll is only 2.26 square miles, and while some of the land of the atoll was destroyed in atomic tests, it was never large.

Herman Obermayer believed that the livable space on Eniwetok was so small that if there were any German scientists present there in July 1950, they were bound to recognize Woods, whose photos had appeared worldwide in 1946. Thus, they would have had motive, means, and opportunity to assassinate him; not all the Germans would have been aware of the attempt against Woods—a small group or even a single individual could have killed him in revenge for his execution of Germans after the war. And so "Obe" scoured

the archives and submitted numerous Freedom of Information Act (FOIA) requests to find answers to three questions:

1. What German technicians were present on Eniwetok on July 21, 1950?

2. Were any of these Germans disciplined for any infraction during this period or were they transferred off the atoll after this date?

3. Where are the personnel files of these men and how could they be examined?

Herman Obermayer, biographer and close friend of Chief Justice William Rehnquist, former owner and publisher of the *Long Branch* (New Jersey) *Daily Record* and the *Northern Virginia Sun*, and cum laude graduate from Dartmouth College, was stonewalled. It wasn't malicious, more like benign neglect in collecting and maintaining the files. Attempt after attempt to obtain information on Operation Paperclip personnel on Eniwetok ended more with a whimper than a bang. Since the operation had formally ended in 1990, many of the documents and files associated with it were still under wraps. And although several Operation Paperclip personnel were later investigated because of their wartime activities, no German scientist or engineer was found guilty of any crime, in the United States or Germany—or Eniwetok. The personnel files are available today but are not organized concerning where each man worked; visits to the National Archives could not find any lists of German engineers at the atoll.

During the years that I knew him, "Obe" did not mention if he had any electrical experts weigh in on the findings of 1Lt. Forest K. Weaver and his voltmeter. I did not question the findings then, since I had not read the investigation report cover to cover in research for *The Fifth Field* because Woods's fate was not part of that effort.

However, during the interview with senior electricians John and Rich Closs, I showed them information concerning the level of expertise of the German scientists and engineers on Operation Paperclip. I then posed a question to them: Could one of these German electrical specialists have been behind the electrocution of Woods—in other words, could this incident have been intentionally caused? The brothers looked skyward, whistled, and began thinking out loud:[81]

Well, the perpetrator would need to have access to the switch beforehand so he could modify it so that the current would flow through it regardless of the position to which it was set. Then he would have to have another device—maybe some kind of circuit breaker along the line between the generator and the line break in the quarry that he could use to turn the current off when he wanted it and on when he wanted. He would have to know that Woods was the guy who was splicing the line, so he would have to know the routine of who fixed generator current issues at night. And he would have to be able to be close enough to see it was Woods on the line, so he could turn on his own switch and let the current flow to the break as soon as Woods started splicing the wire.

Right now, nothing in the report suggests that, so right now it was most likely that it was a mechanical fault in the switch, not a human error of the corporal who turned the switch on. *Having said that, a swift German electrical engineer could have come up with something like this or even something we would never think of to make it look like an accident* [emphasis added].

It all comes down to means, motive, and opportunity. This study concludes that all three were present on Eniwetok Atoll that late night in July 1950. What is lacking, however, is more than a general category of perpetrator, and currently we cannot identify those Operation Paperclip personnel who were present that night on Eniwetok, or any individual ever suspected of murdering the American hangman.

The American Hangman. Iconic photograph of MSgt. John C. Woods. *Source: public domain*

Just a year ago Master Sergeant John C. Woods did the most famous hanging job in history. Strictly a business man he's still on the job

Hangman

Top of the world. After the Nürnberg executions, Woods became well known around the world. This first page of an article in *True, The Man's Magazine*, with the bright-red title "Hangman," was seen by millions. The seahorse patch on his right breast was a pocket badge by US Engineer amphibious personnel, and the shoulder patch is the Engineer Special Brigade sleeve insignia; Woods served in the 5th Engineer Special Brigade at Normandy. *Source: Original photograph taken by* Wichita Beacon; *subsequently used by* True; *photos appear courtesy of the* Wichita Eagle / www.Kansas.com

Sgt. Richard Mosley. Serving as a prisoner escort for six executions in which Woods worked as the assistant hangman, he tragically died in 1953. *Source: Mosley family*

Period photograph of Wichita High School. Woods attended the school for one year. *Source: public domain*

Hazel Chilcott in high school. Photo taken about 1930. *Source: Linda Clark and Carol Stark, nieces of Hazel*

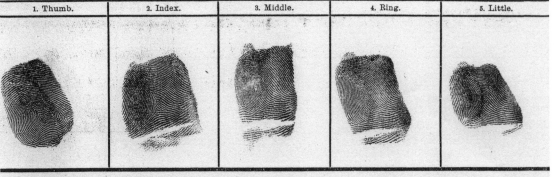

Classification No. _____

RIGHT HAND.

4—1128

1. Thumb.	2. Index.	3. Middle.	4. Ring.	5. Little.

LEFT HAND.

6. Thumb.	7. Index.	8. Middle.	9. Ring.	10. Little.

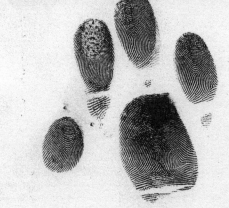

LEFT HAND.
Plain impression of the four fingers taken simultaneously and of the thumb.

RIGHT HAND.
Plain impression of the four fingers taken simultaneously and of the thumb.

Apprentice Seaman John C. Woods's fingerprints, taken while Woods was in the US Navy in 1929–30. *Source: US Navy personnel file on Apprentice Seaman John C. Woods*

Lt. Col. Lionel F. Smith. The brave officer, killed in action on Omaha Beach on June 6, 1944, commanded of the 37th Engineer Combat Battalion, to which Woods was assigned. *Source: Susan Keener on Find A Grave website*

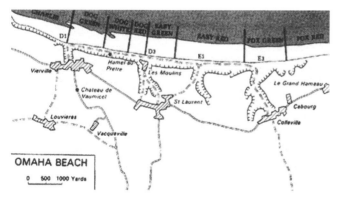

Map of Omaha Beach for June 6, 1944. Woods's unit assaulted Easy Red beach, but nothing about the operation was easy. *Source: US Army Center for Military History*

Grave of Paul M. Kluxdal. Woods served as the assistant hangman for the seriously botched hanging. Grave is located adjacent to the American Military Cemetery of Oise-Aisne at Seringes-et-Nesles, France, in what is called "Plot E" and "the Fifth Field." *Source: author, 2011*

Sgt. Earl E. Mendenhall. Mendenhall (*top left*) had the stressful duty of escorting five prisoners to the gallows in 1944; photo taken in 1942 in Iceland. *Source: Bruce Mendenhall*

Execution site of Leo Valentine Sr. and Oscar Newman. Woods served as the assistant hangman for both men at Beaunay, France, on November 29, 1944. *Source: author, 2011*

Execution site of Walter James Baldwin. Woods hanged Baldwin on January 17, 1945, at Beaufay, France, for the crime of murder. It took Baldwin seventeen minutes to die. *Source: author, 2011*

Execution site of John David Cooper and J. P. Wilson. For Wilson, the trapdoor would not open immediately, but Woods acted quickly and Wilson dropped. *Source: author, 2011*

Execution site of Amos Agee, John C. Smith, and Frank Watson. Woods hanged all three at La Saussaye, France, on March 3, 1945, for rape. *Source: author, 2011*

Execution site of William C. Downes. Woods hanged Downes at Étienville, France, on February 28, 1945. *Source: author, 2011*

Execution site of Olin W. Williams. Woods hanged Williams at Le Chene Daniel, France, on March 29, 1945, for rape and murder. It took Williams thirteen minutes to die. *Source: author, 2011*

Execution site of John Williams, James L. Jones, and Milbert Bailey. Woods hanged all three on April 19, 1945, at La Pernelle, France, for rape and murder. *Source: author, 2011*

HEADQUARTERS
LOIRE DISCIPLINARY TRAINING CENTER
APO 562, U.S. Army

26 March 1945

AG 300.4

SUBJECT : Orders.

TO   : Officers and Enlisted Men Concerned.

The following named O and EM, Hq Loire Dis Tng Cen, 286th MP Co, and 94th QM Trk Bn, WP, o/a 27 Mar 1945, to Le Chene Daniel, A'Cherence Le Heron, France, and thence to Prise Guinment, France, on temp dy not to exceed four (4) days, to carry out the instructions of the Commanding General, Hq ETOUSA. Upon completion of such dy, these O and EM will return to proper sta. Govt T atzd.

Lt Col	HENRY L. PECK,	O-289263, CMP
Capt	MILTON B. ASBELL,	O-472209, DC
M/Sgt	John C. Woods,	37540591
Tec 3	Thomas F. Robinson,	32555124
Sgt	Russell E. Boyle,	36721587
Sgt	Jack D. Briscoe,	38051551
Sgt	Alfonso Girvalo,	32316672
Tec 5	George H. Garnand,	38395128
Pvt	William Reynolds,	35655164

(Auth: Cir 113, Hq ETOUSA, dtd 22 Nov 1944.)
TDN TCNT 60-114 P 432-02 A 212/50425.

By order of Lt Colonel PECK:

K. M. CASHION, JR.
Captain, CMP,
Adjutant.

OFFICIAL:

K. M. CASHION, JR.
Captain, CMP,
Adjutant.

DISTRIBUTION: 2 - CG, NBS
               1 - PM, NBS
               1 - CO, Southern Dist.
               1 - CO, 286th MP Co
               1 - CO, 94th QM Trk Bn
               2 - Ea O and EM conc
               1 - File

Orders sending personnel to an execution. There is no mention of an execution, only to "carry out the instructions of the commanding general." Woods hanged Tommie Davison and Olin Williams on March 29, 1945. *Source: US Army records*

Grave of Benjamin F. Hopper. Woods hanged Hopper on April 11, 1945, at the Loire DTC at Le Mans, France, for murder; it took Hopper twenty-three minutes to die. *Source: author, 2011*

Grave of Matthew Clay, Jr. Woods hanged Clay on June 4, 1945, at Fontenay-sur-Mer, France, for murder. "The condemned man cried, whimpered and faltered during the march to the gallows." *Source: author, 2011*

Peter Kohn, murderer of an American airman, is led to the gallows. Photograph taken about 5:00 a.m. on June 29, 1945, at Rheinbach Prison. Woods hanged Kohn five minutes later. *Source: courtesy AP Images / photographer Peter Carroll / ID #450704042*

Execution of German war criminal Peter Kohn. Woods cannot be seen but is placing a black hood over Kohn's head. On the small platform to the right, the trapdoor release rope can be seen. This was the mechanism primarily used by Woods prior to the Landsberg executions. *Source: courtesy AP Images / photographer Peter Carroll / ID #450629099*

Execution of German war criminal Mathias Gierens. Execution occurred at 5:50 a.m. on June 29, 1945, at Rheinbach Prison. Woods's right hand can be seen cutting the release rope with a knife, which would release the trapdoor. *Source: courtesy AP Images / photographer Peter Carroll / ID #4506290107*

Body of Peter Back hangs beneath the scaffold. Execution occurred at 6:35 a.m. on June 29, 1945, at Rheinbach Prison. Prison authorities previously removed the condemned man's shoe laces so he could not hang himself in his cell. *Source: courtesy AP Images / photographer Peter Carroll / ID #4506291162*

Thomas F. Robinson. Thomas, *far left*, attended brother Robert's wedding to Gloria; in the middle is their father, John Michael. Technician Third Grade Robinson assisted in thirty-two hangings. *Source: courtesy Ashley Robinson Skala, grandniece of Thomas F. Robinson*

Woods checking hanging rope at Bruchsal Prison. Photo taken on November 10, 1945, when he hanged five German war criminals for murdering downed American airmen. *Source: courtesy AP Images / photographer Henry Burroughs / ID #451116015*

Execution of German war criminal Johannes Seipel at Bruchsal Prison. Hanging occurred on November 10, 1945. Woods, *in center*, is adjusting the black hood around the neck of the condemned. Soldier in soft cap, holding the noose (*to the left*), is assistant executioner Vincent J. Martino. *Source: NARA, Record Group 111, Box 305, Photo SC 215808*

MSgt. John C. Woods examining the swinging body of Johannes Seipel. Photo was taken about 2:55 p.m. on November 10, 1945, at Bruchsal Prison. *Source: courtesy AP Images / photographer Henry Burroughs / ID #4511100101*

Body of Johannes Seipel being placed in coffin. Three civilians are German prison workers. Technician Fifth Grade Vincent J. Martino, on scaffold, is preparing the next rope for Johann Opper. Photo was taken about 3:00 p.m.
Source: courtesy AP Images / photographer Henry Burroughs / ID #4511100119

Execution orders being read to Johann Opper. Soldier in soft cap behind MP on the left is Vincent J. Martino. Order was first read in English and then in German. Photo was taken about 3:05 p.m. at Bruchsal Prison. *Source: courtesy AP Images / photographer Henry Burroughs / ID #4511100168*

Execution of German war criminal Phillip Gütlich at Bruchsal Prison on November 10, 1945. Woods is standing behind the MP on the right and has just actuated the trapdoor through which Gütlich is now falling. *Source: NARA, Record Group 111, Box 306, SC 215977*

Execution of German war criminal Josef Hartgen at Bruchsal Prison on November 10, 1945. Prisoner is being led to the gallows, where Woods is waiting for him. *Source: NARA, Record Group 111, Box 307, Photo SC 216207*

Execution of German war criminal Clemens Wiegand at Bruchsal Prison on January 11, 1946. Wiegand murdered American airman Anthony Martin after Martin's aircraft was shot down. Vincent J. Martino is holding the noose. *Source: United States Holocaust Memorial Museum (Photo #78933), courtesy of Ron Leidelmeyer*

Preparation of execution of German war criminal Dominikus Thomas at Bruchsal Prison on January 12, 1946. Noose is placed over a side railing of the scaffold while Vincent J. Martino checks that Thomas's ankles are bound. Woods is partially hidden to the rear. *Source: NARA, Record Group: 319-CE, Box 8, Photo SC 237251*

Execution of German war criminal Dominikus Thomas at Bruchsal Prison on January 12, 1946. Woods has to stretch to get the hood on correctly. There is some confusion concerning which Signal Corps photos are correct for which of the condemned. On the basis of comparisons and background lighting, this study concludes these are the right identifications. *Source: NARA, Record Group: 319-CE, Box 8, Photo SC 237248*

Walk to the gallows for German war criminal Wilhelm Dieterman at Bruchsal Prison on January 12, 1946. *Source: NARA, Record Group: 319-CE, Box 8, Photo SC 237247*

Execution of German war criminal Wilhelm Dieterman at Bruchsal Prison on January 12, 1946. Woods adjusts the hood; he was shorter than almost all of the condemned, which could have caused some of the problems at executions. Dieterman realizes he will be hanged in less than a minute. *Source: NARA, Record Group: 319-CE, Box 8, Photo SC 237250*

Bruchsal Prison, 2017. Nicknamed "Café Eight Corners," the facility was based on an American design. Woods executed thirteen German war criminals here in 1945–46. *Source: author, 2011*

Eerie photograph of Karl Willig, executed at Bruchsal Prison. Woods hanged Willig on March 14, 1946. The condemned man had murdered numerous victims at the Hadamar euthanasia center. The black hood apparently was damp, and Willig's facial features can be seen. *Source: US Army Signal Corps photo, found in the public domain*

German Bruchsal Prison officials place body of Karl Willig in coffin. Photo taken about 1:45 p.m. on March 14, 1946.
Source: courtesy AP Images / ID #450521196

Landsberg Prison. US military aerial photo of Landsberg prison taken at night in late 1945 or 1946. *Source: US Army Signal Corps photo, found in the public domain*

Gallows at Landsberg Prison, showing trapdoor lever. Steel lever that actuated trap is shown behind the condemned man. Photo is cropped from larger print showing execution of German war criminal in 1947. *Source: NARA, Record Group: 319-CE, Box 9, US Army Signal Corps photo, SC283435*

Gallows at Landsberg Prison, showing trapdoor. Trapdoor in open position is visible just behind the body of German war criminal in 1947. *Source: NARA, Record Group: 319-CE, Box 9, US Army Signal Corps photo, SC283441*

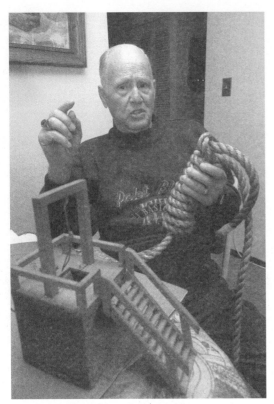

Joseph "Dirty Dom" Malta in later years. "It was a pleasure doing it. I'd do it all over again." This study could not confirm the legend that "Dirty Dom" occasionally took this scale model scaffold to show condemned men the evening before their execution. Photo taken in October 1996. *Source: courtesy AP Images / photographer Steven Senne / ID #96101501292*

German war criminal Friedrich Wilhelm Ruppert. *Source: US Army Signal Corps photo, found in the public domain*

Execution of German war criminal Friedrich Wilhelm Ruppert at Landsberg Prison on May 28, 1946. American soldier slightly behind Ruppert (*to the left*) is Joseph Malta, who assisted Woods in twenty-five hangings. Woods is obscured directly behind Ruppert; all that is visible are his arm and master sergeant stripes. *Source: NARA, Record Group: 319-CE, Box 8, US Army Signal Corps photo, SC241815*

German war criminal Otto Förschner. *Source: United States Holocaust Memorial Museum (Photo #49678), courtesy of Stuart McKeever*

Woods the instant he activates the trapdoor in execution of Otto Förschner. Förschner is in center of the photograph, snapped about 10:05 a.m. on May 28, 1946. Woods, *on far right*, has his right hand on the lever. *Source: courtesy AP Images / photographer Robert Clover / ID #4605280140*

Grave of German war criminal Otto Förschner at Landsberg. Physicians declared Förschner dead at 10:22 a.m. Witnesses claimed that he was responsible for the brutal conditions and execution of prisoners at Kaufering, a subcamp of Dachau. *Source: author, 2011*

Execution of German war criminal Engelbert Valentin Niedermeyer. Woods is almost completely hidden behind the condemned man, with only the stripes on his uniform sleeve visible. *Source: courtesy AP Images / photographer Robert Clover / ID #4605281114*

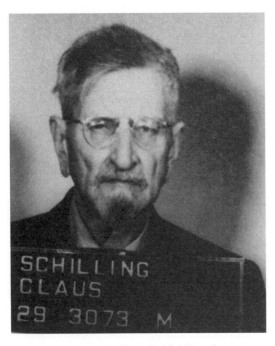

German war criminal Dr. Klaus Karl Schilling. *Source: NARA, Record Group: 549, Entry Number A-1 2243, Box 11*

German war criminal Walter Langleist. *Source: NARA, Record Group: 242, Berlin Document Center, SS Officer Personnel Files, A3343, SSO-Roll 242A (Langleist Walter)*

Execution of German war criminal Klaus Karl Schilling at Landsberg Prison on May 28, 1946. Woods hanged him right after lunch; physicians pronounced Schilling dead at 1:37 p.m. *Source: NARA, US Army Signal Corps photo*

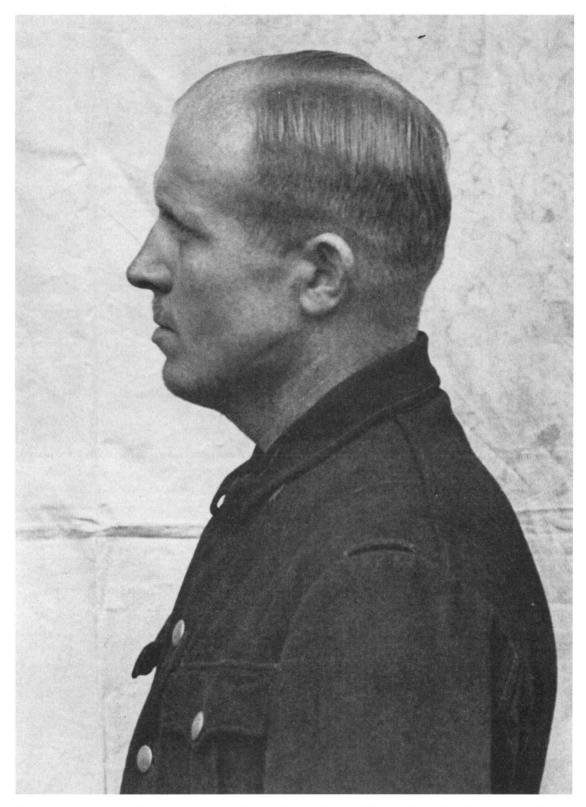

German war criminal Otto Moll. *Source: United States Holocaust Memorial Museum (Photo #49681), courtesy of Stuart McKeever*

Rough caskets for Nazi war criminals executed at Landsberg Prison on May 28, 1946. *Left to right*: Rudolph Suttrop, Engelbert Niedermeyer, and Otto Förschner. *Source: NARA, Record Group: 319-CE, Box 8, US Army Signal Corps photo, SC241821*

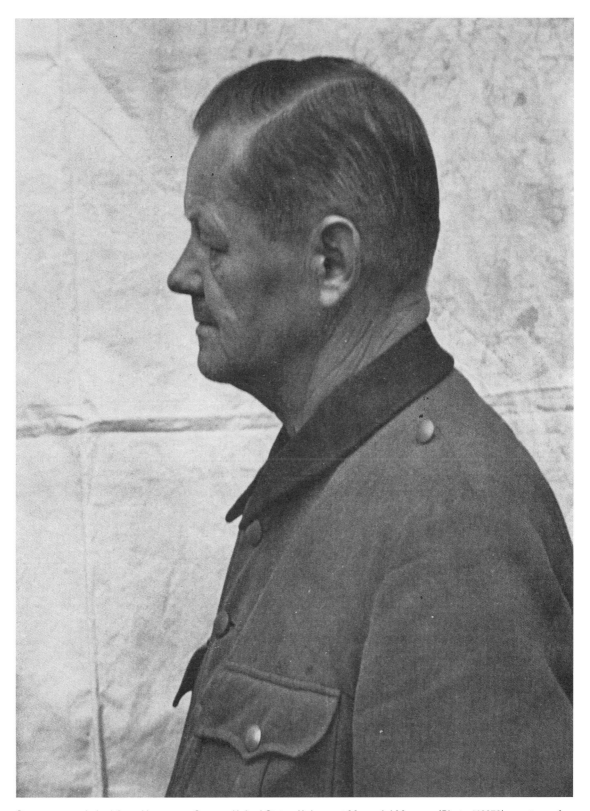

German war criminal Arno Lippmann. *Source: United States Holocaust Memorial Museum (Photo #49672), courtesy of Stuart McKeever*

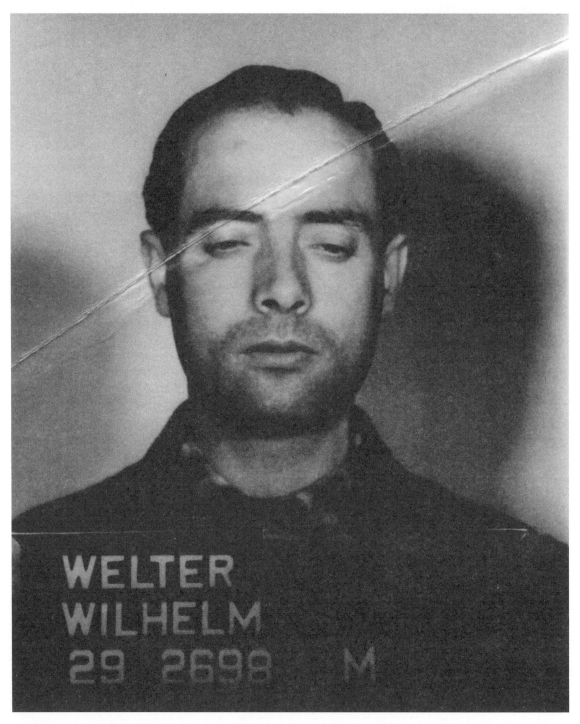

German war criminal Wilhelm Welter. *Source: NARA, Record Group: 549, Entry Number A-1 2243, Box 14*

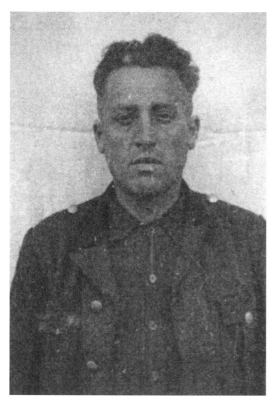

German war criminal Wilhelm Wagner. *Source: US Army Signal Corps photo, public domain*

Grave of German war criminal Johann Kick at Landsberg. Woods hanged Kick on May 29, 1946; physicians declared him dead at 1:19 p.m. *Source: author, 2011*

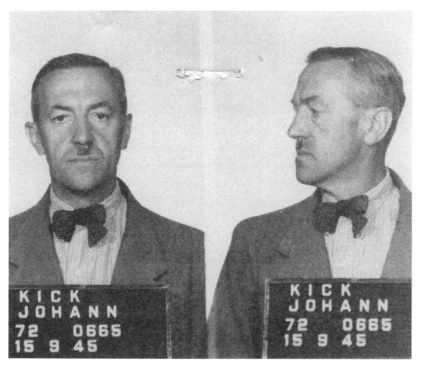

German war criminal Johann Kick. *Source: NARA, Record Group: 549, Entry Number A-1 2243, Box 7*

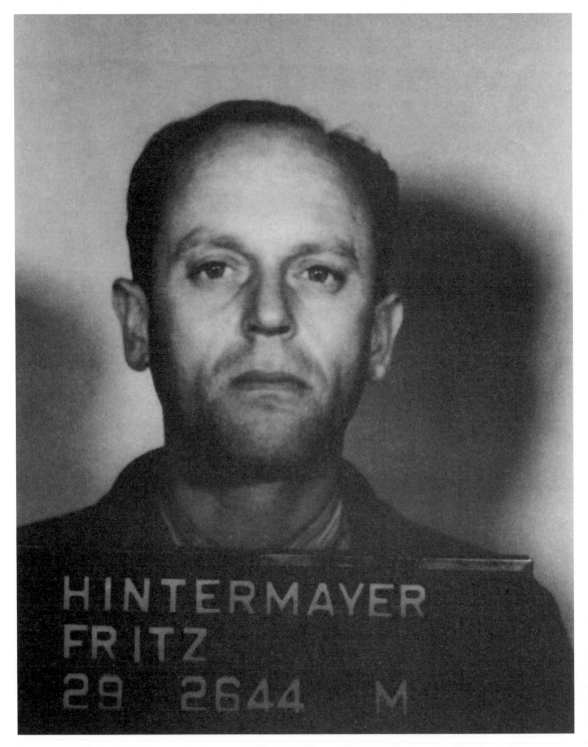

German war criminal Fritz Hintermayer. *Source: NARA, Record Group: 549, Entry Number A-1 2243, Box 6*

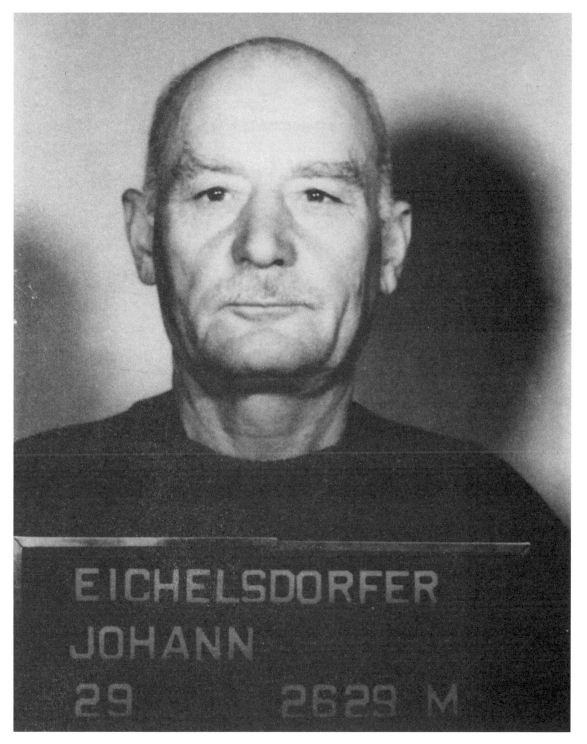

German war criminal Johann Baptist Eichelsdörfer. *Source: NARA, Record Group: 549, Entry Number A-1 2243, Box 3*

German war criminal Leonhard Anselm Eichberger. *Source: NARA, Record Group: 549, Entry Number A-1 2243, Box 3*

Grave of German war criminal Leonhard Eichberger at Landsberg. Woods hanged Eichberger on May 29, 1946; he was declared dead at 2:26 p.m. Eichberger had his lower left leg amputated during the war and had to hop on one leg up the thirteen steps of the gallows. *Source: author, 2011*

Execution of German war criminal Martin Weiss. Civilian with gray hair, wearing a suit with white handkerchief and holding the rope (*on far left*), is Johann Reichhart. Photos of men executed by Reichhart at Landsberg indicate their hands were secured with steel handcuffs. *Source: NARA, Record Group: 319-CE, Box 8, US Army Signal Corps photo, SC241826*

Grave of Johann Reichhart. Reichhart died in a nursing home at Dorfen near Erding, Bavaria, on April 26, 1972, from dementia. His remains are buried in the Ostfriedhof in this family grave. *Source: author, 2011*

Inside Nürnberg International Military Tribunal courtroom. Accused sat on the far left of the photo, judges on the far right; photo taken in 1945–46. *Source: US Army Signal Corps photo, now found in public domain*

View into a cell corridor of the Nürnberg Prison. Photo taken on December 8, 1945. Cell #5 was that of Hermann Göring. *Source: courtesy AP Images, photo #640439394316*

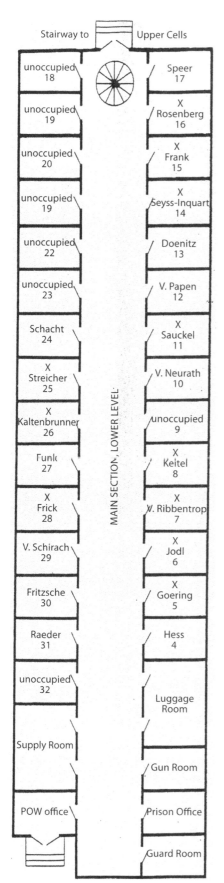

Stairway to   Upper Cells

unoccupied 18	Speer 17
unoccupied 19	X Rosenberg 16
unoccupied 20	X Frank 15
unoccupied 19	X Seyss-Inquart 14
unoccupied 22	Doenitz 13
unoccupied 23	V. Papen 12
Schacht 24	X Sauckel 11
X Streicher 25	V. Neurath 10
X Kaltenbrunner 26	unoccupied 9
Funk 27	X Keitel 8
X Frick 28	X V. Ribbentrop 7
V. Schirach 29	X Jodl 6
Fritzsche 30	X Goering 5
Raeder 31	Hess 4
unoccupied 32	Luggage Room
Supply Room	
	Gun Room
POW office	Prison Office
	Guard Room

MAIN SECTION, LOWER LEVEL

Nürnberg Prison layout of prisoner cells. One prisoner was assigned to each cell; a guard was required to observe the prisoner twenty-four hours a day through a small observation opening in the door. Even so, Hermann Göring successfully took poison hours before his scheduled hanging. *Source: US Army drawing by way of Memorium Nuremberg Trials, Museen der Stadt Nürnberg*

Nürnberg Prison exercise yard. Photo taken in the winter of 1945–46. *Source: US Army Signal Corps photo, found in public domain*

Nürnberg Prison: the last walk. Condemned men, one by one, walked under guard from their prison cell in the first floor of the large building (*on the left*), went down the stairs, turned left, and then walked to the doors of the smaller building (*on the right*), where Woods had assembled three gallows. *Source: public domain*

Nürnberg Prison gymnasium, where Nazi war criminals were hanged early on October 16, 1946. The floor was dusty and the walls were dirty gray; it was a shabby place to die. The building was demolished in 1983. *Source: Oberlandesgericht Nürnberg-Fürth by way of Memorium Nuremberg Trials, Museen der Stadt Nürnberg*

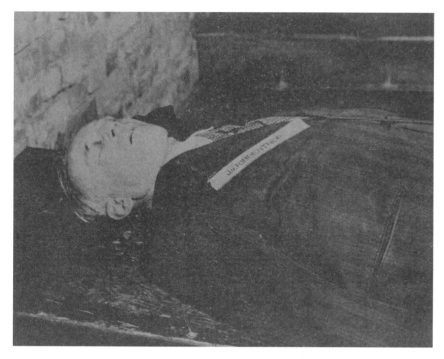

Nürnberg Prison: Joachim von Ribbentrop. Woods hanged him at 1:13 a.m.; he was pronounced dead at 1:32 a.m. *Source: NARA, Record Group 111, Box 472, US Army Signal Corps Photo SC 262452*

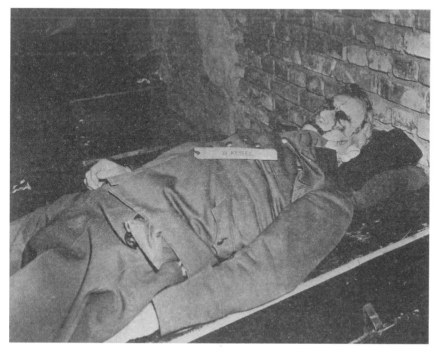

Nürnberg Prison: Wilhelm Keitel. Woods hanged him at 1:20 a.m.; he was pronounced dead at 1:44 a.m. *Source: NARA, Record Group 111, Box 472, US Army Signal Corps Photo SC 262459*

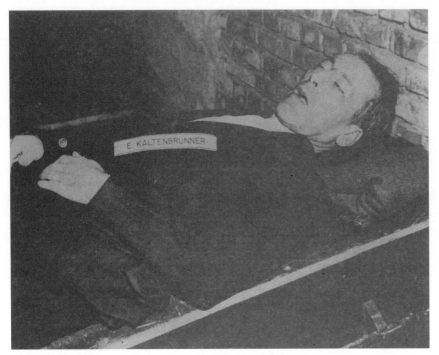

Nürnberg Prison: Ernst Kaltenbrunner. Woods hanged him at 1:39 a.m.; he was pronounced dead at 1:52 a.m. *Source: NARA, Record Group 111, Box 472, US Army Signal Corps Photo SC 262457*

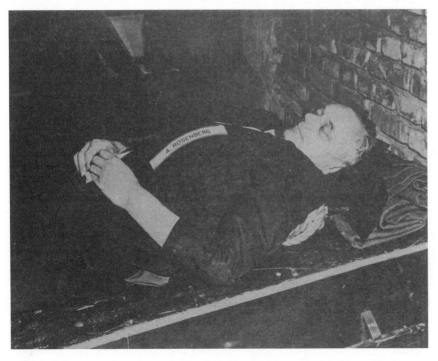

Nürnberg Prison: Alfred Rosenberg. Woods hanged him at 1:49 a.m.; he was pronounced dead at 1:59 a.m. *Source: NARA, Record Group 111, Box 472, US Army Signal Corps Photo SC 262461*

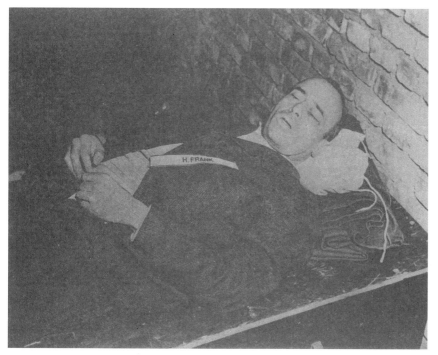

Nürnberg Prison: Hans Frank. Woods hanged him at 1:58 a.m.; he was pronounced dead at 2:09 a.m. *Source: NARA, Record Group 111, Box 472, US Army Signal Corps Photo SC 262462*

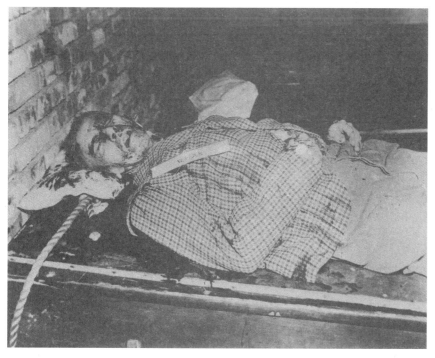

Nürnberg Prison: Wilhelm Frick. Woods hanged him at 2:08 a.m.; he was pronounced dead at 2:20 a.m. *Source: NARA, Record Group 111, Box 472, US Army Signal Corps Photo SC 262456*

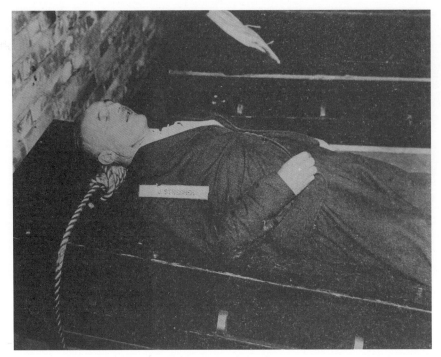

Nürnberg Prison: Julius Streicher. Woods hanged him at 2:14 a.m.; he was pronounced dead at 2:28 a.m. *Source: NARA, Record Group 111, Box 472, US Army Signal Corps Photo SC 262458*

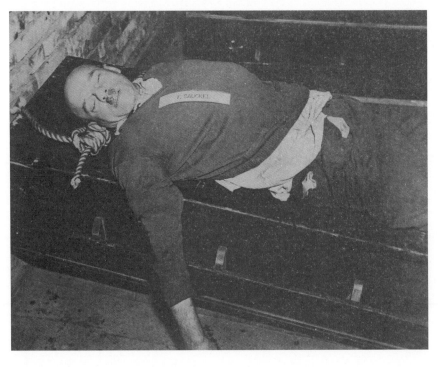

Nürnberg Prison: Fritz Sauckel. Woods hanged him at 2:26 a.m.; he was pronounced dead at 2:40 a.m. *Source: NARA, Record Group 111, Box 472, US Army Signal Corps Photo SC 262460*

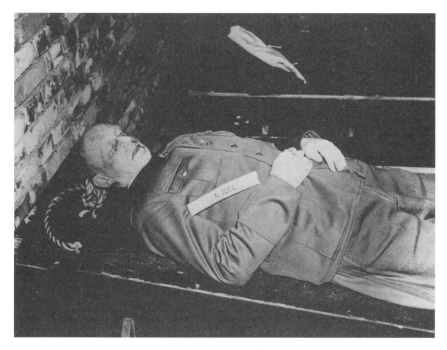

Nürnberg Prison: Alfred Jodl. Woods hanged him at 2:34 a.m.; he was pronounced dead at 2:50 a.m. *Source: NARA, Record Group 111, Box 472, US Army Signal Corps Photo SC 262453*

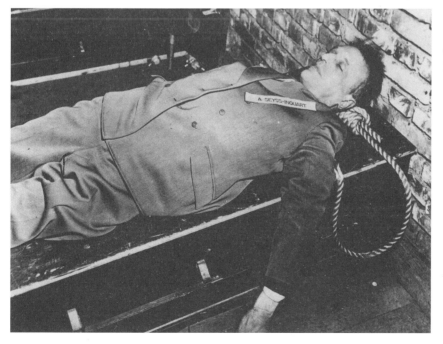

Nürnberg Prison: Arthur Seyss-Inquart. Woods hanged him at 2:45 a.m.; he was pronounced dead at 2:57 a.m. *Source: NARA, Record Group 111, Box 472, US Army Signal Corps Photo SC 262454*

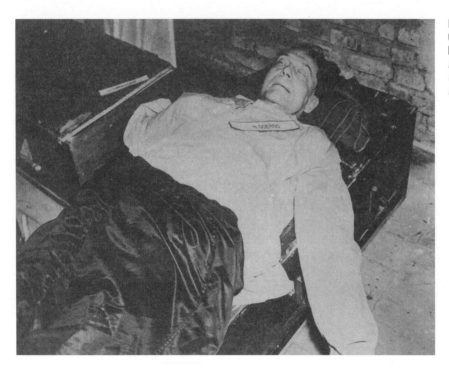

Nürnberg Prison: Hermann Göring. He cheated the hangman. *Source: NARA, Record Group 111, Box 472, US Army Signal Corps Photo SC 2624545*

Crematoria at the East Cemetery (Ostfriedhof) in Munich in 2017. Even though the bodies of the executed Nürnberg war criminals were cremated here more than seventy years ago, current crematory supervisors would not allow the author to photograph inside the facility. *Source: author, 2011*

Hazel Woods, 1946. Photo taken on October 17, 1946, in Wichita, when reporters mobbed her after initial stories of the Nürnberg executions revealed John to be the hangman. *Source: courtesy AP Images / ID #383778836934*

Woods (*right*) celebrating with TSgt. Gibilante at Heidelberg. Photo probably taken October 18, 1946. *Source: courtesy AP Images / ID #461018013*

Woods with his dog at Heidelberg, Germany. Photo taken October 18, 1946. *Source: courtesy AP Images / ID #591964686296*

Woods interviewed by the Associated Press. Photo taken morning of October 18, 1946, in Heidelberg; interviewer is Don Doane. *Source: courtesy AP Images / photographer Gerhard F. Baatz / ID #572433174700*

Woods on troopship *St. Albans Victory*. Photo taken upon ship's arrival at Brooklyn, New York, on November 19, 1946. *Source: courtesy AP Images / photographer Anthony Camerano / ID #895762799650*

Woods with Hazel in Wichita. Photo taken November 28, 1946. The couple is leaving a church service. *Source: courtesy AP Images / ID #701658476156*

Woods as "editor for the day" at the *Wichita Beacon*. Photo taken November 29, 1946, during his furlough. *Source:* Wichita Beacon*; photos appear courtesy of the* Wichita Eagle / *www.Kansas.com*

Woods with niece. Photo taken between December 1946 and February 1947, while he was on furlough in Wichita; location is in front of 621 North Emporia, where Hazel lived. *Source: Anna Dale Chilcott Cole*

Lt. Charles Rexroad. Rexroad executed some 130 Japanese war criminals after the war, making him the US Army's preeminent hangman. Photo taken June 10, 1949, at Camp Chaffee, Arkansas. *Source: NARA, US Army Signal Corps Photo, SC-333338*

Woods with his sister in 1947. Photo taken at Wichita, Kansas, in February 1947 before Woods reported back to duty following a furlough. Mary Woods Dye lived in Wichita at the time. *Source:* Wichita Beacon; *photos appear courtesy of the* Wichita Eagle / *www. Kansas.com*

Herbert A. Kleinbeck Jr. Kleinbeck served as an assistant hangman for Woods for one execution. Photograph taken in 1939 at the University of Illinois, Lambda Chi Alpha fraternity. *Source:* The Illio 1939 (*University of Illinois Yearbook, 1939*)

Woods in 1948. Photo taken November 28, 1948, at the *Wichita Beacon*, when Woods returned from Germany. Hoping to report to the Far East to hang Hideki Tojo, he was assigned to Fort Belvoir, Virginia. *Source:* Wichita Beacon; *photos appear courtesy of the* Wichita Eagle / *www.Kansas.com*

Woodses' residence in 1948. The apartment building was located at 428 North Emporia, Wichita. Military veterans live there now. *Source: author, 2011*

MORNING REPORT

ENDING 2400	DAY 21	MONTH Jul	YEAR '50

ORGANIZATION (HQ, CO, DET, ETC.)	(PARENT UNIT)	(ARM OR SERVICE)
Hq & Hq Company 7th Engineer Brigade		CE

STATION OR LOCATION
APO 187 c/o Postmaster San Francisco Calif

NAME	SERIAL NUMBER	GRADE	MOS	CODE
Woods John C	RA37540591	M Sgt		96

Dy to died by electric shock sustained
at Rock Quarry Eniwetok Marshall Islands
LD Yes

	ASGD (2)	Gains UNASGD (3)	TOTAL Losses (4)	ATCHD FR.OTHER ORG'S (5)	PRESENT FOR DUTY (6)	PRESENT NOT FOR DUTY (7)	ABSENT T D D S (8)	SK (9)	CONF (10)	LV FUR (11)	AWOL (12)	MISSING (13)
GEN				1	1							
COL	1				1							
LT COL	8			1	7	2						
MAJ	7			1	8							
CAPT	12				11	1						
1ST LT	4			1	5							
2ND LT	1			1	2							
TOTAL	33			5	35	3						
WO	1				1							
MSGT 1ST	7				7							
SGT	11				10	1						
SSGT	26			1	25	2						
	55		2		55	2						
	58			28	60	5	1					
	10			22	31		1					
TOTAL	147		1	53	188	10	2					

I CERTIFY THAT THIS MORNING REPORT IS CORRECT: PAGE 1 OF 1 PAGES

SIGNATURE *Willard C Taft*

NAME TYPED OR PRINTED WILLARD C TAFT

GRADE CAPT   ARM OR SERVICE CE

WD AGO FORM 1
1 NOVEMBER 1944   W. D. COPY THRU MRU OR SCU

THIS FORM SUPERSEDES WD AGO FORM NO. 1, 1 MAY 1944 WHICH MAY BE USED UNTIL EXISTING STOCKS ARE EXHAUSTED

Company morning report. Headquarters and Headquarters Company of the 7th Engineer Brigade, daily personnel strength report: July 21, 1950. Lower portion of image shows numbers of soldiers by rank assigned, present for duty and absent. *At top*, the company clerk made special annotations. Death of John Woods is shown, going from duty status (Dy) to "died by electrical shock sustained at Rock Quarry Eniwetok Marshall Islands." Although the report of investigation had not been completed, the clerk noted that the death occurred in the line of duty (LD). *Source: National Archives, Office of the Adjutant General Morning Reports, Headquarters & Headquarters Company, 7th Engineer Brigade*

Woods's obituary photo. Photo was used in some articles announcing his death. *Source: probably US Army, now public domain*

JTF-3 Headquarters on Eniwetok. Photo taken on June 14, 1951. Gen. "Pete" Quesada, JTF-3 commander, is on the right. *From left*: Representative F. Edward Hebert, Gordon Dean (chairman, Atomic Energy Commission), and RAdm. Tom E. Hill (deputy commander, JTF-3). *Source: public domain*

Sign on Eniwetok Atoll showing athletic field named after John Woods. The sign, with incorrect birth date, indicates that Woods was in Europe in 1947–48, later confirmed by company morning reports. *Source: photograph presented to Hazel Woods, now in possession of the family*

Grave of TSgt. Vincent J. Martino. Martino, buried at the Florida National Cemetery at Bushnell, Florida, in Plot 1100 of Section 329, served as assistant hangman to John Woods for eighteen executions. *Source: author, 2011*

Grave of John and Hazel Woods [37°47'30" N, 95°56'38" W]. Hazel's parents (Chilcott) are in the next grave. *Source: author, 2011*

EPILOGUE

The remains of Lt. Col. Lionel F. Smith, who was killed in action on Omaha Beach on June 6, 1944, and was commander of the 37th Engineer Combat Battalion, to which John Woods was assigned, were reinterred on December 14, 1947, in Carthage, Missouri, at Park Cemetery (plot: bl 33, lot 59, sp 6). Smith was posthumously awarded a Purple Heart, Bronze Star, and the French *Croix de Guerre* with Palms.

Capt. Stuart O. Greig, Apprentice Seaman John C. Woods's commanding officer on the USS *Hovey*, died on November 13, 1949. He is buried at Arlington National Cemetery in section 8, site 504.

Richard A. Mosley, who had served as a prisoner escort for six executions in which MSgt. John C. Woods worked as the assistant hangman, took his own life on January 5, 1953, in Hanford, California—most likely the victim of posttraumatic stress disorder. He is buried at Grangeville Cemetery in Armona, California.

Mortimer Heth Christian, commandant of Seine Disciplinary Training Center and the de facto trainer of John Woods as a hangman, died on November 1, 1955. He is buried at Arlington National Cemetery in section 1, site 931-B.

Lee Roy Woods, John Woods's father, died in Arkansas City, Kansas, in November 1955 and is buried there next to his second wife, Mildred Luella Martin, at Parker Cemetery.

Maj. Gen. Iona T. Nikitchenko, senior Soviet official at the International Tribunal at Nürnberg, who asked Woods to explain and demonstrate the gallows shortly before the executions there, died on April 22, 1967, in Moscow.

Martha "Mattie" Wootrus/Woods/Green/Cooper, John Woods's mother, appears to have died on June 30, 1967; she is buried in an unmarked grave (space 4, lot 178, section H) at the Old Mission Cemetery in Wichita, Kansas.

Johann Reichhart, German hangman at Landsberg Prison for the May 28–29, 1946, executions, died in a nursing home at Dorfen, Bavaria, on April 26, 1972. His remains are buried in Munich's Ostfriedhof (section 47, row 2, #21).

Brig. Gen. Theodore F. Wessels, former provost marshal for the European theater of operations, who once referred to Woods as "that ungrateful son-of-a-bitch," died on May 1, 1974, in San Antonio, Texas. He is buried at the Ft. Sam Houston National Cemetery in section V, site 219.

Capt. Paul M. Robinett, who signed Woods up for the Civilian Conservation Corps, went on to command Combat Command B of the US 1st Armored Division in North Africa in 1943. He died on February 5, 1975, at Mountain Grove, Missouri, and is buried at the Hillcrest Cemetery, in plot SE 1st 43-6 at Mountain Grove.

Wichita detective Floyd R. Gunsaullus, who apprehended Woods in December 1939 for writing a fraudulent $50 check and who later served as a pallbearer at John Woods's funeral, died in August 1978. He is buried at the Wichita Park Cemetery at the Acacia Annex D, in lot 192, grave 4-5.

James M. Woods, John's brother, died in August 1983 in Wichita.

Cornelius T. Morris, former US Army major who supervised Woods's news media interviews at Ft. Dix in November 1946, died on April 29, 1986, in Hamilton, Massachusetts.

Thomas F. Robinson, an assistant hangman to Woods, died on February 14, 1990, in Geauga, Ohio. He is buried at Burton Township's Welton Cemetery.

Sgt. Billy Ford, the forgotten assistant to Woods at the Nürnberg executions, died on August 14, 1991, in Clark, Nevada.

Elwood Richard "Pete" Quesada, commander of Joint Task Force Three on Eniwetok Atoll, died at Jupiter, Florida, on February 9, 1993. He was buried with full military honors in section 30 (grave 439) at Arlington National Cemetery.

Henry L. Peck, commandant, Loire Disciplinary Training Center, later worked for the Veteran's Administration. He died on December 5, 1996, in Boca Raton, Florida, of lung cancer; he is buried in Silver Springs, Maryland.

Anthony J. Gibilante, army buddy of Woods, died on August 3, 1999, in Abington, Pennsylvania. He is buried at St. John Neumann Cemetery in Chalfont, Pennsylvania.

Charles C. Rexroad, the US Army's preeminent hangman of the postwar period, died of cancer on December 23, 1992, at the Department of Veterans Affairs Medical Center in Augusta, Georgia. He is buried at the Hillcrest Memorial Park Cemetery in Augusta.

After the executions at Nürnberg, Joseph "Dirty Dom" Malta picked up another nickname, "Hangman 10." The former assistant hangman under Woods died in Revere, Massachusetts, on January 6, 1999. He is buried at Holy Cross Cemetery in Malden, Massachusetts.[1]

Stanley Tilles, who supervised Woods at the Nürnberg executions, died on February 16, 2000, at Yorba Linda, California. He is buried at the Riverside National Cemetery.

Herbert Kleinbeck, assistant hangman to Woods for one execution, died on February 21, 2000, in East La Mirada, Los Angeles County, California.

Forest K. Weaver, the first lieutenant who examined the power source at Eniwetok associated with the electrocution of Woods and found equipment failure, went on to have a distinguished military career; his fitness reports praised his technical expertise in all his positions until he retired as a major. He died on August 31, 2000, in Seattle, Washington, and is buried at the Tahoma National Cemetery in section 9B, site 173.[2]

Hazel Chilcott Woods lived most of her life, after her husband died, in Wichita and Toronto, Kansas. Toronto then had a population of about four hundred people and had two grocery stores, three cafés, one beer joint, one pool hall, one bank, two gas stations, and a funeral home. She never remarried and she never spoke much about her husband after his death. In 1953, she was listed as a nurse's aide at St. Francis Hospital in Wichita, residing at 618 North Topeka Avenue. She later worked at Parkers Café in Toronto but had her own brush with death when a coffeepot exploded, sending shards of glass and metal into her face and body. She recovered and later worked the Toronto Meat Locker wrapping meat; she was finally employed at the Yates Center Nursing Home at nearby Yates Center. Most of the people in the small town knew her as "Aunt Hazel." On May 20, 2000, Hazel Woods died in Toronto. She is buried next to her husband in the Toronto Cemetery, southeast of town.[3]

Vincent J. Martino, former assistant hangman for Woods, died on October 14, 2003, in Naples, Florida. He is buried at the Florida National Cemetery at Bushnell in plot 1100 of section 329. His wife, Sylvia, died on October 11, 2011.[4]

The Spöttinger Cemetery, in which rest the remains of nine German war criminals who were hanged by John C. Woods in 1945–46, was the oldest cemetery in Landsberg am Lech. Actually, more than 140 war criminals are buried in this former prison cemetery, which belonged to Bavaria since 1923. From 1945 to 1951, 259 death sentences from various war crimes trials were carried out by hanging and twenty-nine by shooting in the War Criminal Prison No. 1, the Allied name for the Landsberg Prison, but the families of more than one hundred of the executed requested that the remains be transferred to their home cities.

In 1984, Spöttinger Cemetery was closed for future burials. On January 22, 2003, the Bavarian minister of justice, Dr. Manfred Weiß, declared that the cemetery was closed and no longer sacred ground, which allowed the graveyard to go into disrepair. On February 13, 2003, workers removed the inscriptions from the simple wooden crosses, in part to erase public memory of those executed and their crimes. The Bavarian state ministry of justice had planned to completely clear the cemetery in order to rid the problem of German war guilt once and for all. However, the state legislature finally caved in to political pressure from groups that wanted the Spöttinger Cemetery to remain as a "document of modern history." A recent visit to the cemetery revealed that the rate of decay of the abandoned terrain indicates that it will be completely cleared sooner rather than later.

• • •

Another cemetery, 443 miles west of Landsberg, also contains the handiwork of John Woods. Designed to be secret in existence and inaccessible to the general public, it is called "Plot E" by the American Battle Monuments Commission; others often refer to it as "the Fifth Field." The size of a basketball court, the plot of land is adjacent to—but technically outside—the First World War American Military Cemetery of Oise-Aisne at Seringes-et-Nesles, France. There are ninety-six grave markers here, and as at the Spöttinger Cemetery, none of the markers have a name, since these ninety-six executed men did not represent "the service, achievements, and sacrifice" of the 416,800 American military dead in World War II. Thirty-four of the dull white, flat, marble stones sunken below ground level mark the final resting place of those American soldiers hanged by Master Sergeant Woods. Each stone has a number between one and ninety-six; there is no rhyme or reason why each grave has a particular number. The remains of the ninety-six, originally buried in plots from England to Algeria, were consolidated in 1949, transported without fanfare to the American Military Cemetery of Oise-Aisne, and reinterred there.[5]

• • •

The final ten men whom Woods hanged do not have even nameless markers to designate their passing. These condemned men were the infamous top Nazis war criminals tried and sentenced to death by the International Military Tribunal at Nürnberg in 1946. These individuals were determined to be so evil that their remains were taken by American military trucks in the dead of night on October 16, 1946—just hours after their execution—to the cradle of Nazism, Munich, to be cremated in that city's East Cemetery. US Army personnel surreptitiously took the ashes of these dead to a bridge across the nearby Isar River in downtown Munich and dumped the detritus into the swiftly flowing water—to ensure that no future memorial of any kind could ever be erected.

In the last few seconds of John C. Woods's life, he was probably not thinking of these two cemeteries or the men whom he had caused to be there. Perhaps he thought for a moment that the Nazis had finally exacted their revenge on him, and that maybe they were behind the electrical malfunction, but now he just didn't care. He was only a few ticks of the clock from death, and his passing was happening exactly as he had described to "Obe" Obermayer five years before: "clean, painless, and traditional."

He wasn't going to die by inches as would some old alcoholic. He wasn't going to cough his lungs out in a dank, depressing VA hospital after a lifetime of smoking. He wasn't going to be put out to pasture, as the Army moved from hanging to electrocution. And the hell with Lt. Rexroad and his 130 Japanese war criminals; the big show had been Europe and the Nazi big shots.

No, in that last instant of his life, Master Sergeant John C. Woods probably had much-grander thoughts. Once the broadcast boys in Washington—and Chicago—and New York—and Berlin—and Paris—and London—and even Moscow—found out about his death, they would put that breaking news on "Page 1." Just like at Nürnberg, once again little Johnny Woods would be on top of the world.

Who would have thought it? Five foot, four and a half inches tall, a high-school drop-out;

someone who had been abandoned by his mother, who had washed out of the Civilian Conservation Corps, who once could find only work driving a casket delivery truck, who the United States Navy had said suffered from moral degeneration, and who had dodged an avalanche of Nazi bullets and shells on "Bloody Omaha" beach at Normandy on June 6, 1944—John Clarence Woods had beaten them all.

APPENDIXES

Appendix 1
Executive Biography
of John C. Woods

John C. Woods served as the US Army's principal hangman in the European theater of operations (ETO) in the last seven months of World War II. After the war, he continued in this position through October 1946 with the Office of Military Government, United States, in the American occupation zone of Germany. His most significant achievement was to serve as the executioner at the International Military Tribunal at Nürnberg, where, on October 16, 1946, he hanged ten senior Nazis, including Joachim von Ribbentrop (foreign minister), Wilhelm Keitel (chief of staff of the armed forces), Wilhelm Frick (minister of the interior), Ernst Kaltenbrunner (head of the Reich security main office), Hans Frank (governor-general of Occupied Poland), Alfred Jodl (operations chief of the armed forces), Alfred Rosenberg (Reichs minister for the Occupied Eastern Territories), Julius Streicher (Nazi anti-Semitic publisher and *Gauleiter* of Franconia), Fritz Sauckel (plenipotentiary general for the allocation of labor), and Arthur Seyss-Inquart (Reich commissioner for Occupied Netherlands).

Woods was born in Wichita, Kansas, on June 5, 1911, in hardscrabble conditions. He completed freshman year of high school but then dropped out. Woods enlisted in the Navy in 1929 but quickly deserted. Authorities apprehended him; a summary court-martial convicted him of an unauthorized absence, and the Navy dismissed him for being mentally unstable and unsuitable for military service. Woods received a dishonorable discharge from the Civilian Conservation Corps after six months in 1933, when he refused to work

and went AWOL, and he married Hazel Chilcott on September 30, 1933, in Eureka, Kansas; the couple had no children. For the next ten years, prior to his enlistment in the Army on August 30, 1943, he lived in Eureka and Wichita, Kansas, working on and off.

Listed as having blue eyes and brown hair, with a ruddy complexion, and standing 5'4½" tall and weighing 130 pounds, he reported to Fort Leavenworth, Kansas, to begin training on September 19, 1943; he was assigned to Company B of the 37th Engineer Combat Battalion in the 5th Engineer Special Brigade on March 30, 1944. Woods participated in the landings on Omaha Beach on June 6, 1944, with his unit. Three months later, lying to get out of the combat engineers and into the position of Army hangman, he was attached to the 2913th Disciplinary Training Center and promoted directly from private to master sergeant.

During his career as a hangman, Woods reportedly executed 347 men, but this is a large exaggeration. In late 1946, he estimated that he had hanged two hundred men, of which 134 were in Europe; this, too, was a gross embellishment. From October 1944 to October 1946—the full extent of his grim career—Woods first served as an assistant hangman for fourteen executions (one Waffen-SS soldier and thirteen American soldiers) and subsequently as the primary hangman in seventy-six executions (thirty-five American soldiers and forty-one German war criminals) throughout these two years. After Nürnberg, John Woods never hanged another man.

During his Army career, Master Sergeant John C. Woods was awarded the European–African–Middle Eastern Campaign Medal (with one campaign star), the Good Conduct Medal, the Occupation (Germany) Medal, the World War II Victory Medal, and a Distinguished Unit Badge. He was listed by the US Army as accidentally electrocuted at 10:55 p.m. on July 21, 1950, on Eniwetok Atoll (today Enewetak Atoll) in the Pacific, although mysterious circumstances surrounding his death have continued to this day and have led some to believe that he was murdered. John C. Woods is buried in the city cemetery in Toronto, Kansas, a small town 60 miles east of Wichita.

Appendix 2
John Woods's Quotes

"It's traditional with hangmen to hang themselves when they get old" (said to Herman Obermayer and other soldiers, November 1945).[1]

"Told you it would be all right, Lieutenant!" (said to Stanley Tilles after Soviet delegation inspected the gallows at Nürnberg Prison, October 15, 1946).[2]

"Okay; when's early chow?" (said to an American officer when asked how he was doing after the first five hangings at Nürnberg, October 16, 1946).[3]

"A fellow can't afford to have nerves in this business" (said to news media after the Nürnberg executions, October 19, 1946).[4]

"Ten men in 103 minutes. That's fast work" (said to various news media after the Nürnberg executions, October 18–19, 1946).[5]

"The way I look at this hanging job, somebody has to do it" (said to various news media after the Nürnberg executions, October 18–19, 1946).[6]

"It's hard to remember just what each one did or said. Hanging 10 men one after the other is fast, you know. And that was a rope I had in my hand, not a notebook" (said to various news media after the Nürnberg executions, October 18–19, 1946).[7]

"Even the Russian general came up afterwards and told me it was a first-class job" (said to various news media after the Nürnberg executions, October 23, 1946).[8]

"I always carry two .45s with me. If some German thinks he wants to get me, he better make sure he does it with the first shot, because I was raised with a pistol in my hand and I'm an expert shot with either hand" (said to various news media after the Nürnberg executions, October 23, 1946).[9]

"Hey kid! When are you going to bring the next one up?" (said to *True: The Man's Magazine* at Ft. Dix, New Jersey, in November 1946, concerning that he lost track of how many men had been hanged during the Nürnberg executions).[10]

"I never saw three quarts of whiskey disappear so fast in my life" (said to *True: The Man's Magazine* at Ft. Dix, New Jersey, in November 1946, concerning his team having a few drinks after the Nürnberg hangings).[11]

"I like what I call the Thirteen Knot noose. It's my own invention. Perfected it a good while back in Texas" (said to *True: The Man's Magazine* at Ft. Dix, New Jersey, in November 1946, concerning which noose he preferred when conducting a hanging).[12]

"I guess the clerk thought I was up to some heavy fraternizing" (said to *True: The Man's Magazine* at Ft. Dix, New Jersey, in November 1946, concerning purchasing some girls' black hair ribbons, which he used for the Nürnberg executions).[13]

"I had looked forward to hanging Goering. As a matter of fact, I had stretched a rope for him six months before" (said to Ernest A. Warden of the *Wichita Beacon*, November 29, 1946, concerning disappointment that he was not able to execute Hermann Göring, who had taken poison).[14]

"I don't think I'll ever come back to Wichita alive again" (said to Ernest A. Warden of the *Wichita Beacon*, February 1947).[15]

"I can't think of a better way to die. When the time comes I'll probably save myself a lot of grief and pain that you guys will have" (said to Herman Obermayer and other soldiers concerning how Woods wanted to die, November 1945).[16]

"People seem to think I'm a racketeer or something worse. My job was no worse than any other soldier's" (said to Leslie Sourbeer of the *Wichita Beacon*, November 28, 1946).[17]

"I had no feeling that I was executing human beings when I executed war criminals" (said to Ernest A. Warden of the *Wichita Beacon*, November 29, 1946).[18]

"The Nazis not only were animals—they were training other Germans to become animals and kill. Germany was becoming a whole nation of animals waiting for their prey" (said to Ernest A. Warden of the *Wichita Beacon*, November 29, 1946).[19]

ENDNOTES

Foreword by French L. MacLean

1. Herman J. Obermayer, "Clean, Painless, and Traditional," *Dartmouth Jack O Lantern*, Christmas Issue, December 1946: 24.

Preface

1. Carl B. Wall, "Hangman," *True: The Man's Magazine*, November 1947: 62.

Chapter 1

1. Ancestry.com: John C. Woods.
2. Ibid.
3. Ibid.
4. Ibid.
5. 1880 US Federal Census for Marion County, Illinois.
6. 1885 Kansas Census, Sedgwick County.
7. 1900 US Federal Census for Reno County, Illinois.
8. Ancestry.com: John C. Woods.
9. "Week in Wichita Society," *Wichita Daily Eagle*, December 24, 1905: 9.

Chapter 2

1. *Polk-McAvoy Directory Company's Wichita City Directory, 1912* (Wichita, KS: Polk-McAvoy Directory Company, 1912), 312, on Ancestry. com.
2. *Polk-McAvoy Directory Company's Wichita City Directory, 1914* (Wichita, KS: Polk-McAvoy Directory Company, 1914), 312, on Ancestry. com.
3. 1915 Kansas Census, Sedgwick County; *Polk-McAvoy Directory Company's Wichita City Directory, 1915* (Wichita, KS: Polk-McAvoy Directory Company, 1915), 276, 277, on Ancestry.com.

4. *Polk-McAvoy Directory Company's Wichita City Directory, 1916* (Wichita, KS: Polk-McAvoy Directory Company, 1916), 297, on Ancestry. com.
5. *Polk-McAvoy Directory Company's Wichita City Directory, 1918* (Wichita, KS: Polk-McAvoy Directory Company, 1918), 263, on Ancestry. com.
6. Memo for Commanding Officer, probably dated from 1929, US Navy Personnel File, John C. Woods, NPRC, St. Louis, MO.
7. *R. L. Polk's Wichita City Directory, 1922* (Wichita, KS: R. L. Polk, 1922), 342, on Ancestry.com.
8. Ernest A. Warden, "Suicide of Goering Was 'Biggest Disappointment' at Nazi Hangings," *Wichita Beacon*, November 29, 1946: 1.
9. Discussion with Paul Oberg, McCormick School Museum, Wichita, KS, February 24, 2015.
10. Interview with Janice Leitch, Alvin Morris Administration Center and Gwen Leivian, Wichita East High School, on September 14, 2017, at Wichita, KS.
11. *Polk's Wichita City Directory, 1928* (Kansas City, MO: R. L. Polk, 1928): 307, on Ancestry.com.
12. Application for Enlistment and NRB Form 16, US Navy recruiting documents, US Navy Personnel File, John C. Woods, NPRC.

Chapter 3

1. Application for Enlistment and NRB Form 16, US Navy recruiting documents, US Navy Personnel File, John C. Woods, NPRC.
2. Service Record of Woods, John Clarence, 341-73-98, US Navy Personnel File, John C. Woods.
3. Consent, Declaration, and Oath of Parent or Guardian in the Enlistment of a Minor under Twenty-One Years of Age for John C. Woods, US Navy Personnel File.

4. Application for United States Government Life Insurance, US Navy Personnel File, John C. Woods.

5. Service Record of Woods, John Clarence, 341-73-98, US Navy Personnel File, John C. Woods.

6. Declaration and Reward for Straggler from United States Naval Service (John Clarence Woods), signed by S. O. Greig, February 25, 1930, US Navy Personnel File, John C. Woods.

7. Service Record of Woods, John Clarence, 341-73-98, US Navy Personnel File, John C. Woods.

8. Ibid.

9. United States Fleet, Destroyer Squadrons, Battle Fleet, USS *Hovey*, letter from commanding officer to Bureau of Navigation, Woods, John Clarence, #341-73-98, apprentice seaman, US Navy—removal of mark of desertion—Report of, US Navy Personnel File, John C. Woods.

10. Board of Medical Survey, Report of Medical Survey, Woods, John Clarence, April 23, 1930, US Navy Personnel File, John C. Woods.

11. Ibid.

12. Ibid.

13. Service Record of Woods, John Clarence, 341-73-98, US Navy Personnel File, John C. Woods.

Chapter 4

1. Letter from Mr. John C. Woods to Bureau of Navigation concerning his discharge, May 17, 1931, US Navy Personnel File, John C. Woods.

2. Application for Certificate in Lieu of Discharge, May 25, 1931, US Navy Personnel File, John C. Woods.

3. Beccy Tanner, "Civilian Conservation Corps Built Woodson State Fishing Lake in Kansas," *Wichita Eagle* May 20, 2012.

4. Civilian Conservation Corps file, John C. Woods.

5. Ibid.

6. Tanner, "Civilian Conservation Corps Built Woodson State Fishing Lake in Kansas."

7. "Married, Chilcott-Woods," *Toronto Republican* (Toronto, KS), October 1–7, 1933.

8. 1920 US Federal Census for Woodson County, Kansas; 1930 US Federal Census for Woodson County, Kansas; and Ancestry.com: Hazel Marie Chilcott.

9. Interview with Linda Clark and Carol Stock, daughters of Helen Chilcott (Hazel Chilcott's sister) and Jerry Clark, on September 14, 2017, Toronto, KS.

10. Interview with relatives of Hazel Woods; "Married, Chilcott-Woods."

11. Civilian Conservation Corps file, John C. Woods.

12. Copy of marriage license for John C. Woods and Hazel Marie Chilcott, courtesy Linda Clark.

13. "Married, Chilcott-Woods."

14. Interview with relatives of Hazel Woods.

15. "Married, Chilcott-Woods"; and *Polk's Wichita City (Kansas) Directory, 1935* (Vol. XLIV) (Kansas City, MO: R. L. Polk, 1935), 288, on Ancestry.com.

16. Letter from Mr. John C. Woods to Bureau of Navigation concerning his discharge, July 1, 1936, US Navy Personnel File, John C. Woods.

17. *Polk's Wichita City (Kansas) Directory, 1941* (Vol. L) (Kansas City, MO: R. L. Polk, 1941), 307, on Ancestry.com.

18. Ancestry.com; Kansas, City and County Census Records, 1919–1961.

19. Interview with relatives of Hazel Woods.

20. Copy of journal entry, The State of Kansas vs. John C. Woods, dated 22nd day of December 1939, courtesy Linda Clark.

21. 1940 US Federal Census for Greenwood County, Kansas.

22. Ancestry.com; Kansas, City and County Census Records, 1919–1961.

23. "9 from Greenwood Called to Army Service July 8," *Eureka Herald* (Eureka, KS), June 26, 1941: 1; interview with Marilyn Bogle and Hazel Russell, Greenwood County Historical Society and Museum, September 14, 2017, Eureka, KS.

24. "Six to Leave Eureka for Fort Leavenworth," *Eureka Herald* (Eureka, KS), August 21, 1941: 1; interview with Marilyn Bogle and Hazel Russell.

25. *Polk's Wichita (Sedgwick County, Kansas), City Directory, 1942* (Vol. LI) (Kansas City, MO: R. L. Polk, 1942), 371, 383, on Ancestry.com.

26. Interview with Anna Dale Chilcott Cole, daughter of Dale Chilcott, Hazel Chilcott's brother, October 2, 2017.

27. *Polk's Wichita (Sedgwick County, Kansas), City Directory, 1943* (Vol. LII) (Kansas City, MO: R. L. Polk, 1943), 848, on Ancestry.com; and George Lancaster, "Wife Stunned to Know of Husband 'Executioner,'" *Wichita Beacon*, October 17, 1946: 1.

28. The United States Army Air Corps was designated the United States Army Air Forces on June 20, 1941.

29. Robert A. Mann, *The B-29 Superfortress Chronology, 1934–1960* (Jefferson, NC: McFarland, 2009), 26–29.

Chapter 5

1. "More Men Leave for the Armed Service," *Eureka Herald* (Eureka, KS), August 26, 1943: 1.

2. "Men Accepted Are Home on Furlough," *Eureka Herald* (Eureka, KS), September 2, 1943: 1.

3. Interview with Anna Dale Chilcott Cole.

4. Office of the Adjutant General Morning Reports, Company B, 37th Engineer (C) Battalion, March 31, 1944.

5. Alfred M. Beck, Abe Bortz, Charles W. Lynch, Lida Mayo, and Ralph F. Weld, "Preparing for D-day Landings," in *The Corps of Engineers: The War against Germany* (Washington, DC: Center of Military History, US Army, 1985), 302–316.

6. Beck et al., "The Landings on OMAHA and UTAH," in *The Corps of Engineers: The War against Germany*, 1, 327, 328, www.history.army. mil/html/reference/Normandy/TS/COE/COE15. html

Chapter 6

1. War Department, the Adjutant General's Office, "Pamphlet: Execution of Death Sentences," 31 March 1943; War Department, the Adjutant General's Office, SUBJECT: Execution of Death Sentences, 8 July 1943.

2. HQ, Normandy Base Section, Communications Zone, ETO, Memorandum, SUBJECT: Report of Personnel Experienced as Hangmen, 10 September 1944.

3. Experienced Hangman, 15 September 1944; Message, Survey concerning Qualified Hangman, from Major General John C. H. Lee to All Base Sections, 16 September 1944; Message from Loire Section to ETO ref identification of a potential hangman, 27 September 1944; Message from Normandy Base Section to ETO ref Private John C. Woods and Private First Class Thomas S. Robinson, 2 October 1944; all in Records Group 0498, HQ, ETO, US Army (World War II), Entry # UD1028, Judge Advocate Section, General Correspondence, Decimal File, 1942–1945, 250.451 Court-Martial Changes August 1945– December 1945 through GCM Reviews by Staff Judge Advocates of Subordinate Commands, Box 4726.

4. Note from ETO through the provost marshal to the judge advocate concerning the use of enlisted hangmen, 12 October 1944, in Records Group 0498, HQ, ETO, US Army (World War II), Entry # UD1028, Judge Advocate Section, General Correspondence, Decimal File, 1942–1945, 250.451 Court-Martial Changes August 1945–

December 1945 through GCM Reviews by Staff Judge Advocates of Subordinate Commands, Box 4726; HQ, ETO, "Standing Operating Procedure, No. 54, Execution of Death Sentences Imposed by Courts-Martial," 14 December 1944, Records Group 338, Records of US Army Operations, Tactical and Support Organizations (World War II and Thereafter), War Department, VIII Corps, Decimal Subject Files, 1940–1945, Entry UD 42882, Adjutant General Section 247 to Adjutant General Section 250 (Discipline, January 1944–May 1945), Box 7; Army Personnel File John C. Woods; HQ, ETO, Office of the Theater Provost Marshal, APO 887, Memorandum to General Lord concerning Hangmen, 28 September 1944.

Chapter 7

1. HQ, Seine DTC, APO 887, Report of Proceedings in the Death Chamber [*Rottenführer* Gunther Ohletz, 21st *SS Panzer Grenadier Regiment*, German army,] 9 October 1944; multiple email and telephone discussions with Frederic L. Borch III, regimental historian & archivist, Judge Advocate General's Corps, US Army, Judge Advocate General's Legal Center and School, Charlottesville, VA, 2017–2018.
2. Report of Proceedings in the Death Chamber [*Rottenführer* Gunther Ohletz].
3. Wall, "Hangman," 64.
4. Personnel file, James B. Sanders.
5. Personnel file, Roy W. Anderson.
6. HQ, ETO, Review of Staff Judge Advocate, *United States v. Technician Fifth Grade James B. Sanders, 34124233, Company B, 29th Signal Construction Battalion and Private Roy W. Anderson, 35407199, Company B, 29th Signal Construction Battalion*, undated.
7. HQ, ETO, General Court-Martial Order Number 91 [Technician Fifth Grade James B. Sanders and Private Roy W. Anderson], 21 October 1944.
8. HQ, Seine DTC, APO 887, Report of Proceedings in the Death Chamber [General Prisoner James B. Sanders], 26 October 1944.
9. Ibid.
10. Ibid.
11. HQ, Seine DTC, APO 887, Report of Proceedings in the Death Chamber [General Prisoner Roy W. Anderson], 26 October 1944.
12. Ibid.
13. Service Record, Paul M. Kluxdal, March 17, 1942–October 31, 1944.
14. HQ, ETO, General Court-Martial Order Number 94 [Private First Class Paul M. Kluxdal], 26 October 1944.
15. HQ, Seine DTC, APO 887, Report of Proceedings in the Death Chamber, 1 November 1944.
16. Ibid.
17. Ibid.
18. Personnel Files, Willie Wimberley Jr. and Joseph Watson.
19. Branch Office of the Judge Advocate General with the ETO, APO 871, Board of Review No. 1, *United States v. Private Joseph Watson (39610125) and Technician Fifth Grade Willie Wimberley Jr. (36392154), Both of 257th Signal Construction Company*, 11 October 1944.
20. HQ, Seine DTC, APO 887, Report of Proceedings in the Death Chamber [Willie Wimberly], 10 November 1944.
21. Ibid.
22. Ibid.
23. HQ, Seine DTC, APO 887, Report of Proceedings in the Death Chamber [Joseph Watson], 10 November 1944.
24. Ibid.
25. Personnel File, Richard Bunney Scott.
26. General Court-Martial Order Number 106.
27. HQ, Guard House Overhead Detachment Number 5, US Army, APO 562, Report of Proceedings at the Execution of General Prisoner, Richard B. Scott, 38040012 (formerly Technician 5th Grade, 229th Quartermaster Salvage Collecting Company), 18 November 1944.
28. Ibid.
29. Ibid.
30. Personnel File, William D. Pennyfeather.

31. Branch Office of the Judge Advocate General with the ETO, APO 871, Board of Review No. 1, *United States v. Private William D. Pennyfeather, 32801627, 3868th Quartermaster Truck Company,* 4 November 1944.

32. HQ, Guard House Overhead Detachment Number 5, US Army, APO 562, Report of Proceedings at the Execution of General Prisoner, William D. Pennyfeather, 32801627 (formerly Private, 3868th Quartermaster Truck Company), 18 November 1944.

33. Ibid.

34. The General Board, United States Forces, European Theater, Judge Advocate Section, the Military Offender in the Theater of Operations, Study 84, 5. Report cited Eugene S. Sernans, executive secretary of the General Howard Association, quoted in *Stars & Stripes* on October 10, 1945.

35. Personnel File, Theron W. McGann.

36. HQ, First United States Army, APO 230, Review of the Staff Judge Advocate of the Record of Trial by General Court-Martial of McGann, Theron W., 39332102, Private, Company A, 32nd Signal Battalion, 21 September 1944.

37. HQ, ETO, General Court-Martial Order Number 104 [Private Theron W. McGann], 15 November 1944.

38. HQ, Normandy Base Section, Communications Zone, ETO, APO 562, Execution of General Prisoner Theron W. McGann, 17 November 1944; HQ, Normandy Base Section, Communications Zone, ETO, APO 562, Report of Proceedings at the Execution of General Prisoner Theron W. McGann, 39332102, 20 November 1944.

39. Ibid.

40. Ibid.

41. HQ, Third United States Army, Office of the Judge Advocate, Review of the Staff Judge Advocate, *United States v. Private Arthur E. Davis, 36788637, 3326th Quartermaster Truck Company, and Private Charles H. Jordan, 14066430, 3327th Quartermaster Truck Company,* 28 August 1944.

42. Branch Office of the Judge Advocate General with the ETO, APO 887, Board of Review No. 2, *United States v. Private Arthur E. Davis, 36788637, 3326th Quartermaster Truck Company, and Private Charles H. Jordan, 14066430, 3327th Quartermaster Truck Company,* 2 November 1944.

43. HQ, ETO, General Court-Martial Orders Number 105 [Private Arthur E. Davis and Private Charles H. Jordan], 15 November 1944.

44. HQ, VIII Corps, APO 308, Review of Staff Judge Advocate, *United States v. Private First Class James E. Hendricks, 33453189, 3326th Quartermaster Truck Company,* 18 September 1944.

45. Ibid.

46. Ibid.

47. Ibid.

48. Ibid.

49. HQ, ETO, General Court-Martial Orders Number 109 [Private First Class James E. Hendricks], 19 November 1944.

50. Report of Proceedings at the Execution of General Prisoner James E. Hendricks, 33453189, 24 November 1944.

51. Ibid.

52. Ibid.

53. Branch Office of the Judge Advocate General with the ETO, APO 887, Board of Review No. 1, *United States v. Sergeant Johnnie E. Hudson (34741799) and Technician Fifth Grade Leo Valentine Sr. (32954278), Both of 396th Quartermaster Truck Company, and Technician Fifth Grade Oscar N. Newman (35226382), Headquarters and Headquarters Company, 712th Railway Operation Battalion,* 18 November 1944.

54. Army Personnel File, Leo Valentine.

55. Service Record for Oscar N. Newman from August 13, 1943, to November 29, 1944.

56. HQ, ETO, General Court-Martial Order Number 115 (Technician Fifth Grade Oscar N. Newman), 25 November 1944.

57. HQ, Oise Section, Communications Zone, APO 513, Report of Proceedings at the Execution of General Prisoner Leo Valentine Sr., 32954278 (formerly Technician Fifth Grade, 396th Quartermaster Truck Company), 29 November 1944.

58. Ibid.

59. Ibid.

60. HQ, Oise Section, Communications Zone, APO 513, Report of Proceedings at the Execution of General Prisoner Oscar N. Newman, 35226382 (formerly Technician Fifth Grade, Headquarters and Headquarters Company, 712th Railway Operating Battalion), 29 November 1944.

61. Branch Office of the Judge Advocate General with the ETO, APO 887, Board of Review No. 1, *United States v. Privates First Class William E. Davis (33541888) and J. C. Potts (34759592), Both of 3121st Quartermaster Service Company*, 29 November 1944.

62. HQ, ETO, General Court-Martial Order Number 146 (Private First Class William E. Davis), 21 December 1944.

63. HQ, Loire DTC, APO 517, Report of Proceedings at the Execution of General Prisoner William E. Davis, formerly Private First Class, 3121st Quartermaster Service Company, 28 December 1944.

64. Ibid.

65. Ibid.

66. Receipt for Remains of General William E. Davis, 27 December 1944.

67. Branch Office of the Judge Advocate General with the ETO, APO 887, Board of Review No. 2, *United States v. Private First Class John David Cooper (34562464) and Private J. P. Wilson (32484756), Both of 3966th Quartermaster Truck Company*, 28 December 1944.

68. HQ Loire DTC, APO 517, Report of Proceedings at the Execution of General Prisoner John D. Cooper, formerly Private First Class, 3966th Quartermaster Truck Company, 12 January 1945.

69. HQ, Loire DTC, APO 517, Report of Proceedings at the Execution of General Prisoner Walter J. Baldwin, formerly Private, 574th Ordnance Ammunition Company, 17 January 1945.

70. Personnel File, Walter J. Baldwin

71. Record of Trial General Court-Martial, Private Walter J. Baldwin, Palais de Justice, Le Mans, France, October 6, 1944.

72. Ibid.

73. HQ, Loire DTC, APO 517, Report of Proceedings at the Execution of General Prisoner Walter J. Baldwin.

74. Ibid.

75. Record of Trial, Teton, Wilford, and Farrell, Arthur J., both of Troop C, 17th Cavalry Reconnaissance Squadron, Rennes, Brittany, France, 16 and 23 October 1944.

76. Ibid.

77. HQ, ETO, General Court-Martial Order Number 11, 10 January 1945.

78. HQ, Loire DTC, APO 517, Report of the Proceedings at the Execution of General Prisoner Arthur J. Farrell, formerly Private, Troop C, 17th Cavalry Reconnaissance Squadron, 20 January 1945.

79. Ibid.

80. Ibid.

81. HQ, Normandy Base Section, Communications Zone, Review by the Staff Judge Advocate, *United States v. Private James W. Twiggs, 38265086, Company F, 1323rd Engineer General Services Regiment*, 18 November 1944.

82. HQ, Loire DTC, Report of Proceedings at the Execution of General Prisoner James W. Twiggs, 38265086, formerly Private, Company F, 1323rd Engineer General Service Regiment, 22 January 1945.

83. Ibid.

84. Ibid.

85. Master Sergeant Patrick V. Garland, Retired, "Penal Institutions in the European Theater of Operations," *Military Police: The Professional Bulletin of the Military Police Corps*, Spring 2012 (Ft. Leonard Wood, MO), 65.

86. Branch Office of the Judge Advocate General with the ETO, APO 887, Board of Review No. 1, *United States v. Privates Mervin Holden (38226564) and Elwood J. Spencer (33739343), Both of 646th Quartermaster Truck Company*, 11 January 1945.

87. Ibid.

88. Ibid.

89. HQ, ETO, General Court-Martial Order Number 20 and 21, 20 January 1945.

90. HQ, Loire DTC, APO 517, Report of Proceedings at the Execution of General Prisoner Mervin Holden, formerly Private, 646th Quartermaster Truck Company, 6 February 1945.

91. Ibid.

92. HQ, Loire DTC, APO 517, Report of Proceedings at the Execution of General Prisoner Elwood J. Spencer, formerly Private, 646th Quartermaster Truck Company, 6 February 1945.

93. Ibid.

94. HQ Loire DTC, APO 517, Report of Proceedings at the Execution of General Prisoner J. P. Wilson, formerly Private, 3966th Quartermaster Truck Company, 6 February 1945.

95. Ibid.

96. Ibid.

97. Ibid.

98. HQ, XII Corps, Office of the Provost Marshal, APO 312, Report on Investigation of Shooting and Alleged Rape in Hameau-Pigeon on 1 August 1944.

99. HQ, Normandy Base Section, Communications Zone, ETO, APO 562, Review by the Staff Judge Advocate, *United States v. Private Waiters Yancy, 35802328, 1511th Engineer Water Supply Company, APO 403*, 25 November 1944; HQ, ETO, Review by the Staff Judge Advocate, *United States v. Private Robert L. Skinner, 35802328,*

1511th Engineer Water Supply Company, APO 403, 29 December 1944.

100. HQ, ETO, Confirmation of Sentence, Private Waiters Yancy, 37499079, 1511th Engineer Water Supply Company, 23 December 1944.

101. HQ, Loire DTC, APO 517, Report of Proceedings at the Execution of General Prisoner Waiters Yancy, formerly Private, 1511th Engineer Water Supply, 11 February 1945.

102. Ibid.

103. HQ, Loire DTC, APO 517, Report of Proceedings at the Execution of General Prisoner Robert L. Skinner, formerly Private, 1511th Engineer Water Supply, 11 February 1945.

104. Army Personnel File, John C. Woods.

105. Personnel File, William Mack.

106. Branch Office of the Judge Advocate General with the ETO, APO 887, Board of Review No. 1, *United States v. Private William Mack (32620461), Battery A, 578th Field Artillery Battalion*, 30 January 1945.

107. Ibid.

108. Branch Office of the Judge Advocate General with the ETO, APO 887, Board of Review No. 1, *United States v. Private William Mack (32620461), Battery A, 578th Field Artillery Battalion*, 30 January 1945; HQ, ETO, General Court-Martial Order Number 40 (Private William Mack), 9 February 1945.

109. HQ, Loire DTC, APO 562, Report of Proceedings at the Execution of General Prisoner William Mack, formerly Private, 578th Artillery Battalion, 17 February 1945.

110. Ibid.

111. Ibid.

112. Branch Office of the Judge Advocate General with the ETO, APO 887, Board of Review No. 1, *United States v. Privates James R. Parrott (32483580), Grant U. Smith (35688909) and William C. Downes (33519814), All of 597th Ordnance Ammunition Company*, 9 February 1945.

113. Ibid.

114. HQ, ETO, APO 562, General Court-Martial Order Number 51 [William C. Downes], 23 February 1945.

115. HQ, ETO, APO 562, General Court-Martial Order Number 50 [William C. Clifton], 23 February 1945.

116. Ibid.

117. HQ, Loire DTC, APO 562, "Orders," 25 February 1945.

118. HQ, Loire DTC, APO 562, Report of Proceedings at the Execution of General Prisoner William C. Downes, formerly Private, 597th Ordnance Ammunition Company, 1 March 1945.

119. Ibid.

120. Ancestry.com: Herbert A. Kleinbeck Jr., multiple sources.

121. Branch Office of the Judge Advocate General with the ETO, APO 887, Board of Review No. 2, *United States v. Privates Amos Agee (34163762), Frank Watson (34793522) and John C. Smith (33214953), All of 644th Quartermaster Troop Transport Company*, 14 February 1945.

122. Ibid.

123. HQ, Loire DTC, APO 562, Report of Proceedings at the Execution of General Prisoner Amos Agee, formerly Private, 644th Quartermaster Troop Transport Company, 5 March 1945.

124. Ibid.

125. Ibid.

126. HQ, Loire DTC, APO 562, Report of Proceedings at the Execution of General Prisoner John C. Smith, formerly Private, 644th Quartermaster Troop Transport Company, 5 March 1945.

127. HQ, Loire DTC, APO 562, Report of Proceedings at the Execution of General Prisoner Frank Watson, formerly Private, 644th Quartermaster Troop Transport Company, 5 March 1945.

128. Branch Office of the Judge Advocate General with the ETO, APO 887, Board of Review No. 1, *United States v. Private Olin W. Williams, 34649494, 4194th Quartermaster Service Company*, 14 March 1945.

129. Ibid.

130. HQ, ETO, Confirmation Order for Private Olin W. Williams, 4194th Quartermaster Service Company, 4 March 1945; HQ, ETO, General Court-Martial Order Number 85, 24 March 1945.

131. HQ, Loire DTC, APO 562, Report of Proceedings at the Execution of General Prisoner Olin W. Williams, formerly Private, 4194th Quartermaster Service Company, 31 March 1945.

132. Ibid.

133. HQ, Normandy Base Section, Communications Zone, ETO, APO 562, Review by the Staff Judge Advocate, *United States v. Private Tommie Davison, 34485174, 427th Quartermaster Troop Transport Company*, 25 January 1945.

134. Ibid.

135. Ibid.

136. Ibid.

137. HQ, Loire DTC, APO 562, Report of Proceedings at the Execution of General Prisoner Tommie Davison, formerly Private, 427th Quartermaster Troop Transport Company, 31 March 1945.

138. Ibid.

139. Ibid.

140. War Department, the Adjutant General's Office, SUBJECT: Method of execution of death sentences, 9 April 1945 in Records Group 0498, Headquarters, ETO, US Army (World War II), Entry # UD1028, Judge Advocate Section, General Correspondence, Decimal File, 1942–1945, 250.4 Court-Martial.

141. HQ, First United States Army, APO 230, Review of the Staff Judge Advocate, Case of Private Benjamin F. Hopper, 32720571, 3170th Quartermaster Service Company, 12 December 1944.

142. Ibid.

143. HQ, ETO, General Court-Martial Order Number 107, 7 April 1945.

144. HQ, Loire DTC, APO 562, Report of Proceedings at the Execution of General Prisoner Benjamin F. Hopper, Formerly Private, 3170th Quartermaster Service Company, 12 April 1945.

145. Ibid.

146. Death Book ledger at US Army Clerk of the Court in Ballston, Virginia; final dispositions of rape and/or murder charges tried by General Courts-Martial, December 1941 to April 1946, and analysis of evidence establishing identity of accused in such cases as resulted in death of the accused.

147. Ibid.

148. HQ, ETO, General Court-Martial Order Number 116 [Bailey, Jones & Williams], 15 April 1945.

149. HQ, Loire DTC, APO 562, Report of Proceedings at the Execution of General Prisoner James L. Jones, formerly Private, 434th Port Company, 501st Port Battalion, 21 April 1945.

150. Ibid.

151. Ibid.

152. Ibid.

153. HQ, ETO, Review by Staff Judge Advocate, *United States v. Private George Green Jr., 38476751, 998th Quartermaster Salvage Collecting Company*, 25 February 1945.

154. Ibid.

155. Ibid.

156. HQ, ETO, General Court-Martial Order Number 129, Private George Green Jr., 38476751, 998th Quartermaster Salvage Collecting Company, 1 May 1945.

157. HQ, Loire DTC, APO 562, Report of Proceedings at the Execution of General Prisoner George Green Jr., formerly Private 998th Quartermaster Salvage Collecting Company, 15 May 1945.

158. Ibid.

159. Ibid.

160. Ibid.

161. Death Book ledger

162. Ibid.

163. HQ, ETO, General Court-Martial Order Number 137 [Haze Heard], 11 May 1945.

164. HQ, Loire DTC, APO 562, Report of Execution, Haze Heard, 34562354, 23 May 1945.

165. Ibid.

166. Ibid.

167. HQ, XX Corps, APO 340, Review of the Staff Judge Advocate, Private First Class William J. McCarter, 34675988, 27 February 1945.

168. Ibid.

169. Ibid.

170. HQ, ETO, General Court-Martial Order Number 138, 12 May 1945.

171. Interview with Thomas J. Ward Jr., April 10, 2013, Harrisburg, PA.

172. HQ, Loire DTC, APO 562, Report of Execution, William J. McCarter, 34675988, 29 May 1945.

173. Ibid.

174. Ibid.

175. Service Record, Norris, Clete O., 25 September 1941–31 May 1945.

176. Ibid.

177. HQ, ETO, General Court-Martial Order Number 174, 26 May 1945.

178. HQ, Loire DTC, APO 562, Report of Execution, Clete O. Norris, 31 May 1945.

179. Ibid.

180. Ibid.

181. Ibid.

182. Ibid.

183. HQ, ETO, Office of the Staff Judge Advocate, Review of Record of Trial by General Court-Martial, *United States vs. Alvin R. Rollins, 34716953, Private First Class, 306th Quartermaster Railhead Company*, 25 April 1945.

184. Ibid.

185. HQ, Loire DTC, APO 562, Report of Proceedings at the Execution of General Prisoner Alvin R. Rollins, formerly Private First Class, 306th Quartermaster Railhead Company, 1 June 1945.

186. Branch Office of the Judge Advocate General with the ETO, APO 887, Board of Review No. 2, *United States v. Private First Class Matthew Clay Jr. (38490561), 3236th Quartermaster Service Company*, 18 May 1945.
187. Ibid.
188. Ibid.
189. HQ, Loire DTC, APO 562, Report of Proceedings at the Execution of General Prisoner Matthew Clay Jr., formerly Private First Class, 3236th Quartermaster Service Company, 5 June 1945.
190. Ibid.
191. Ibid.
192. Ibid.
193. Ibid.
194. HQ, Channel Base Section, Communications Zone, ETO, APO 228, Review of the Staff Judge Advocate, Ortiz, Victor, 30405077, 22 March 1945.
195. Ancestry.com: Victor Ortiz
196. Review of the Staff Judge Advocate, Ortiz, Victor, 30405077, 22 March 1945.
197. Branch Office of the Judge Advocate General with the ETO, APO 887, Board of Review, *United States v. Private Victor Ortiz, 30405077, 3269th Quartermaster Service Company*, 8 June 1945; HQ, ETO, General Court-Martial Order Number 213, 16 June 1945.
198. HQ, Loire DTC, APO 562, Report of Proceedings at the Execution of General Prisoner Victor Ortiz, formerly Private, 3269th Quartermaster Service Company, 23 June 1945.
199. Ibid.
200. Ibid.
201. Ibid.
202. Branch Office of the Judge Advocate General with the ETO, APO 887, Board of Review Number 3, *United States v. Private Willie Johnson 38270465, 3984th Quartermaster Truck Company*, 11 June 1945.
203. Ibid.
204. HQ, 165th General Hospital, APO 562, Insanity Board Proceedings for Johnson, Willie, Private, 38270465, 3984th Quartermaster Truck Company, 23 January 1945.
205. Branch Office of the Judge Advocate General with the ETO, APO 887, Board of Review Number 3, *United States v. Private Willie Johnson, 38270465.*
206. HQ, Loire DTC, APO 562, Report of Proceedings at the Execution of General Prisoner Willie Johnson, formerly Private, 3984th Quartermaster Truck Company, 26 June 1945.
207. Ibid.
208. Ibid.
209. Ibid.
210. HQ, Seventh Army, Office of the Staff Judge Advocate, Review of the Staff Judge Advocate in the Case of Gordon, Tom, 34091950, Private, 3251st Quartermaster Service Company, 30 March 1945.
211. Ibid.
212. Ibid.
213. HQ, ETO, Confirmation Order in the Case of Private Tom Gordon, 34091950, 3251st Quartermaster Service Company, 6 May 1945.
214. HQ, Loire DTC, Report of Proceedings at the Execution of General Prisoner Tom Gordon, 34091950, formerly Private, 3251st Quartermaster Service Company, 12 July 1945.
215. Ibid.
216. Ibid.
217. HQ, Army Service Forces, Office of the Provost Marshal General, SUBJECT: Observers Report, ETOUSA in Records Group 0498, HQ, ETO, US Army (World War II), Entry #UD1028, Judge Advocate Section, General Correspondence, Decimal File, 1942–1945, 250.4 Court-Martial.
218. Ibid.
219. Ibid.
220. Ibid.
221. HQ, Seventh Army, SJA, APO 758, Review of the Staff Judge Advocate of the Record of Trial for Wray, Robert (NMI), 34461589, Private, 3299th Quartermaster Service Company, 6 May 1945.

222. HQ, ETO, Review by the Staff Judge Advocate, *United States v. Private Robert Wray, 34461589, 3299th Quartermaster Service Company*, 19 June 1945.

223. HQ, ETO, Confirmation Order in the Case of Private Robert Wray, 34461589, 3299th Quartermaster Service Company, 26 June 1945.

224. HQ, Seventh Army, SJA, APO 758, Review of the Staff Judge Advocate of the Record of Trial for Wray, Robert (NMI), 34461589, Private, 3299th Quartermaster Service Company, 6 May 1945.

225. HQ, Loire DTC, APO 562, Report of Proceedings at the Execution of Robert Wray, formerly Private, 3299th Quartermaster Service Company, 22 August 1945.

226. Ibid.

227. Ibid.

228. Ibid.

229. Office of the Division Judge Advocate, APO 454, Review of Record of Trial by Division Judge Advocate, *United States v. Private Charles M. Robinson, 38164425, 667th Quartermaster Truck Company*, 3 May 1945; and Branch Office of the Judge Advocate General with the ETO, APO 887, Board of Review Number 2, *United States v. Private Charles M. Robinson, 38164425, 667th Quartermaster Truck Company*, 1 September 1945.

230. Ibid.

231. Ibid.

232. HQ, Loire DTC, APO 562, Report of Proceedings at the Execution of Charles M. Robinson, formerly Private, 667th Quartermaster Truck Company, 30 September 1945.

233. Ibid.

234. Branch Office of the Judge Advocate General with the ETO, APO 887, Board of Review Number 3, *United States v. Private First Class Blake W. Mariano (38011593), Company C, 191st Tank Battalion*, 6 September 1945.

235. HQ, Loire DTC, APO 562, Report of Proceedings at the Execution of Blake W. Mariano, 38011593, formerly Private First Class, Company C, 191st Tank Battalion, 10 October 1945.

236. Ibid.

237. Ibid.

238. Ibid.

239. Personal interview with Thomas J. Ward Jr., April 10, 2013 at Harrisburg, PA.

240. Ibid.

241. Personnel File, Thomas J. Ward Jr.

242. HQ, US Forces, ETO, 19 December 1945, General Court-Martial Order No. 626.

243. HQ, Loire DTC, APO 562, 4 January 1946, Special Order Number 4, HQ, Loire DTC, APO 562, 3 January 1946, Memorandum: Special Time Schedule for Execution on 5 January 1946 and signed Certificate concerning the physical and mental condition of Ellsworth Williams.

244. Induction Record for Ellsworth Williams

245. HQ, Loire DTC, APO 562, 5 January 1946, Report of Proceedings at the Execution of Ellsworth Williams, 34200976, formerly Private, Company "E", 1346th Engineer General Service Regiment.

246. Ibid.

Chapter 8

1. *Stars & Stripes*, Mediterranean (Rome) 2, no. 20 (June 30, 1945): 1, 8.

2. "US Army Justice Falls on Germans," *Life Magazine* 19, no. 3 (July 16, 1945): 17–21.

3. Ibid.

4. Ibid.

5. Ibid.

6. Ibid.

7. Technician third grade was often addressed as staff sergeant.

8. Email conversations with Ashley Robinson Skala, grandniece of Thomas F. Robinson, January 1, 2018.

9. "Miss Decker Married to Thomas Robinson," *Herald Statesman* (Yonkers, NY), June 16, 1942: 7.

10. Ancestry.com search; NARA, World War II Army Enlistment Records, Record Group 64; US Social Security Applications and Claims Index; Find-a-Grave: Thomas F. Robinson.

11. Ibid.

12. "5 Germans Hanged for Killing Fliers," *New York Times*, November 10, 1945: 8.

13. *Stars & Stripes*, Mediterranean (Rome) 2, no. 133 (November 12, 1945): 2.

14. "14-Point. GI Hangman Sizes Up Goering, Decides to Stay On," *Stars & Stripes* (European Edition), November 13, 1945: 5.

15. *Stars & Stripes*, Mediterranean (Rome) 2, no. 152 (December 4, 1945): 2.

16. Gregory A. Freeman, *The Last Mission of the Wham Bam Boys: Courage, Tragedy and Justice in World War II* (New York: Palgrave Macmillan, 2011), ix, 197, 198, 199.

17. Ibid.

18. Ibid.

19. Ibid.

20. Ibid.

21. Final [Pay] Statement of Woods, John C., 37540591, 21 January 1946, Personnel File, John C. Woods.

22. *Stars & Stripes*, Mediterranean (Rome) 2, no. 188 (January 15, 1946): 2.

23. Johann Dachs, *Tod durch das Fallbeil: Der deutsche Scharfrichter Johann Reichhart (1893–1972)* (Regensburg, Germany: Mittelbayerische Druck- und Verlags-Gesellschaft, 2001), 10–13.

24. Ibid.

25. Ibid., 13.

26. Ibid., 22–24.

27. Ibid., 26–28.

28. Ibid., 28.

29. Ibid., 30–31.

30. Office of the Adjutant General, War Department, *Histories of Two Hundred and Fifty-One Divisions of the German Army Which Participated in the War (1914–1918)* (Washington, DC: Government Printing Office, 1920), 275–276.

31. Ibid., 276, 600, 601.

32. Ibid., 601–602.

33. Herbert von Sydow, *Das Infanterie-Regiment Hamburg "2. Hanseatisches" Nr. 76 im Weltkriege 1914/18*, Erinnerungsblätter deutscher Regimenter, Ehemals preußische Truppenteile 52 (Oldenburg, Germany, and Berlin: G. Stalling, 1922).

34. Dachs, *Tod durch das Fallbeil*, 32.

35. Ibid., 35–59.

36. Ibid., 59.

37. Ernst Klee, *Das Personenlexicon zum Dritten Reich* (Hamburg, Germany: Nikol Verlag, 2016), 557.

38. Deputy Theater Judge Advocate's Office, War Crimes Branch, United States Forces, European Theater, Review and Recommendations, Case No. 12-793, *United States v. Heinrich Flauaus and Nikolaus Fachinger, German Civilians*, 16 January 1946.

39. NARA, Record Group: 549, Records of Headquarters, United States Army Europe, US Army War Crimes Trials in Europe, T-1078, Hadamar Trial, Roll 2: Report on Executions by Hanging in the Bruchsal Prison, Military Commission Order Number 4.

40. Hadamar Trial, Roll 2: Report on Executions by Hanging in the Bruchsal Prison.

41. Ibid.

42. Ibid.

43. Ibid.

44. Ibid.

45. Report of proceedings regarding the execution by hanging of August Kobus at Bruchsal Prison, Bruchsal Germany on 15 March 1946.

46. Personnel File, Vincent J. Martino.

47. Joseph H. Williams, *Captor—Captive* (Jacksonville, FL: Girtman, 1986), 57.

48. Ibid., 58.

49. Ibid.

50. Ibid., 58–59.

51. Thomas Raithel, *Die Strafenstalt Landsberg am Lech und der Spöttinger Friedhof (1944–1958)* (Munich: R. Oldenbourg Verlag, 2009), 50–53.

52. Stanley Tilles and Jeffrey Denhart, *By the Neck until Dead: The Gallows of Nuremberg* (Bedford, IN: JoNa Books, 1999), 45–46.

53. "Common design" was best explained by Robert E. Conot in *Judgment at Nuremberg*: "The crimes and atrocities were not single or unconnected, but were the inevitable outcome of the basic criminal conspiracy of the Nazi party. This conspiracy, based on the Nazi doctrine of racism and totalitarianism, involved murder, terrorism, and the destruction of peaceful populations in violation of the laws of war. A conspiracy is criminal either because it aims at the accomplishment of lawful ends by unlawful means, or because it aims at the accomplishment of unlawful ends by lawful means. Therefore, such technicalities as the question whether the extermination of fellow Germans by Nazis perpetrated before there was a state of war, would be unimportant, if you recognize as the basic crime the Nazi conspiracy which required for success the killing of dissident liberal Germans and the extermination of German (and non-German) Jews before and after the war had begun." Many Germans strongly disagreed with "common design," preferring only to blame those men who actually pulled the triggers or dumped the poison gas pellets. Had postwar trials adopted the latter rationale, almost no one would have been convicted, let alone sentenced to death.

54. Tilles and Denhart, *By the Neck*, 42.

55. Ibid., 43, 45.

56. "14 Germans Pay for Dachau Crimes," *Stars & Stripes*, Mediterranean (Rome) 2, no. 304 (May 30, 1946): 2.

57. "A German War Criminal Pays the Penalty for His Acts," *New York Times*, May 30, 1946: 10.

58. "Dachau's Last Torturers Die on the Gallows," *Chicago Tribune*, May 30, 1946: 6.

59. Holger Lessing, *Der erste Dachauer Prozess (1945/46)* (Baden-Baden, Germany: Nomos Verlagsgesellschaft, 1993), 268, 269, 270, 271, 367, 394.

60. Irving Dilliard, "28 Dachau Killers Are Hanged at Landsberg," *Stars & Stripes* (European Edition), May 30, 1946: 5.

61. Lessing, *Der erste Dachauer Prozess*, 394; Raithel, *Die Strafenstalt Landsberg*, 55, 141.

62. HQ, Third US Army and Eastern Military District, Office of the Judge Advocate, Review of Proceedings of General Military Court in the Case of *United States vs. Martin Gottfried Weiss*, 18–20.

63. Williams, *Captor—Captive*, 156.

64. 1920 US Federal Census; 1930 US Federal Census; 1940 US Federal Census (on Ancestry.com).

65. Joshua A. Resnik, "Der Henker von Nürnberg," *Zeit* Online, October 18, 1996.

66. NARA, World War II Army Enlistment Records, Record Group 64.

67. John Marcus, "Nuremberg Executioner Says, 'It Was a Pleasure,'" *Los Angeles Times*, November 24, 1996.

68. Online footage, TV interview with Joseph Malta, Part 6; Resnik, "Der Henker."

69. Online footage, TV interview with Joseph Malta, Part 7.

70. Williams, *Captor—Captive*, 156.

71. Resnik, "Der Henker."

72. Marcus, "Nuremberg Executioner Says, 'It Was a Pleasure.'"

73. Review of Proceedings, *United States vs. Martin Gottfried Weiss*, 52, 111.

74. Raithel, *Die Strafenstalt Landsberg*, 139; Review, *United States vs. Martin Gottfried Weiss*, 52, 111. Kiern's remains were buried in Munich.

75. Heinrich Pflanz, *Die Hingerichteten von Landsberg und der Spöttinger Friedhof* (Beltheim-Schnellbach, Germany: Bublies Verlag, 2004), 56–58, Raithel, *Die Strafenstalt Landsberg*, 138;

NARA, Record Group 242, NARA, Collection of
Foreign Records Seized; Berlin Document Center
(BDC), SS Officer Personnel Files, A3343,
SSO-Roll 214; Klee, *Das Personenlexicon*, 158.

76. NARA, Record Group 549: Records of
Headquarters, United States Army Europe,
Records of War Criminal Prison #1 at Landsberg,
Records Relating to Executed Prisoners, Entry
Number A-1 2243, Trenkle-Box 13; Raithel, *Die
Strafenstalt Landsberg*, 150.

77. Pflanz, *Die Hingerichteten*, 59; Raithel, *Die
Strafenstalt Landsberg*, 138; BDC, SS Officer
Personnel Files, A3343, SSO-Roll 170B; Review,
United States vs. Martin Gottfried Weiss, 58, 115.

78. NARA, Record Group 549, Jarolin-Box 6; BDC,
SS Officer Personnel Files, A3343, SSO-Roll
135A; Review, *United States vs. Martin Gottfried
Weiss*, 22-24; NARA, Record Group 549, Records
of Headquarters, United States Army Europe,
Records of War Criminal Prison #1 at Landsberg,
Records Relating to Executed Prisoners, Entry
Number A-1 2243, Jarolin-Box 6.

79. Pflanz, *Die Hingerichteten*, 61–63; Review,
United States vs. Martin Gottfried Weiss, 26.

80. BDC, SS Officer Personnel Files, A3343,
SSO-Roll 097B; Review, *United States vs. Martin
Gottfried Weiss*, 66; Klee, *Das Personenlexicon*,
556.

81. NARA, Record Group 549, Schilling-Box 11;
Review, *United States vs. Martin Gottfried Weiss*,
46, 104; Klee, *Das Personenlexicon*, 535.

82. Pflanz, *Die Hingerichteten*, 64; Review, *United
States vs. Martin Gottfried Weiss*, 27–28.

83. BDC, SS Officer Personnel Files, A3343,
SSO-Roll 242A; Review, *United States vs. Martin
Gottfried Weiss*, 73–74; Klee, *Das
Personenlexicon*, 357.

84. Review, *United States vs. Martin Gottfried Weiss*,
51, 111.

85. NARA, Record Group 549, Records of
Headquarters, United States Army Europe,
Records of War Criminal Prison #1 at Landsberg,
Records Relating to Executed Prisoners, Entry
Number A-1 2243, Moll-Box 9.

86. Pflanz, *Die Hingerichteten*, 66–67; Klee, *Das
Personenlexicon*, 414.

87. Pflanz, *Die Hingerichteten*, 68–69; Review,
United States vs. Martin Gottfried Weiss, 63, 69,
122.

88. Pflanz, *Die Hingerichteten*, 70–72; Review,
United States vs. Martin Gottfried Weiss, 118.

89. BDC, SS Officer Personnel Files, A3343,
SSO-Roll 267A; Pflanz, *Die Hingerichteten*, 73.

90. Review, *United States vs. Martin Gottfried Weiss*,
61, 116; Pflanz, *Die Hingerichteten*, 74.

91. NARA, Record Group 549, Records of
Headquarters, United States Army Europe,
Records of War Criminal Prison #1 at Landsberg,
Records Relating to Executed Prisoners, Entry
Number A-1 2243, Welter-Box 14; Review of
Proceedings of General Military Court in the
Case of *United States vs. Martin Gottfried Weiss*,
55, 114.

92. BDC, SS Officer Personnel Files, A3343,
SSO-Roll 031B; Review, *United States vs. Martin
Gottfried Weiss*, 53, 112; Klee, *Das
Personenlexicon*, 484.

93. Review, *United States vs. Martin Gottfried Weiss*,
32.

94. BDC, SS Officer Personnel Files, A3343,
SSO-Roll 231B; French L. MacLean, *2,000 Quotes
from Hitler's 1000-Year Reich* (Atglen, PA:
Schiffer, 2007), 336; Review, *United States vs.
Martin Gottfried Weiss*, 16–17; Klee, *Das
Personenlexicon*, 664.

95. BDC, SS Officer Personnel Files, A3343,
SSO-Roll 166A; Review, *United States vs. Martin
Gottfried Weiss*, 32-38; Klee, *Das Personenlexicon*,
306; NARA, Record Group 549, Records of
Headquarters, United States Army Europe,
Records of War Criminal Prison #1 at Landsberg,
Records Relating to Executed Prisoners, Entry
Number A-1 2243, Kick-Box 7.

96. Review, *United States vs. Martin Gottfried Weiss*,
63–65, 120.

97. NARA, Record Group 549, Records of Headquarters, United States Army Europe, Records of War Criminal Prison #1 at Landsberg, Records Relating to Executed Prisoners, Entry Number A-1 2243, Hintermayer-Box 6.

98. BDC, SS Officer Personnel Files, A3343, SSO-Roll 100A; Review, *United States vs. Martin Gottfried Weiss*, 35-38; Klee, *Das Personenlexicon*, 257.

99. BDC, SS Officer Personnel Files, A3343, SSO-Roll 178; Review, *United States vs. Martin Gottfried Weiss*, 39, 102; Klee, *Das Personenlexicon*, 128.

100. Review, *United States vs. Martin Gottfried Weiss*, 49, 109–110.

101. NARA, Record Group 549, Records of Headquarters, United States Army Europe, Records of War Criminal Prison #1 at Landsberg, Records Relating to Executed Prisoners, Entry Number A-1 2243, Eichberger-Box 3.

102. The US Army hanged American soldier Solomon Thompson at 6:24 a.m. on September 11, 1946, at the Delta DTC outside Marseilles, France; too difficult for the Army to then transport Woods to get ready for an execution the following morning. Additionally, Lieutenant Stanley Tilles saw Woods at Landsberg the morning of September 11.

103. NARA, Record Group 549, Records of Headquarters, United States Army Europe, Records of War Criminal Prison #1 at Landsberg, Records Relating to Executed Prisoners, Entry Number A-1 2243, Gerstenberg-Box 4.

104. Online footage, TV interview with Joseph Malta, Part 6.

105. Tilles and Denhart, *By the Neck*, 58.

106. Tilles and Denhart, *By the Neck*, 56–58, 60–62; Pflanz, *Die Hingerichteten*, 88–90.

107. Raithel, *Die Strafenstalt Landsberg*, 138.

Chapter 9

1. Tilles and Denhart, *By the Neck*, 56, 58, 59, 113.

2. Kingsbury Smith, "The Execution of Nazi War Criminals," *International News Service* (Nürnberg, Germany), October 16, 1946.

3. Tilles and Denhart, *By the Neck*, 112–113.

4. Wall, "Hangman," 64, 99.

5. Ibid., 63.

6. Tilles and Denhart, *By the Neck*, 111–123.

7. Ibid., 124–127.

8. Ibid., 126–127.

9. "Hangman to Go Back to Texas," *Stars & Stripes* (European Edition), October 19, 1946.

10. Ancestry.com search; NARA, World War II Army Enlistment Records, Record Group 64.

11. Ancestry.com search: Pennsylvania World War II Veteran's Compensation Form No. 1 for Anthony J. Gibilante; US Social Security Death Index, 1935–2014; US WWII Draft Cards, 1940–1947 for Anthony J. Gibilante; New York Passenger Lists, Manifest for Alien Passengers, August 10, 1948, for Katherine and James Gibilante.

12. General Court Martial Order 131, HQ, First US Infantry Division, in Personnel File, Anthony J. Gibilante, 33582004.

13. Dana Adams Schmidt, "Guilt Is Punished: No. 2 Nazi a Suicide Two Hours before the Execution Time," *New York Times*, October 16, 1946.

14. "International: War Crimes; Night without Dawn," *Time Magazine*, October 28, 1946: 34.

15. "Time Schedule of 10 Hanging at Nuernberg," *Chicago Tribune*, October 16, 1946: 11.

16. Hal Poust, "Icy Pall over City," *Chicago Tribune*, October 16, 1946: 10.

17. Colonel Burton C. Andrus, *I Was the Nuremberg Jailer* (New York: Coward-McCann, 1960), 193.

18. Tilles and Denhart, *By the Neck*, 129–130.

19. Online footage, TV interview with Joseph Malta, Part 2.

20. Andrus, *Nuremberg Jailer*, 194.

21. Tilles and Denhart, *By the Neck*, 130–132.

22. Smith, "The Execution of Nazi War Criminals"; Tilles and Denhart, *By the Neck*, 130–132.

23. Tilles and Denhart, *By the Neck*, 130–132; "Time Schedule of 10 Hanging at Nuernberg," *Chicago Tribune*, October 16, 1946: 11.

24. MacLean, *2,000 Quotes*, 275.

25. Online footage, TV interview with Joseph Malta, Part 3.

26. Andrus, *Nuremberg Jailer*, 195.

27. Smith, "The Execution of Nazi War Criminals."

28. Andrus, *Nuremberg Jailer*, 196; Tilles and Denhart, *By the Neck*, 134.

29. Warden, "Suicide of Goering," 23.

30. MacLean, *2,000 Quotes*, 217.

31. Andrus, *Nuremberg Jailer*, 196; Tilles and Denhart, *By the Neck*, 134; MacLean, *2,000 Quotes*, 214.

32. Online footage, TV interview with Joseph Malta, Part 6.

33. Andrus, *Nuremberg Jailer*, 196; Tilles and Denhart, *By the Neck*, 134.

34. MacLean, *2,000 Quotes*, 288.

35. Andrus, *Nuremberg Jailer*, 196.

36. Tilles and Denhart, *By the Neck*, 134.

37. Smith, "The Execution of Nazi War Criminals."

38. Wall, "Hangman," 99.

39. Tilles and Denhart, *By the Neck*, 135.

40. MacLean, *2,000 Quotes*, 72.

41. G. M. Gilbert, *Nuremberg Diary* (New York: Farrar, Straus, 1947), 75, 420; Smith, "The Execution of Nazi War Criminals."

42. Smith, "The Execution of Nazi War Criminals."

43. Andrus, *Nuremberg Jailer*, 197; Smith, "The Execution of Nazi War Criminals."

44. Smith, "The Execution of Nazi War Criminals."

45. Tilles and Denhart, *By the Neck*, 135–136

46. Warden, "Suicide of Goering," 23.

47. Gilbert, *Nuremberg Diary*, 75. Remark made to Dr. G. M. Gilbert, prison psychologist.

48. Andrus, *Nuremberg Jailer*, 197; Tilles and Denhart, *By the Neck*, 136–137.

49. MacLean, *2,000 Quotes*, 295.

50. Smith, "The Execution of Nazi War Criminals."

51. Andrus, *Nuremberg Jailer*, 197; Tilles and Denhart, *By the Neck*, 137.

52. MacLean, *2,000 Quotes*, 309.

53. Wall, "Hangman," 99; Smith, "The Execution of Nazi War Criminals."

54. Lancaster, "Wife Stunned to Know of Husband 'Executioner,'" 1.

55. "Take 2 Pictures of Each Nazi after Hanging," *Chicago Tribune*, October 17, 1946: 3.

56. M/Sgt John C. Woods, "GI Hangman Tells Story of Top Nazis' Executions," *Stars & Stripes* (by way of the Associated Press), October 20, 1946: 12.

57. Robert L. Gunnarsson Sr., *American Military Police in Europe, 1945–1991: Unit Histories* (Jefferson, NC, McFarland, 2011), 285.

58. NARA, World War II Army Enlistment Records, Record Group 64; Ancestry.com: US Social Security Applications and Claims Index, 1936–2007; US World War II Draft Cards, Young Men, 1940–1947; Nevada, Death Index, 1980–2012; US Department of Veterans Affairs BIRLS Death File, 1850–2010.

59. "Comrades Greet GI Hangman with Steak, Bottle, Curiosity," *Stars & Stripes*, October 21, 1946: 12.

60. Ibid.

61. "Nazis' Executioner 'Never Missed One,'" *Stars & Stripes* (European Division), October 24, 1946: 7.

62. Leonora Klein, *A Very English Hangman: The Life and Times of Albert Pierrepoint* (London: Corvo Books, 2006), 14; Albert Pierrepoint, *Executioner: Pierrepoint—the Amazing Autobiography of the World's Most Famous Executioner* (London: Hodder and Stoughton, 1974), 63.

63. Klein, *A Very English Hangman*, 18.

64. Klein, *A Very English Hangman*, 81, 228, 229; Pierrepoint, *Executioner: Pierrepoint*, 149.

65. Pierrepoint, *Executioner: Pierrepoint*, 155.

66. John Thompson, "Nazi Hangings Bungled, Says British Report," *Chicago Tribune*, October 30, 1946: 3.

67. Online footage, TV interview with Joseph Malta, Part 6.

Chapter 10

1. "Wichitan Who Hanged Nazis Back in US," *Wichita Beacon*, November 19, 1946: 1.
2. "Missed Death Twice, Army Hangman Says," *New York Times*, November 20, 1946: 16.
3. Online footage, TV interview with Joseph Malta, Part 6.
4. Ibid.
5. Ibid.
6. Wall, "Hangman," 62.
7. Ibid., 63, 99.
8. Ibid., 63, 64.
9. Ibid., 63, 64
10. Ibid., 99.
11. "Nuernberg Hangman Proud of Executions," *Wichita Beacon*, November 20, 1946: 1.
12. Ibid.
13. Leslie Sourbeer, "Executioner of Nazis Goes to Church," *Wichita Beacon*, November 28, 1946: 1; Warden, "Suicide of Goering," 1.
14. Warden, "Suicide of Goering," 1.
15. Ibid.
16. Ibid.
17. M/S John C. Woods, "Hanging Nazis Didn't End All Their Ideals," *Wichita Beacon*, November 29, 1946: 1.
18. Discussions with otolaryngologists indicate that this could have been possible only if John had a perforated eardrum.
19. Interview with relatives of Hazel Woods.
20. Ernest A. Warden, "Nazi Hangman Going Back to Army Career, *Wichita Beacon*, February 15, 1947: 2A.
21. Ernest A. Warden, "Wichitan, Hangman of Nazi War Chiefs, Is Killed in Pacific," *Wichita Beacon*, July 23, 1950: 1.
22. Headquarters and Service Company, 1st Engineer Combat Battalion, Morning Report, 24 September 1948.
23. 507th Engineer Service Company, Morning Report, 2 May 1947.
24. 507th Engineer Service Company, Morning Report, 8 May 1947 and 16 May 1947.
25. 507th Engineer Service Company, Morning Report, 22 May 1947.
26. HQ, Area Engineer Second Military District, 555th Engineer Composite Service Group, Special Orders Number 126, 10 September 1947; HQ & HQ Company, 1103rd Engineer Combat Group, Morning Report, 6 March 1947.
27. Company B, 1st Engineer Combat Battalion, Morning Report, 1 October 1947.
28. Company B, 1st Engineer Combat Battalion, Morning Report, 28 April 1948.
29. Company B, 1st Engineer Combat Battalion, Morning Report, 17 May 1948 and 19 May 1948.
30. Headquarters and Service Company, 1st Engineer Combat Battalion, Morning Report, 24 September 1948,
31. "Furlough for Famed US Hangman," *Wichita Beacon*, November 20, 1948: 1.
32. Ernest A. Warden, "Noted Wichita Hangman Eyes Tojo Execution," *Wichita Beacon*, November 28, 1948: 1.
33. Ibid.
34. Ibid.
35. Interview with Anna Dale Chilcott Cole.
36. Ibid.
37. HQ, 795th Military Police Battalion, Luzon Prisoner of War Camp #1, APO 75, SUBJECT: Award for Army Commendation Ribbon, 14 September 1946.
38. Charles Clarence Rexroad was born on April 22, 1904, in Harrisburg, Oregon. He attended college for just over three years, majoring in sociology at Spokane University. Prior to active military service, to which he entered from San Rafael, California, he was a guard at San Quentin Prison from 1932 to 1936 and served in the National Guard. He began his overseas service on April 22, 1942, later serving as a military prison guard in Australia. Rexroad was a large man, standing 6'3" and weighing 245 pounds. An Army photograph from 1949 has a description stating that Rexroad executed 130 men, mostly Japanese war criminals, including General Tomoyuki Yamashita—hanged February 23, 1946, at the Los

Baños, Laguna Prison, in the Philippines; Rexroad likely hanged former premier Hideki Tojo and six other warlords at Sugamo Prison, Japan, on December 23, 1948. He also hanged Japanese war criminals in the Marianas Islands and hanged seven American soldiers at Oro Bay, New Guinea. He married Dorothy L. Sammons on September 12, 1949, in Sebastian, Arkansas. Rexroad retired from the Army on May 1, 1962, in Augusta, Georgia. He died on December 23, 1992, of cancer at the Department of Veterans Affairs Medical Center in Augusta, Georgia. He is buried at the Hillcrest Memorial Park Cemetery in Augusta. Sources: David Jackson, "Executioner's Role Turned US Soldier into Celebrity," *Augusta Herald* (Augusta, GA), November 7, 1982: 4B; FOIA Request, NARA, St. Louis, MO, First Lieutenant Charles C. Rexroad, which generated HQ, 795th Military Police Battalion, Luzon Prisoner of War Camp #1, APO 75, SUBJECT: Award for Army Commendation Ribbon, 14 September 1946 and Officers and Warrant Officers Qualification Card, Charles C. Rexroad, among several other documents.

39. HQ & HQ Company, 7th Engineer Brigade, Morning Report, October 22, 1948 (Box 17).

40. NARA, Record Group 338, Records of US Army Tactical and Support Organizations (World War II and Thereafter), Unit Histories, 7th Engineer Brigade, Entry # UD 37042, General Orders 1949–1953, General Order 3, General Order 5; interview with Florian Waitl, command historian at US Army Engineer School, Fort Leonard Woods, MO, October 26, 2017.

41. HQ & HQ Company, 7th Engineer Brigade, Morning Report, 12 January 1950.

42. HQ, the Engineer Center and Fort Belvoir, Fort Belvoir, VA, Roster, Movement Order #1, HQ TEC & FB dated 4 January 1950 as amended.

43. NARA, Record Group 338, 7th Engineer Brigade, Entry # UD 37042, General Orders 1949–1953.

44. HQ & HQ Company, 7th Engineer Brigade, Morning Report, 4 March 1950.

45. Photograph of a sign on Eniwetok dedicating an athletic field in memory of Master Sergeant John C. Woods.

46. NARA, Record Group 338, 7th Engineer Brigade, Entry # UD 37042, General Orders 1949–1953.

47. Defense Technical Information Center (DTIC), www.dtic.mil/dtic/tr/fulltext/u2/a078576.pdf AD-A078 576, Joint Task Force Three, Washington, DC, Operation Greenhouse, 80-04, 1951, 1.

48. Headquarters, Task Group 3.2, APO 187, Report of Claims Officer concerning the Circumstances Surrounding the Death of Master Sergeant John C. Woods, RA 37540591, in Personnel File, Master Sergeant John C. Woods.

49. Ibid.

50. Ibid.

51. Headquarters, Task Group 3.2, APO 187, Report of Claims Officer concerning the Circumstances Surrounding the Death of Master Sergeant John C. Woods, RA 37540591 and Special Order Number 102, in Personnel File, Master Sergeant John C. Woods.

52. Testimony of Ernest L. Blanchard, RA11146666, Corporal, in Personnel File, Master Sergeant John C. Woods.

53. Testimony of Richard G. Griffen, RA17260969, Private, in Personnel File, Master Sergeant John C. Woods.

54. Testimony of Thomas W. Sanders, RA3294040, Private First Class, in Personnel File, Master Sergeant John C. Woods.

55. Testimony of Jacob H. Rasely, RA13316288, Private First Class, in Personnel File, Master Sergeant John C. Woods.

56. Certificate of the Medical Officer, Eniwetok, Marshall Islands, in Personnel File, Master Sergeant John C. Woods.

57. Testimony of Justin C. Smith, RA12287414, Private, in Personnel File, Master Sergeant John C. Woods.

58. Testimony of Calvin H. Malone, RA13121182, Corporal, in Personnel File, Master Sergeant John C. Woods.

59. HQ & HQ Company, 7th Engineer Brigade, Morning Report, 21 July 1950.

60. Report of Investigation in the Cause of Death of Woods, John C., 22 July 1950, in Personnel File, Master Sergeant John C. Woods.

61. Testimony of Forest K. Weaver, 1st LT, CE, 02033075, in Report of Investigation in the Cause of Death of Woods, John C., 22 July 1950, in Personnel File, Master Sergeant John C. Woods.

62. Ibid.

63. Ibid.

64. Personal interview with Rich Closs and John Closs, co-owners Closs Electric, on September 18, 2017, at Decatur, IL.

65. Ibid.

66. Ibid.

67. Ibid.

68. Warden, "Wichitan, Hangman of Nazi War Chiefs, Is Killed in Pacific," 1.

69. Interview with Anna Dale Chilcott Cole.

70. Summary Statement by John K. Frost, Captain, Medical Corps, Chief of Autopsy and Pathology Section, Tripler Army Hospital, in Personnel File, Master Sergeant John C. Woods.

71. Preparation Room Report, US Army Mortuary, Tripler Army Hospital, in Personnel File, Master Sergeant John C. Woods.

72. "Armed Forces: Hangman's End," *Time*, August 7, 1950: 16.

73. Interview with Anna Dale Chilcott Cole.

74. "Sergeant Woods Funeral Held," *Wichita Beacon*, August 15, 1950.

75. Email from Linda Clark, December 22, 2014.

76. "Sie mögen schuldig sein," *Der Spiegel*, February 28, 1951: 5.

77. Bob Considine, "On the Line with Bob Considine," *Daily Times from New Philadelphia* (OH), June 14, 1956: 13.

78. Discussions with Herman Obermayer.

79. Defense Technical Information Center, AD-A078 576, Joint Task Force Three, 2 and 8.

80. Ibid., 4.

81. Interview with Rich Closs and John Closs.

Epilogue

1. Ancestry.com: US Veterans' Gravesites, ca. 1775–2006.

2. Interview with Dean Gall, senior archivist, NPRC, January 16, 2018.

3. Interview with relatives of Hazel Woods.

4. Ancestry.com: US Social Security Applications and Claims Index, 1936–2007; US Veterans' Gravesites, ca. 1775–2006; US World War II Army Enlistment Records, 1938–1946.

5. French L. MacLean, *The Fifth Field: The Story of the 96 American Soldiers Sentenced to Death and Executed in Europe and North Africa in World War II* (Atglen, PA: Schiffer, 2013), 7–10.

Appendix 2

1. Herman J. Obermayer, "Clean, Painless, and Traditional," 24.

2. Tilles and Denhart, *By the Neck*, 126–127.

3. Wall, "Hangman," 99.

4. Woods, "GI Hangman Tells Story of Top Nazis' Executions," 12.

5. Ibid.

6. Ibid.

7. Ibid.

8. "Nazis' Executioner 'Never Missed One,'" *Stars & Stripes* (European Division), October 24, 1946: 7.

9. Ibid.

10. Wall, "Hangman," 99.

11. Ibid., 99.

12. Ibid., 64.

13. Ibid.

14. Warden, "Suicide of Goering," 1.

15. Warden, "Wichitan, Hangman of Nazi War Chiefs, Is Killed in Pacific," 1.

16. Obermayer, "Clean, Painless, and Traditional," 24.

17. Sourbeer, "Executioner of Nazis Goes to Church," 1; Warden, "Suicide of Goering," 1.

18. Warden, "Suicide of Goering," 1.

19. Ibid.

BIBLIOGRAPHY

Primary Sources

National Archives and Records Administration (NARA), National Personnel Records Center (NPRC), St. Louis, MO

CM Case # 287315 / Personnel File	Agee, Amos	34163762	PVT
CM Case # 285969 / Personnel File	Anderson, Roy W.	35497199	PVT
Personnel File	Bailey, Milbert	34151488	PVT
CM Case # 287413 / Personnel File	Baldwin, Walter J.	34020111	PVT
CM Case # 286393	Clay, Matthew, Jr.	38490561	PFC
CM Case # 287064	Cooper, John David	34562464	PFC
CM Case # 283439 / Personnel File	Davis, William E.	33541888	PFC
CM Case # 287135 / Personnel File	Davison, Tommie	34485174	PVT
CM Case # 285325 / Personnel File	Downes, William C.	33519814	PVT
CM Case # 286064	Farrell, Arthur J.	32559163	PVT
Personnel File	Gibilante, Anthony J.	33582004	PVT
CM Case # 286910 / Personnel File	Gordon, Tom E.	34091950	PVT
CM Case # 287605 / Personnel File	Green, George, Jr.	38476751	PFC
Personnel File	Heard, Haze	34562354	PFC
CM Case # 287773	Holden, Mervin	38226564	PVT
CM Case # 288114 / Personnel File	Hopper, Benjamin F.	32720571	PVT
CM Case # 288384 / Personnel File	Johnson, Willie	38270465	PVT
Personnel File	Jones, James L.	34221343	PVT
Personnel File	Kleinbeck, Herbert A., Jr.	16100440	T/5
CM Case # 288505 / Personnel File	Kluxdal, Paul M.	36395076	PFC
CM Case # 288771 / Personnel File	Mack, William	32620461	PVT
CM Case # 296582 / Personnel File	Mariano, Blake W.	38011593	PFC
Personnel File	Martino, Vincent J.		
CM Case # 288535 / Personnel File	McCarter, William J.	34675977	PFC
CM Case # 287783 / Personnel File	Newman, Oscar N.	35226382	T/5
CM Case # 289745 / Personnel File	Norris, Clete O.	37082314	SGT
CM Case # 289785 / Personnel File	Ortiz, Victor	30405077	PVT

CM Case # 298666 / Personnel File	Philpot, Henry C.	39080069	PVT
CM Case # 303097 / Personnel File	Robinson, Charles M.	38164425	PVT
CM Case # 300615 / Personnel File	Rollins, Alvin R.	34716953	PFC
CM Case # 285969 / Personnel File	Sanders, James B.	34124233	T/5
CM Case # 289454 / Personnel File	Skinner, Robert L.	35802328	PVT
CM Case # 287315 / Personnel File	Smith, John C.	33214953	PVT
CM Case # 287773 / Personnel File	Spencer, Elwood J.	33739343	PVT
CM Case # 291296 / Personnel File	Twiggs, James W.	38265086	PVT
CM Case # 287783	Valentine, Leo, Sr.	32954278	T/5
Personnel File	Ward, Thomas	33515563	SGT
CM Case # 287315 / Personnel File	Watson, Frank	34793522	PVT
CM Case # 303439	Williams, Ellsworth	34200976	PVT
Personnel File	Williams, John	32794118	PVT
CM Case # 291944 / Personnel File	Williams, Olin W.	34649494	PVT
Personnel File	Woods, John C.	37540591	MSG
US Navy Personnel File	Woods, John C.	3417398	AS
Civilian Conservation Corps File	Woods, John C.		
CM Case # 296038 / Personnel File	Wray, Robert	34461589	PVT
CM Case # 293448	Yancy, Waiters	37499079	PVT

Office of the Adjutant General Morning Reports, Company B, 37th Engineer (C) Battalion
March 31, 1944
October 7, 1944
November 6, 1944
Office of the Adjutant General Morning Reports, Headquarters & Headquarters Company, 7th Engineer Brigade
October 22, 1948 (Box 17)
January 4, 1950 and January 12, 1950 (Box 37; Reel 31.28)

March 4, 1950 (Box 62; Reel 33.85)
July 21, 1950 (Box 59; Reel 34.280)
Office of the Adjutant General Morning Reports, 1st Engineer Combat Battalion
May 1947 (Box 82; Reel 14.1007)
September 1947 (Box 54; Reel 17.1091)
October 1947 (Box 34; Reel 1.1217)
February 1948 (Box 22; Reel 7.929)
April 1948 (Box 34; Reel 28.168)
May 1948 (Box 19; Reel 16.1265)
September 1948 (Box 59; Reel 19.1003)
October 1948 (Box 59; Reel 3.980)

Office of the Adjutant General Morning Reports, 507th Engineer Service Company May 1947 (Box 88; Reel 14.1013)

Office of the Adjutant General Morning Reports, 555th Engineer Composite Service Group March 1947 (Box 106; Reel 10.931)

Office of the Adjutant General Morning Reports, 7801st Station Complement Unit, 2nd Military District, Wetzlar, Germany, October 1947 (Box 46; Reel 2.1056)

National Archives and Records Administration, College Park, MD

NARA, Record Group 111, Records of the Office of the Chief Signal Officer, World War II.

NARA, Record Group 242 National Archives Collection of Foreign Records Seized; Berlin Document Center, SS Officer Personnel Files, A3343, SSO.

NARA, Record Group 319-CE, Records of the US Army Staff Prints: Photographs of the US and Foreign Nations, 1942–64.

NARA, Record Group 338, Records of US Army Tactical and Support Organizations (World War II and Thereafter), Unit Histories, 7th Engineer Brigade, Entry # UD 37042, General Orders 1949–1953.

NARA, Record Group 498, Headquarters, European Theater of Operations, US Army (World War II), Entry # UD1028, Judge Advocate Section, General Correspondence, Decimal File, 1942–1945, 250.4 Court-Martial.

NARA, Record Group 549, Records of Headquarters, United States Army Europe, Records of War Criminal Prison #1 at Landsberg, Records Relating to Executed Prisoners, Entry Number A-1 2243.

NARA, Record Group: 549, T-1021, German Documents among the War Crimes Records of the Judge Advocate Division Headquarters, United States Army, Europe.

NARA, Record Group 498, Roll: MP63-9-0106

Other Primary Source Documents

HQ, Seine DTC, APO 887, Report of Proceedings in the Death Chamber [*Rottenführer* Gunther Ohletz, 21st *SS Panzer Grenadier Regiment*, German Army,] 9 October 1944, linked to the Cornell University Library.

The General Board, United States Forces, European Theater, Judge Advocate Section, the Military Offender in the Theater of Operations, Study 84.

Copy of journal entry, *The State of Kansas vs. John C. Woods*, dated 22nd day of December 1939, Sedgwick County, KS, in possession of Linda Clark.

Copy of marriage license for John C. Woods and Hazel Marie Chilcott, Greenwood County, KS, dated 30th day of September 1933, in possession of Linda Clark.

Published Works

Andrus, Colonel Burton C. *I Was the Nuremberg Jailer*. New York: Coward-McCann, 1960.

Beck, Alfred M., Abe Bortz, Charles W. Lynch, Lida Mayo, and Ralph F. Weld. *The Corps of Engineers: The War against Germany*. US Army in World War II. Washington, DC: Center of Military History, US Army, 1985. www.history.army.mil/html/reference/Normandy/TS/COE/COE15.html

Berthold, Will. *Vollstreckt: Johann Reichhart, der letzte deutsch Henker*. Munich: Wilhelm Goldmann Verlag, 1982.

Dachs, Johann. *Tod durch das Fallbeil: Der deutsch Scharfrichter Johann Reichhart (1893–1972)*. Regensburg, Germany: Mittelbayerische Druck- und Verlagsgesellschaft, 2001.

Freeman, Gregory A. *The Last Mission of the Wham Bam Boys: Courage, Tragedy and Justice in World War II*. New York: Palgrave Macmillan, 2011.

Gilbert, G. M. *Nuremberg Diary*. New York: Farrar, Straus, 1947.

Greene, Joshua. *Justice at Dachau: The Trials of an American Prosecutor*. New York: Broadway Books, 2003.

Gunnarsson, Robert L., Sr. *American Military Police in Europe, 1945–1991: Unit Histories*. Jefferson, NC: McFarland, 2011.

Klee, Ernst. *Das Personenlexicon zum Dritten Reich*. Hamburg, Germany: Nikol Verlag, 2016.

Klein, Leonora. *A Very English Hangman: The Life and Times of Albert Pierrepoint*. London: Corvo Books, 2006.

MacLean, French L. *The Camp Men: The SS Officers Who Ran the Nazi Concentration Camp System*. Atglen, PA: Schiffer, 1999.

MacLean, French L. *The Fifth Field: The Story of the 96 American Soldiers Sentenced to Death and Executed in Europe and North Africa in World War II*. Atglen, PA: Schiffer, 2013.

MacLean, French L. *2,000 Quotes from Hitler's 1000-Year Reich*. Atglen, PA: Schiffer, 2007.

Obermayer, Herman J. *Soldiering for Freedom: A GI's Account of World War II*. College Station: Texas A&M University Press, 2005.

Pflanz, Heinrich. *Die Hingerichteten von Landsberg und der Spöttinger Friedhof*. Beltheim-Schnellbach, Germany: Bublies Verlag, 2004.

Pierrepoint, Albert. *Executioner: Pierrepoint—the Amazing Autobiography of the World's Most Famous Executioner*. London: Hodder and Stoughton, 1974.

Raithel, Thomas. *Die Strafenstalt Landsberg am Lech und der Spöttinger Friedhof (1944–1958)*. Munich: R. Verlag, 2009.

Taylor, Richard T., ed. *The Illio 1939*. University of Illinois Yearbook. Champaign and Urbana: University of Illinois, 1939.

Tilles, Stanley, and Jeffrey Denhart, *By the Neck until Dead: The Gallows of Nuremberg*. Bedford, IN: JoNa Books, 1999.

Williams, Joseph H. *Captor—Captive*. Jacksonville, FL: Girtman, 1986.

Magazine Articles

"Armed Forces: Hangman's End." *Time*, August 7, 1950.

Garland, Master Sergeant Patrick V., Retired. "Penal Institutions in the European Theater of Operations." *Military Police: The Professional Bulletin of the Military Police Corps*, Spring 2012. Fort Leonard Wood, Missouri.

Obermayer, Herman J. "Clean, Painless, and Traditional." *Dartmouth Jack O Lantern*, Christmas Issue, December 1946.

Resnik, Joshua A. "Der Henker von Nürnberg." *Zeit* Online, October 18, 1996. www.zeit.de/1996/43/Der_Henker_von_Nuernberg

"Sie mögen schuldig sein." *Der Spiegel*, 28 February 28, 1951.

Wall, Carl B. "Hangman." *True: The Man's Magazine*, November 1947.

Newspaper Articles

"3 Germans Hanged for Slaying Airman." *New York Times*, June 30, 1945.

"5 Germans Hanged for Killing Fliers." *New York Times*, November 10, 1945.

"9 from Greenwood Called to Army Service July 8." *Eureka Herald* (Eureka, KS), June 26, 1941.

"14 Germans Pay for Dachau Crimes." *Stars & Stripes* 2, no. 304, Mediterranean (Rome), May 30, 1946,

"14-Point. GI Hangman Sizes Up Goering, Decides to Stay On." *Stars & Stripes* (European Edition), November 13, 1945.

"Army Executioner Electrocuted on Eniwetok Atoll." *Montana Standard* (Butte, MT), July 27, 1950.

Becker, Jens, and Gunnar Dedio. "Der Henker von Nürnberg." *Der Tagesspiel*, April 21, 2002.

"Comrades Greet GI Hangman with Steak, Bottle, Curiosity." *Stars & Stripes*, October 21, 1946.

Considine, Bob. "On the Line with Bob Considine." *Daily Times from New Philadelphia* (OH), June 14, 1956.

Dillard, Irving. "28 Dachau Killers Are Hanged at Landsberg." *Stars & Stripes* (European Edition), May 30, 1946.

"Eniwetok Base, Atom Proving Site, Depicted as Normal Town of 8,000: Representative Hebert, Witness at Blast, Describes 'Thriving Community' in Which Tests Have Caused No Deaths." *New York Times*, June 16, 1951.

"Furlough Ends." *Wichita Beacon*, December 19, 1948.

"Furlough for Famed US Hangman." *Wichita Beacon*, November 20, 1948.

"A German War Criminal Pays the Penalty for His Acts." *New York Times*, May 30, 1946.

"Germans Executed for Killing American Airmen." *New York Times*, November 22, 1945.

"Hangman to Go Back to Texas." *Stars & Stripes* (European Edition), October 19, 1946.

Jackson, David. "Executioner's Role Turned US Soldier into Celebrity." *Augusta Herald* (Augusta, GA), November 7, 1982.

Lancaster, George. "Wife Stunned to Know of Husband 'Executioner.'" *Wichita Beacon*, October 17, 1946.

Marcus, John. "Nuremberg Executioner Says, 'It Was a Pleasure.'" *Los Angeles Times*, November 24, 1996.

"Married, Chilcott-Woods." *Toronto Republican* (Toronto, KS), October 1–7, 1933.

"Men Accepted Are Home on Furlough." *Eureka Herald* (Eureka, KS), September 2, 1943.

"Miss Decker Married to Thomas Robinson." *Herald Statesman* (Yonkers, NY), June 16, 1942.

"Missed Death Twice, Army Hangman Says." *New York Times*, November 20, 1946.

"More Men Leave for the Armed Service." *The Eureka Herald* (Eureka, KS), August 26, 1943.

"Nazis' Executioner 'Never Missed One,'" *Stars & Stripes* (European Division), October 24, 1946.

"Nuernberg Hangman Proud of Executions." *Wichita Beacon*, November 20, 1946.

"Nurnberg Hangman Killed in Accident." *Stars & Stripes* (European Edition), July 28, 1950.

Schmidt, Dana Adams. "Guilt Is Punished: No. 2 Nazi a Suicide Two Hours before the Execution Time." *New York Times*, October 16, 1946.

"Sergeant Woods Funeral Held." *Wichita Beacon*, August 15, 1950.

"Six to Leave Eureka for Fort Leavenworth." *Eureka Herald* (Eureka, KS), August 21, 1941.

Smith, Kingsbury. "The Execution of Nazi War Criminals." *International News Service* (Nürnberg, Germany), October 16, 1946.

Sourbeer, Leslie. "Executioner of Nazis Goes to Church." *Wichita Beacon*, November 28, 1946.

Warden, Ernest A. "Nazi Hangman Going Back to Army Career." *Wichita Beacon*, February 15, 1947.

Warden, Ernest A. "Noted Wichita Hangman Eyes Tojo Execution." *Wichita Beacon*, November 28, 1948.

Warden, Ernest A. "Suicide of Goering Was 'Biggest Disappointment' at Nazi Hangings," *Wichita Beacon*, November 29, 1946.

Warden, Ernest A. "Wichitan, Hangman of Nazi War Chiefs, Is Killed in Pacific." *Wichita Beacon*, July 23, 1950.

"Week in Wichita Society." *Wichita Daily Eagle*, December 24, 1905: 9.

"Wichitan Who Hanged Nazis Back in US." *Wichita Beacon*, November 19, 1946.

Woods, M/Sgt John C. "GI Hangman Tells Story of Top Nazis' Executions." *Stars & Stripes* (by way of the Associated Press), October 20, 1946.

Woods, M/S John C. "Hanging Nazis Didn't End All Their Ideals." *Wichita Beacon*, November 29, 1946.

Interviews

Email conversations with Ashley Robinson Skala, grandniece of Thomas F. Robinson, 2017–2018.

Personal interview with Thomas J. Ward Jr., April 10, 2013, Harrisburg, PA.

Personal interview with Linda Clark and Carol Stock, daughters of Helen Chilcott, and Jerry Clark, Linda's husband, September 14, 2017, Toronto, KS.

Personal interview with Marilyn Bogle and Hazel Russell, Greenwood County Historical Society and Museum, September 14, 2017, Eureka, KS.

Personal interview with Janice Leitch, Alvin Morris Administration Center and Gwen Leivian, Wichita East High School, September 14, 2017, Wichita, KS.

Personal interview with Rich Closs and John Closs, co-owners of Closs Electric, September 18, 2017, Decatur, IL.

Personal discussions with Herman Obermayer, 2007–2013, Virginia, the National Archives at College Park, MD.

Multiple email and telephonic discussions with Frederic L. Borch III, regimental historian & archivist, the Judge Advocate General's Corps, US Army, the Judge Advocate General's Legal Center and School, Charlottesville, VA, 2017–2018.

Multiple email and personal interviews with Dean Gall, senior archivist at the National Personnel Records Center, St. Louis, MO, 2016–2018.

Telephone interview with Anna Dale Chilcott Cole, daughter of Dale Chilcott, Hazel Chilcott's brother, October 2, 2017, and personal interview on November 16, 2017.

Telephone interview with Florian Waitl, command historian, US Army Engineer School, Fort Leonard Woods, MO, October 26, 2017.

Websites

AD-A078 576, Joint Task Force Three, Washington, DC, Operation Greenhouse, 80-04, 1951.

Beck, Alfred M., Abe Bortz, Charles W. Lynch, Lida Mayo, and Ralph F. Weld. *The Corps of Engineers: The War against Germany, US Army in World War II*, chapter XV, "The Landings on OMAHA and UTAH." www.history.army.mil/html/reference/Normandy/TS/COE/COE15.html.

Defense Technical Information Center (DTIC). www.dtic.mil/dtic/tr/fulltext/u2/a078576.pdf.

Online footage, TV interview with Joseph Malta. www.onlinefootage.tv/stock-video-footage/42239/nuremberg-trials-interview-with-joseph-malta-part7.

Third US Army and Eastern Military District, Office of the Judge Advocate, Review of Proceedings of General Military Court in the Case of *United States vs. Martin Gottfried Weiss, et al.*, January 24, 1946. www.jewishvirtuallibrary.org/jsource/Holocaust/dachautrial/d3.pdf HQ.

INDEX OF SELECTED PERSONNEL